T0301722

LEADERSHIP WITH
SOUL

André Lacroix

André Lacroix

Leadership with Soul

Putting people at the heart
of your growth strategy...

 World Scientific

 ESKA
PUBLISHING

Published by

ESKA Publishing
12 rue du Quatre Septembre
75002 Paris

and

World Scientific Publishing Co. Pte. Ltd.
5 Toh Tuck Link, Singapore 596224
USA office: 27 Warren Street, Suite 401-402, Hackensack, NJ 07601
UK office: 57 Shelton Street, Covent Garden, London WC2H 9HE

British Library Cataloguing-in-Publication Data
A catalogue record for this book is available from the British Library.

LEADERSHIP WITH SOUL
Putting People at the Heart of Your Growth Strategy

Copyright © 2023 by André Lacroix

ISBN 978-981-126-688-1 (hardcover)
ISBN 978-981-126-689-8 (paperback)

For any available supplementary material, please visit
https://www.worldscientific.com/worldscibooks/10.1142/13157#t=suppl

Desk Editor: Nicole Ong

Printed in Singapore

Contents

Preface
Time for change

'I am the wisest man alive, for I know one thing, and that is that I know nothing'.
(Socrates, c. 470–399 BC)

When the established rules and received wisdom on which society is built receive a shock of sufficient strength, the old truths and beliefs that guide how people think, behave and plan their lives quickly become obsolete.

I believe we are at one of those points in history.

Of course, not everything is bad.

Looking back over the last eight decades, it's incredible to see the global progress that has been made since WWII.

New powers have emerged in the shape of China, Russia, the Middle East and Eastern Europe and others are flexing across Africa, Latin America and Southeast Asia.

But since the beginning of the 21st century, we have been hit by a series of consecutive shocks that throw into question some of the most important foundations on which the success of the global economy has been built.

Taming risk for a better world

My view is pretty straightforward: recent failures by leaders to recognise and mitigate emerging risks in the world have led to just about every major crisis we've faced this century.

Maybe 9/11 wouldn't have happened if the aviation industry had taken a broader and better view of safety risks.

The financial crisis in 2008/2009 would perhaps never have occurred if banks had not failed to manage borrowing risks properly.

Trust in corporations would not be as desperately low as it is today if companies did not so often ignore the importance of delivering sustainable growth to focus on short-term results, the direct cause of so many quality, safety and ethical scandals.

Outside the corporate world, governmental and institutional failures to anticipate and defuse risk with the right governance are why so much of the Middle East has been in a state of crisis for so many years and why we started 2022 with a war in Ukraine.

Demonstrations, civil wars and other conflicts in multiple countries are often the result of a failure to understand the need to share progress equally across society. Movements like MeToo and Black Lives Matter only exist because too many people in prominent and powerful social positions fail to appreciate the importance, the value and the justice of diversity.

Perhaps above all, the climate emergency is a direct consequence of a collective failure to balance the short-term benefits of global growth with the long-term risks to the Earth as a whole. In short, too few people genuinely care about the future of our planet and the generations to come.

For some people (and I am possibly one of them) the COVID-19 pandemic and its global social and economic impact has crystallised views on many of these issues.

Looking back to early 2020, our global healthcare systems failed to put the right early-warning systems and action plans in place. This has resulted in the pandemic's impact on people's lives being far, far greater than it should have been.

The economic impact, while closely related, has been further exaggerated by companies' failures to ensure they had the right processes to ensure business continuity in their supply chains, employee safety in the workplace and consumer safety in public places.

All these factors are failures of leadership.

But the great thing about a crisis – any crisis – is the opportunity it gives us to learn, adapt and improve.

That's never been clearer than it is today, in the aftermath of COVID-19.

It's time for the world's leaders, including those of governments and companies, institutions and regulators, to work together to create something bigger and better for everybody.

Our planet is under tremendous pressure and the young population is right to be so vocal about the crisis we face.

Young people might represent circa 20% of the world but they are 100% of the future.

We cannot wait!

Enough is enough.

It's time for change.

Those of us who are leaders of large or small companies, private or public enterprises, big or small business units, profit or non-profit organisations, have an essential role to play to build back a better society.

Around 3.3 billion people across the world work every day.

We corporate leaders, have a huge responsibility to make the workplace a better, safer and more sustainable environment for each and every one of them.

The American analytics and advisory company Gallup is the world authority in measuring engagement in the workplace, asking employees how they feel every day.

The statistics they have to show are alarming.

According to Gallup's latest engagement data, 80% of the global workforce is not engaged.

Making the workplace better for the more than 2.6 billion employees who are not engaged is the opportunity we all share as leaders.

It's a huge opportunity for all of us. It's a huge opportunity for the world!

Grasping the opportunity to make the workplace a better place will make the world a better place. For everybody.

Positive change must start in the workplace

Today's world is an incredibly complex place for any leader.

Right across the planet, institutions everywhere and of every kind are enormously challenged by this complexity.

Operating in a global, demanding and 24/7 environment is hugely challenging for any global CEO.

Leading a big or small business unit in any large company is not easy given the politics that often hinder progress.

Running a small company with limited resources is hard work for the leadership team.

Leading a public institution is extremely complex given the multiple stakeholders to manage.

Being responsible for a non-profit organisation is far from trivial.

Being part of any government is an incredible leadership challenge too.

Notwithstanding these challenges, leaders have to accept the fact that just 20% engagement in the workplace is simply not acceptable for all stakeholders, as it clearly demonstrates that organisations are not reaching their full potential.

It's time for change!

But there is a problem.

Over the years, corporations have made huge progress on multiple fronts and are run much better today than 40 years ago. There is no question about this!

However, I firmly believe that corporations today are not unleashing their full potential.

Why?

Companies and organisations are over-managed and underled!

How can we explain that 2.6 billion employees are not engaged every day at the workplace?

Truly alarming!

It's what I call the 'leadership vacuum'.

Too often, today's leaders do not have the experience, the knowledge, the understanding or the support of their employer to deliver against their leadership responsibility.

Of course, the significant and growing tidal wave of distrust across society when it comes to what is happening in the workplace makes the role of any leader even more challenging. Excess pay and volatile corporate earnings, unethical behaviours, a lack of proper governance, a focus on short-term results – all these factors and more are in the spotlight.

Based on my experience over the years as a leader, I realised that students at business schools are unfortunately not well-trained when it comes to getting the right leadership skills before they start their careers.

There have been many books written on leadership over the years and, having read quite a few of them, I came to the conclusion that none of these books were offering a cutting-edge and systemic leadership model built on proven, real-world experience across multiple industries.

Some of these books have been written by keen students of leadership, typically professors or consultants who have widely acknowledged expertise at an academic level.

Some of the books have been written by those with impressive hands-on CEO experience. Individuals who have been there and done it. Typically, the books will major on a few topics of effective leadership without giving the reader a systemic, end-to-end approach to leading successfully.

Above all, leadership is difficult.

That is where this book fits in. For close to three decades, I have been fortunate enough to hold leadership positions in some great companies, often with a global footprint.

During that time, I have continually reflected on what it means to be a Good Leader. I have taken notes, I have continuously learned new lessons and I have put my growing knowledge and insight into practice.

Despite some inevitable mistakes and false dawns along the way, I think I can say with due modesty that the performance of the organisations I led has demonstrated the value of my learnings and the effectiveness of my leadership approach.

In this book, I have attempted to crystallise my leadership approach into 10 chapters, each looking in detail at a particular aspect of the leadership model I have developed over the years. Wherever possible, I illustrate the points I'm making with my personal experience – with stories that I've lived myself.

For anyone who is too busy to read all 10 chapters, I am prepared to reveal here the single overarching factor that unifies all the information, reflection, stories, guidance and more that follow.

The thinking in this book is based one fundamental belief: the only way to be successful when you lead an organisation of any kind is to always put people at the heart of your growth strategy and day-to-day operational management.

I call my unique leadership approach 'Leadership with Soul'.

It is humanist. It is fair. It works. It is industry and scale-agnostic, equally appropriate for a global corporation as a small one-site hotel, a local government body, or a charitable association. And I believe it is what the world needs right now and into the future as we build back a better society.

Leadership with Soul will provide any leader with a systemic end-to-end approach that will unleash the full potential of any organisation and deliver sustainable results for all stakeholders with a highly engaged workforce.

To get the most from the thinking in this book, never forget that quote from Socrates at the top of this chapter – I never do: 'I am the wisest man alive, for I know one thing, and that is that I know nothing'.

What he was saying was deceptively simple: never stop learning. For leaders, this is particularly important. True leadership is the constant pursuit of perfection, and that means never being satisfied with what you think you know.

The 10 principles at the heart of Leadership with Soul – each the subject of a chapter of its own – will provide plenty to guide you and help you become a better leader every day.

But you will only get the most from them if you use them as a starting point, to help you learn more about yourself and what leadership really means in this incredibly diverse, complex and fast-changing world.

Leadership with Soul has been written for leaders who are willing to learn and change their leadership approach to address the fact that the biggest challenge the world faces today is the lack of Good Leadership in all parts of society.

It is not acceptable that close to 3 billion employees wake up every day to go to work disengaged!

It's not acceptable anymore that companies and organisations are underled and over-managed.

It's time for change.

It's time for Good Leadership.

Introduction
Leadership with Soul...
the early years

When I was a child, I had two great slices of good fortune. The first of these was that I grew up in the South of France in a small and beautiful town on the Mediterranean coast: 'la Grande Bleue', as we say in French.

It was in many ways an idyllic childhood, with much time spent playing on stunning local beaches during the summer and sailing on blustery seas for 12 months a year.

My second slice of luck came in the shape of my parents' values. They were strict with me and my sister particularly around working hard at school, practising sport on a regular basis and, of course, attending Mass every Sunday.

Just as important, they taught me how necessary it is to see and experience other ways of life, to gain an understanding of how people think, feel and act in different environments and new situations.

I'll never forget my first trip abroad with my family at the age of five, to a frozen Madrid at Easter in 1965. It was so different to anything I had seen before, and I remember it as if it were yesterday.

This was followed some years later after me living with a family in Wangen, Bavaria, for three months to learn the German language. And then, every summer until I was 21, my parents would send me to summer camps some-where in Europe to practice sports and learn German, English or Spanish.

These early experiences were vital to my becoming a citizen of the world, which has served me well throughout my career. I've learned to know my way in all parts of the planet, having lived in many countries, including Europe, the USA, the Middle East and Africa, having worked across all continents and having visited more than 120 countries.

Observing new situations never fails to boost my intellectual energy, and I've never stopped trying to learn about this fascinating world and the fascinating people that live in it.

Taking this open-minded approach very early on in my life has convinced me of one thing: that there is always a better way ahead in society, in business and in our personal lives.

It doesn't matter what you achieve, however great your accomplishments have been: there is always a better way to start all over again.

A humanist outlook

I was very young when I started to see my way ahead.

As a child, I was a committed humanist. I decided I wanted to spend my life helping people. I also believed that the best way to make a difference was to become a surgeon.

As far as I was concerned there was no better future for me than saving lives. So, when I reached the age of 14, I decided to study maths and physics, enabling me to get into the right university to become a doctor.

Then, at 18, I changed my mind – literally overnight. I saw there was an even better way to help the world. It happened like this. My school organised an after class careers event, where I and my fellow students could hear experienced women and men talk about their careers in a wide range of fields: lawyers, professors, doctors, scientists, sales executives, marketers, CFOs and CEOs.

For me, this was a life-changing evening. I was incredibly energised, talking to people from a range of backgrounds and organisations as they shared their passions and talked about their achievements.

One executive, in particular, made a deep impression on me. He was the CEO of a medium-sized business, and he was compelling company during the event that evening. In just a few minutes, he taught me how leading people was by far the most important aspect of his role in making his company successful. Not just today and tomorrow, but for the long term too.

So I had a lot on my mind when I went to bed on that warm spring night in 1978. By the time I finally awoke after a restless sleep, I had the clarity of thought I needed to come to a truly life-defining conclusion: that in reality the essential role of a leader is to achieve great things by taking people with you on the journey ahead.

I no longer wanted to be a surgeon. I wanted to be a businessman.

People: the key to sustainable success

That realisation was the launch-pad for a career that's been very different from that of most CEOs. A career in which I've been able to take a direct interest in all the major management disciplines, from marketing, finance and strategy to sales, organisational leadership and development, technology, corporate communications, board governance, risk management and sustainability.

It's given me first-hand exposure to managing start-ups and growing businesses, turnarounds, acquisitions, disposals and restructurings. And it's given me a great deal of experience across sectors, and industries, enabling me to identify leadership patterns and reflect on what works and what does not.

Today, I have been a CEO for more than 25 years. I've been lucky enough to work for and with some great companies in that time and I'm proud that I've delivered significant sustainable growth for all stakeholders and that I've been able to steer them through some challenging moments.

Euro Disney, during the collapse in tourist spending that followed the 9/11 terrorist attacks on New York.

Burger King Germany through the BSE crisis in 1996.

Global car distributor and retailer Inchcape, during the great recession of 2008/09.

And Intertek, the global assurance, inspection, product testing and certification company, as we all faced the biggest crisis in our lifetime, the COVID-19 pandemic.

In all those years, I haven't wavered in my belief that people and how they are led are the two essential factors in achieving sustainable success for organisations. This has always defined my approach as a leader, and it will continue to do so for as long as I am one.

In this time, I have deeply reconciled what I do for all stakeholders with the humanist side that is an essential part of my character.

In fact, having delivered strong earnings growth consistently and sustainably over many decades, I have discovered that my humanism is actually my strongest asset.

It took somebody else, a renowned German journalist called Gretel Weiss, to join those particular dots for me, pointing out that people follow me because I genuinely care for people. I knew immediately that she was right – and also that this was why I so enjoy achieving great things through people. I am enormously grateful for her insight.

But, as I look around at the corporate landscape and the teaching that's available for the leaders of tomorrow, I see little evidence that achieving great things through highly engaged employees is how leaders understand their role.

In fact, despite the enormous progress in the quality of life that so many people across the planet have experienced over the last 10, 30 or 50 years, I am convinced that most corporations are under led and therefore not unleashing their full potential, as evidenced by the Gallup survey on engagement.

Consequently, there is widespread mistrust of businesses, as the evidence of a 'me first' attitude among corporate leaders continues to reveal itself every day. All too often, the focus is sadly, on short-term shareholder value creation at the expense of other important groups, most particularly employees.

The penalty of failure to convert short-term gains into long-term, sustainable success for all is all too often borne by employees in the shape of job losses.

Good Leadership is clearly what's needed.

Learning from the ancients

When the ancient Greek philosophers were looking at the world a long time ago, their thinking was all about making the world ever better.

That's why I started this book with a quote from Socrates. Plato, his disciple, has also given a lot to the world, and I particularly love this quote. 'Good actions give strength to our self and inspire good actions in others'.

Plato was essentially expressing an enormously powerful way to define Good Leadership: it all starts with good actions from ourselves.

Another quote, that I maybe love even more, is from Pericles. It builds further on what Plato said. 'What you leave behind is not what is engraved in stone monuments, but it is what is woven into the lives of others'. For me, this says it all, and is more important than ever today as all corporations seek ways to make sure their organisations create truly sustainable value for all stakeholders.

Sustainability is the movement of our time. We all must do everything we can to protect the planet and make life better for the generations to come.

That's why every leader needs also to consider the sustainability of her or his actions as the most important aspect of Good Leadership.

Essential skills: engagement and motivation

I believe the 'leadership vacuum' problem starts at the universities and business schools where so many of the leaders of tomorrow go to learn essential skills.

Having looked at the programmes of all the leading institutions across the world, I believe that students today are not fully prepared to embrace all aspects of successful leadership when they finish their studies. The discipline being taught is all about the thinking activities of a leader.

This is important, of course, as it is necessary to understand what a strategic planning process is, what a marketing strategy is all about how financial policies work or what the architecture of an organisation should be.

But leadership is far more complex than these disciplines alone. A leader needs to develop and deliver a strategy through an engaged and motivated organisation.

This isn't touched upon in a deep and systematic way at the schools – and neither is it properly addressed by the training that companies provide for their own future leadership talent. Such training currently does not focus on a systemic, end-to-end approach to leadership that delivers sustainable value for all stakeholders for many years to come.

I have also read many books and articles on management and leadership over the years – and I've never found one that had the answers to help define what Good Leadership is all about. They are usually too narrow. They too fail to take a systemic approach to helping leaders deliver sustainable growth for all.

That's what this book aims to do.

In it, I describe my own leadership model, Leadership with Soul, which I've been developing over many years – since 2002 in fact.

Each chapter is devoted to one of the 10 principles that, when applied consistently, deliver superior and sustainable performance in any organisation, no matter its size, geography or business model. It could be a local restaurant or a bookshop, a charity or a non-profit organisation, a school or a global enterprise.

Leadership with Soul is anchored on the following 10 principles to help leaders deeply engage their people to unleash the full potential of their organisation – today, tomorrow and the day after tomorrow.

1. **Lead with emotional intelligence:** how do your employees feel when in the thick of it, both individually and collectively?
2. **Imagine the journey and paint the picture for all:** what is the direction of travel and the destination? Are these crystal clear to everyone?
3. **Energise the organisation to outperform:** how can you inspire the organisation to deliver high performance and eclipse the competition?
4. **Customer intimacy:** how do you create a truly customer-centric organisation?
5. **Reinvent the future:** what needs to be done to out-innovate your competitors?
6. **Master complexity:** how do you create the capabilities needed to deliver the growth agenda?
7. **Embody the strategy at the top:** how do you inspire people to follow the lead set at the top of the organisation?
8. **Laser-focused execution:** what is the most effective way to ensure excellent execution with zero defects?
9. **Ever better branding glo-cally:** how do you create and deliver the right communication strategy that balances global trends with local customer insights?
10. **Sustainable performance for all:** how do you ensure all stakeholders get the performance they're looking for?

These are the building blocks of a leadership model that reconciles the tension that can exist between the owners' or shareholders' interest in sustainable value creation and the employees' desire to make the business a better place to work.

This is fundamental: the organisation will only deliver the results shareholders want if employees feel great as they work towards those results. And this convergence between what employees and shareholders look for from a company has to be sustained for the long term.

Bad CEOs are usually interested in short-term results that make them look good. This soon becomes visible, and CEOs with a short-term mindset will never gain the trust or respect of their people or shareholders.

Good CEOs build to last, positioning the company for continuous growth in the future and delivering sustainable value for all stakeholders. And that takes leading the organisation with soul.

Becoming a Good Leader

It all starts with you, the leader.

Leadership is both thrilling and demanding.

The thrill of achieving great things through people is highly energising.

Leadership is very demanding and becoming a Good Leader takes time, determination and an open mind.

Good Leaders operate with strong values. They lead, based on an inspirational purpose that is meaningful for all.

Good Leaders are visionary and innovative entrepreneurs. They understand how to create sustainable value for all stakeholders.

Good Leaders put people at the heart of their growth strategy and day-to-day operations.

Good Leaders never stop challenging their own approach, asking themselves two simple questions no matter what they do and where they are every day:

Are we doing the right things to deliver our goals?

Are our people truly engaged to take the organisation forward?

In my experience, following the 10 principles that come together to form Leadership with Soul means you can answer 'yes' to both of these critical questions: the 'What' and the 'How'.

If you can say 'yes' one day, ask the same questions the next day. And as soon as you cannot, change something.

As I've already said, there is always a better way.

Socrates implied this more than 2,000 years ago: admitting that you know nothing shows far greater wisdom than never questioning what you are doing.

No one is perfect, and it is high time for many leaders to change the way they lead. We can no longer accept that 80% of the global workforce is disengaged at the workplace every day.

I hope the leadership model in this book will inspire those who are willing to learn and are ready to listen to their humanist side. That's the first step towards reinventing themselves and their organisations, enabling them to become Good Leaders and deliver sustainable value for all stakeholders.

Never stop training

Having worked continuously and vigorously on my leadership approach, I must confess that becoming a Good Leader is not easy.

It takes a lot of work, a very humble mindset and a major time commitment to work on your own leadership style, no matter how powerful or important you are in the organisation.

Applying these 10 principles every day with tenacity, consistency and a commitment to continuous improvement is essential.

And getting the balance right between the 'What' and the 'How' is where the secret of Good Leadership lies.

Good Leadership is like doing sport at the highest level. A leader, like an athlete, has to train hard to be fit for the ride.

Like sporting champions, Good Leaders are not born. They might have an intellectual or physical predisposition to lead others, but they also have to train and work hard if they want to get to the top of their game.

I have had the privilege to experience at first-hand what Good Leadership is and this is highly energising. Truly exhilarating.

Once you have become a Good Leader, it is like being a Formula 1 World Champion. You drive much faster than the competition because your team has built one of the fastest cars on the racetrack. And you know you can accelerate hard because you have full confidence in your team!

I also have learned that, just like in sport, once you have become a Good Leader, you never stop training hard to stay fit.

Becoming a Good Leader is a continuous journey. You never stop improving yourself.

The best way to take the world forward is to create progress and growth opportunities for everyone, starting with yourself!

Acknowledgments and thanks

One final word before you immerse yourselves in the 10 principles of Leadership with Soul.

Leadership with Soul is the project of my life and is meant to help any existing or future leader of any organisation – large, small, private, public, profit and non-profit – to become a Good Leader.

Leadership is a true privilege and is highly rewarding.

Good Leadership for the greater good of any organisation is also hard work and very challenging.

Leadership with Soul is a leadership model that has worked for me and I have written this book to inspire any leader to stop and think on how to become a Good Leader.

Said differently, Leadership with Soul is an invitation to reinvent and strengthen your own leadership style based on a cutting edge and systemic leadership approach that has created a lot of sustainable value for all stakeholders across multiple industries.

Leadership with Soul would not have been possible without all the fantastic colleagues I worked with at Ernst & Young, Colgate, Pepsico, Burger King, Diageo, The Walt Disney Company, Inchcape, Reckitt Benckiser and Intertek, who have inspired and energised me to become an ever better leader every day.

Many thanks to you all!

Leadership Principle 1
Lead with emotional intelligence

Chapter content:

- Recognise the importance of placing individuals at the heart of your strategy and operations.
- Lead your company using a decentralised and co-ordinated operating model that creates genuine empowerment.
- Shape a high-performance culture that embraces the values of Respect, Courage, Passion, Integrity and Responsibility.
- Lead by example to demonstrate emotional intelligence when interacting with people.
- Have the right antennae in place to ensure you never stop sensing the pulse of the organisation.

Too many business leaders don't give enough credit to the engagement of the people who work for them.

I've read many articles about CEOs over the last three or four decades, including interviews on the highs and lows of their careers.

In all that time, I've never come across a CEO who says, 'You know what, this venture failed because I didn't create the right level of engagement and energy behind my strategy'. Equally, I've almost never seen one say: 'The engagement of our people played a massive role in the success of the company'.

I find this extraordinary. In my view it's a key responsibility of the CEO and the senior team to make sure they create the right levels of engagement for success.

It's essential that leaders engage with their people on an emotional level.

Recognise the importance of placing individuals at the heart of your strategy and operations

I have already described in the Introduction the two questions I ask myself every day: 'Are we focusing the company on the right priorities to deliver our goals?' And: 'Are we sure we know how our employees feel?'

OK, this is pretty simplistic. But it's also a straightforward and effective way of making sure I never forget that people are at the heart of our growth strategy and day-to-day operational management.

All my observations of how CEOs and boards operate suggest that this approach is rare – and that's a shame. Every top team recognises that creating and delivering a strategy based on the right business plan is key. But the full impact of this strategy will never be unleashed unless they also put the right levels of motivation, alignment and energy behind it.

Not bringing your people with you, failing to involve them emotionally in the action (both individually and collectively), is incredibly damaging. Even the best strategy will achieve only a fraction of its potential for good. That means a lot of wasted effort and progress that never sees the light of day.

The problem is to do with how companies actually execute their strategy. Too often, they focus on organisational capability: looking at capital allocation processes, technology and people's talents. Capability alone, however, is not enough to drive sustained high performance.

You need to complement the capability of your operations with a high level of engagement inside the organisation. Of course, every successful organisation needs a good pay system (monthly, year-end and long-term) and personal growth opportunities, including attractive career-progression. But this is not enough.

The leadership's ability to inspire motivation, enthusiasm and energy throughout the organisation is mission-critical. This is where I think most companies fail to maximise their potential.

Quite simply, when developing and executing their strategies, CEOs and their senior teams often don't invest enough time in considering the people factor. This has something to do with the strategic planning process. Typically, while developing the content of a strategy or action plan (the 'what' as opposed to the 'how'), the senior team works largely in isolation. They focus on analysing data – both external, in the wider marketplace, and internal, within the boundaries of the company itself. And they spend a lot of time considering the financial implications of their strategies.

When it comes to thinking about the delivery stage (the 'how'), their focus is likely to be above all on technology investments. This is followed by process re-engineering, staffing plans, training needs, pay adjustments and more. But they don't give enough time and thought, in my view at least, to creating the right levels of motivation, alignment and energy behind the strategy. And this is a major failure.

Getting the people agenda right

When evaluating the success or otherwise of a strategy, many leaders tend to claim responsibility as long as the figures look good. But if there are performance issues, management will often look for external causes like market challenges and competitor activities, rather than admit to errors and quality failures.

In short, success has many fathers, failure is an orphan.

Most failures in business are not linked to having the wrong strategy. They are due to poor execution arising from not being able to engage and motivate everyone behind the strategy.

So, it's vital that CEOs and their top teams start to recognise the importance of getting the people agenda right to drive strategic success and avoid poor performance. They must recognise that while the leadership team is important, they are nothing without the support of a highly motivated, aligned and energised organisation. They need, in short, to be more humble.

And you know what? The actions involved in getting the organisation energised about the strategy are not complicated – provided you take a two-step approach.

In step 1, while developing the strategy, you have to create a process to engage the organisation. And then, in step 2, when executing the strategy, you must run a comprehensive internal communications programme. This will keep employees informed and engaged at every level, while gathering the ongoing feedback needed to keep the strategic process going. Every strategy can be improved as the strategic process will continue during the execution phase with the right engagement level.

Strategy development

Developing the strategy is always complicated. But one of its most important components – gathering insights from shareholders, trade partners, franchisees, customers and, above all, employees – is also a powerful part of creating the engagement process. It's extraordinary how much knowledge, understanding and insight you'll find at every level of the organisation. Every time a leader unveils a 'new' strategy, somebody always says: 'Oh, this makes total sense. Tracy in Accounts has been talking about it for years!'

The solution is simple. Use the actual process of gathering insights to engage your stakeholders throughout the organisation. Giving this engagement process the time and attention it deserves will not only provide concrete ideas to help your strategic thinking; it will also make your colleagues a key part of the strategy-development process. Doing so creates a tremendous sense of alignment, resulting in a boost of motivation and energy. It's a vital aspect of leading an organisation with EQ.

I know this. I've seen it first-hand, many times.

Then, when executing the strategy, putting a proper two-way internal communications programme in place is important. This is critical to sustaining and increasing levels of ownership, motivation and passion throughout the organisation, which will be the most powerful success factors behind your plans. Energising the teams to take action will involve a lot of time explaining the strategy's meaning and putting it in the right context. You will also need to make time to listen and gather feedback from everybody to make the strategy ever better, every day.

I'd like to give you a personal example of this sort of thinking in action. It was a key part of an immensely complex and daunting challenge I was asked to help resolve.

Multi-year innovation programme

I first met Michael Eisner, CEO of The Walt Disney Corporation, in 2002 in Los Angeles, where he told me the full story behind Euro Disney. He'd been present at the park's foundation many years before. And he was still extremely passionate about the incredible growth potential it had – if only it could overcome a number of short-term financial challenges. Naturally, I was tremendously excited by the opportunity to re-energise Euro Disney with a strong capital structure and a multi-year innovation programme.

When I arrived, the business was in a challenging financial situation. Partly owned by the Walt Disney Company and partly listed on the stock market, Euro Disney had quite a lot of debt and therefore was operating with a weak balance sheet. At that time, Euro Disney was suffering from the downturn in tourism that followed the 9/11 attacks, making the payment of its debts more difficult.

Euro Disney plays a major role in the economic vitality of the region in the East of Paris, being a major resort for holidays in France and Europe and of course, employing a large workforce. Said differently, it is a very high profile operation, being Europe's number one tourist destination.

Being a prominent operation means that whatever happens with the financial performance of Euro Disney, or inside its operations, is very public. That's why repositioning the company for sustainable growth financed by a balance sheet restructuring was not an easy task.

I was leading Euro Disney with an excellent team and together with the support of the Walt Disney Company, our banks and the French Government, we secured the third financial restructuring, which enabled us to finance a multi-year innovation programme to reposition Euro Disney for sustainable growth.

Our approach proved successful in restructuring and preparing the company for growth, while continuing to run a highly public entertainment business offering magic to every guest, every day. I believe there was one core reason for this success. We led Euro Disney with EQ.

It was the only way of responding successfully to the unique challenges involved in restructuring a highly public company. Negotiating with all stakeholders. Keeping everybody in the company motivated in the face of overwhelming media coverage and public interest. Everything I said as the CEO internally would immediately be reported externally. And everything I said externally would be studied closely by employees as I was regularly on TV, radio and in the newspapers, given the significant interest of all stakeholders in the future of Euro Disney.

So, this is what we said to our 12,000 employees (or 'cast members' as they are called at Disney): 'This is the situation. We cannot fix it alone. We're going to do it together, and we need your help to develop and deliver the strategy that will underpin the financial restructuring and re-energise Euro Disney for future growth.

'Here's the deal. If we develop the strategy together, we will invest in sustainable growth to take Euro Disney to greater heights. We'll build new attractions, launch new shows and start managing the business for future growth.'

We then tapped into the immense power of the 1,200 managers who ran the resort every day. We invited them to a breakfast session, where I asked each of them a very simple question: 'If you were in my position, and you had to make one single change to the resort strategy in the next 12 months, what would it be?'

Every manager responded, giving us an immediate diagnosis of the situation. But we couldn't take what they said at face value – the stakes were too high.

So, in parallel, the Marketing and Strategy departments carried out a fact-based analysis of the challenges involved in re-establishing growth.

Their diagnosis was remarkably close to the insights we received from the resort's 1,200 managers.

This was almost certainly the best piece of market research I've ever done. We had 1,200 individuals, all with first-hand knowledge and deep emotional investments in the business, each coming up with what they saw as the single most important issue for us to address and fix. From these, we identified the 10 largest problem areas we faced or, I should say, the growth opportunities we had.

It had given us the flying start we needed.

Then we decided to take employee involvement and engagement with our strategy to the next level. I wanted all 12,000 cast members also to have a say.

So, we did something that I don't think had ever been attempted before in the corporate world. We asked every single one of them to give us their thoughts, ideas and dreams relating to each of those 10 opportunity areas.

We came up with the idea during a senior-team brainstorming session. 'Why don't we organise a series of roundtables where people can talk them all through?' Roundtables for thousands of people? It was certainly audacious. And it was incredibly successful.

Much of this success was down to the company's culture. Disney cast members don't really see their jobs as work. They love what they do. They love telling stories to their guests, being part of the Disney magic. They care genuinely about their jobs and the company itself. And this was their chance to help secure its future.

We called the events 'Summer Camps', as they took place throughout August 2003. And more than half of our cast members – over 6,000 people – participated, either at a camp or via email.

As well as delivering fantastic insights and creative ideas, the programme injected a massive boost of energy and solidarity just at the time it was most needed. Because our cast members kept hearing in the news that their jobs were at risk, keeping energy levels constantly topped up was vital.

Vital, not just to develop and deliver the strategy, but also to put and keep our people at their very best, all day and every day. After all, we had around 30,000 guests every weekday, rising to around 60,000 at weekends. They were there for the magic. The last thing they wanted was to be bothered by our financial worries and uncertain future. It was more important than ever that the magic was delivered. And our cast members delivered brilliantly.

Astonishing creativity

Just as important, the Summer Camps were also the birthplace of most of the short and long-term strategic initiatives that spearheaded the relaunch of the resort and helped re-establish sustainable growth. The level of creativity and the commercial skills the Camps revealed were astonishing. For me, the experience proved that your loyal, passionate workforce is almost always the best place to look for fresh ideas.

Here are some of the ideas from the Summer Camps that we successfully implemented during the months and years ahead:

- The launch of the Hopper (called 'Passe-partout') that enables guests to visit both Euro Disney parks on the same day
- A new seasonal product strategy, designed to increase innovation during the tougher winter trading environment – this included a stronger focus on Halloween, for which we invented new characters including the Pumpkin Men
- A merchandising strategy that looks at every store independently for innovation and builds on the success of Disney's all-important shows
- An improved hotel and restaurant offering
- Many ideas for future attractions.

Perhaps the most important – and certainly most iconic – new idea was the relaunch of the Space Mountain ride, extending the journey it takes you on from the Moon to the very edge of our Galaxy.

Two-way communication

I was particularly impressed by how quickly the leadership team went back to all employees, with updates on the outcome of the Summer Camps and commitments to act on some of the ideas.

This was a vital part of the deal. The cast members had shown their commitment. Now it was the leadership's turn, showing real determination to turn the cast members' ideas into reality. So, the Summer Camps happened in August. All the short-term initiatives for implementation were identified by October. They were presented to cast members in November, leaving nobody in any doubt that we were committed to driving some quick wins. Over the next 18 months, we issued regular communication updates on the progress of all initiatives, large and small.

And then, in February 2005, we put together a vast internal communication and celebratory event, presenting to all 12,000 cast members the resort's attraction and innovation programme for the next three years. This was a very important moment in the history of Euro Disney. It marked the end of two years of restructuring and strategising, and the beginning of our multi-year innovation programme to re-establish and sustain growth.

Gathering ideas

But it was far from the end of my commitment to engaging people and staying in tune with the pulse of the organisation. This went well beyond Summer Camps. It included a programme of weekly breakfast meetings with 15 to 25 cast members, where I'd listen to their concerns, answer any questions – and, above all, hear about their ideas.

One week I'd meet up with the gardening teams. The next, it might be with the laundry department. And the one after that, I'd meet with people from the restaurants. I can't remember a single time when we failed to generate a good idea to continue to innovate and improve the experience of our resort for employees and guests.

Looking back, I can clearly see that we wouldn't have achieved all this if I and the leadership team had worked in isolation. Capturing the energy and creativity of our passionate cast members was fundamental. To achieve this, it was critical that we demonstrated, through everything we said and did, that we were totally committed to hearing what they had to say.

The restructuring of Euro Disney gave me the perfect opportunity to apply the first of my 10 leadership principles: that it's vital to engage employees in day-to-day operational management and the development of the growth strategy. It has to be real – people have to feel it. Get this right, and the benefits can be huge.

Lead your company using a decentralised and co-ordinated operating model that creates genuine empowerment

Around 99% of the success of any strategy lies in how it is executed. Because of this, the CEO must make sure that the organisational model is structured to address three important goals:

1. Delivering the right level of empowerment for management and employees.
2. Clarifying who is responsible for doing what.
3. Ensuring that the organisation gains the full benefit of scale.

To maximise performance, this empowerment needs to be as close as it can be to the organisation's front end: where it meets the real world. By being close to the market and customers, it will help employees make rapid decisions based on what will make the business more competitive and successful.

Frontline employees must be enabled to make decisions within a framework built on a set of clear rules and policies with a complete understanding who does what, as well as what are the risks and rewards. In other words, getting the balance right.

This approach works at many different levels to get the benefits of scale – globally, across regions, in individual countries and within local markets. It effectively structures the benefits of organisational scale while giving customer-facing individuals a true licence to make a difference.

This is the so-called 'glo-cal' organisational model – decentralised but co-ordinated. In my view, it is the most powerful model there is.

Empowerment and responsibility

Although an increasing number of companies have come to recognise the overwhelming importance of execution to strategic success, there is still a clear trend to operate a 'command and control' model.

In my view, this is the sign of an organisation that does not put its people at the heart of its strategy.

As a result, executives across the world remain frustrated by the need to listen to the output of micro-managed decision-making processes. Worse, these decisions come from headquarters that are sited thousands of miles from the realities that managers, employees and their customers across the world face every day.

Designing and building a glo-cal organisation can only start with the strong belief that empowering people with clear responsibilities will lead to better results. These happen automatically when people are truly at the heart of your thinking and you recognise that people are what make the essential difference when executing your strategy.

But that's not to say it's easy – far from it.

It is very easy to go too far, or not far enough. And it's all too easy to make the rules and policies designed to manage the related risks too lax or too restrictive. In short, it's very easy to get the balance wrong.

That's why – in addition to having the right people mindset at the top of the organisation – to get it right, you need a clear modus operandi with deep understanding of what is global and what is local.

Global versus local

This is a very important item on my personal agenda. At the time of writing, I lead an organisation, Intertek, with 44,000 employees across the world but fewer than 50 people in our global headquarters. The way I see it, roughly, is as follows.

There are several areas that need global alignment across all our operations. These include our global vision and purpose, our values, management accounts, policies, group priorities, scale investments, branding, financial communications and metrics.

Then there are areas that can only be local. These include individual market strategies, customer service, operational plans, people recruitment and training, local investments, product specifications, pricing and channel strategies, local communications and publicity.

Getting the balance right requires a very rigorous way of working, supported and enabled by crystal-clear communication that leaves no room for misunderstanding about responsibilities. This is essential for building a team that is motivated, aligned and empowered with clear responsibilities.

You will also need a precise process for managing glo-cal initiatives, particularly where global initiatives or synergies are to be locally managed and delivered.

This again is not easy. It can only work if the organisation's senior team dedicates management time to frame the glo-cal agenda precisely. This has to include a shared agenda with clearly defined responsibilities for development and implementation at a global or a local level.

Going glo-cal at Burger King

One illustration from my own career involves an operating model that didn't work, and how we changed it.

During the 1990s, Burger King underwent a massive re-engineering exercise that eradicated all country management structures. The company replaced these with a single centralised organisation, based in Miami. That was where functional heads ran their own policies and operations across the entire world.

So, everybody had to report to Miami. If you were a classroom trainer for Burger King Asia Pacific, you reported to somebody in Miami. If you ran a restaurant in Mexico City or Sydney, you reported to Miami. Likewise, if you were an accountant in London, a Quality Assurance person in Buenos Aires or a marketing professional in Munich.

The approach worked in the USA because this was just one country. Unfortunately, the system didn't work in the other 50 countries across the world where the company had restaurants but no general management.

You can imagine some of the challenges involved in running some 10,000 restaurants at this time, across multiple cultures and time zones, without any local or regional decision-making responsibilities. You can picture just how important decisions made by people with no relevant experience were received by the thousands of employees who had to implement them. You can empathise with the frustration of international senior management, whose lack of clout made it tough to attract attention from a global head-quarters that only ever had the time to deal with the very biggest problems. And you can sense how international franchisees must have felt as they tried and failed to communicate with the decision-makers based in Miami.

Overall, the system was a recipe for failure. And this was at a time when the company was struggling outside the USA with a lack of critical mass and very weak business fundamentals. At the end of 1995, the owners, Grand Metropolitan, recognised that this was not the way to build a strong international operation. They brought in local management.

I joined Burger King as General Manager of the German operation in September 1996. This was right at the peak of the first BSE crisis, which did so much damage to consumer trust in beef. I was a member of the newly created European management team, with the mandate from Grand Metropolitan to develop and deliver a truly glo-cal turnaround strategy.

This was based on the glo-cal organisation model I described earlier, looking at the benefits of scale within the European region.

First, we started developing comprehensive bottom-up country plans that addressed all local opportunities; and then we identified all pan-European initiatives where we could leverage the benefits of scale.

Getting everything to work wasn't easy at the time. Grand Metropolitan invested in the design and building of a new European management team with strong talents. Based on a clear, glo-cal modus operandi with laser-focused priorities, we did ultimately succeed in driving an exceptionally strong turnaround in the revenues and profits of all Burger King's European markets.

Formulating our plans

So, how did we do it? Most importantly, we invested a great deal of time in ensuring the highest possible standards of execution for all initiatives, both local and pan-European. This gave us the rigour we needed to ensure we benefitted as much as possible from strong local implementation and regional synergies.

Our secret weapon was identifying what was local and what was European, and then formulating a clear plan. David Williams, then president of Burger King Europe, Middle East and Africa, named the plan for Europe-wide initiatives 'The Value Delivery Programme'. Its work streams covered all the most important areas of the business, from quality to restaurant development, training to innovation, financial management to marketing. The milestones and metrics in place enabled us to track the performance of each initiative. And we ensured these metrics and reporting tools were aligned so we could track and compare performance in every market.

The European management team also met each month to review progress and discuss next steps. One of the most crucial success factors was that each initiative had its own champion on the team, comprising country general managers and functional heads. Sharing an agenda between line and functional managers every month helped create a very positive team spirit.

These efforts collectively turned around our performance. Soon the European division was the star of Burger King worldwide, with outstanding acceleration in like-for-like sales, highly efficient restaurant development, excellent margin improvement, double-digit profit growth and the market's best value proposition for franchisees.

Powerful and effective glo-cal initiatives that sprang directly from the Value Delivery Programme were directly responsible for this turnaround. They enabled Burger King in Europe to enter the 21st century with much stronger fundamentals.

Wide-ranging initiatives

These initiatives were wide-ranging. For example, we achieved millions of savings and synergies in purchasing, simply by putting our volumes together. And we did this while upgrading product specifications. In advertising and marketing, we made a return to product-based advertising focused on superior taste and food innovation. We created a new way of developing the restaurants with lower capex and a faster route to market. And we brought forward a strong pipeline of product innovations across all categories – sandwiches, fries, finger food and desserts.

Perhaps the star initiative was a back-to-basics operational quality programme called 'Make Every Bite Right'. I still think this is one of the most powerful quality programmes I've ever been involved in. With that name, it was obvious to everybody working in our restaurants what it was about. It helped us to open people's minds, to remind them that the Whopper is the world's best-tasting burger – provided it's built correctly. So, we were saying, 'Why don't we spend a little time together to retrain everyone on how to make a Whopper, and how to cook our fries?' And the results, first in quality and consequently in sales and customer loyalty, were remarkable.

These are typical examples of what can be achieved by getting your glo-cal organisational model right. This example is Europe-wide – but it doesn't have to be. You might be running a global company, a country or a department – the same principles always apply.

Getting the balance right

The Burger King turnaround would never have happened if we hadn't taken an approach that was both decentralised and co-ordinated. If it had been entirely decentralised, the individual markets would never have had the strength alone to deliver against their short-term turnaround needs and address certain strategic issues. If it had been entirely centralised, it would have been impossible to achieve strong local performance while building effective initiatives with pan-European impact.

It is hard to get this right. There is always a tension between global and local agendas. I have often seen shareholder value being destroyed when global programmes are implemented blindly, when there is no understanding of local market opportunities or when individual management teams only consider local interests.

So again, it's all about balance – recognising the strength of local empowerment combined with the benefits of teamwork and economies of scale. And all based on a shared agenda and a collective ambition. What we delivered at Burger King clearly shows what can be achieved when you get it right.

Shape a high-performance culture that embraces the values of Respect, Courage, Passion, Integrity and Responsibility

People often call a company's culture its DNA, or the glue that holds it together. For me, it's more than that.

It is the people-based energy you can draw on to fuel sustainable growth. It is how organisations make things happen through people, driving every bit of performance every day. And it's based on a set of strong values: Respect, Courage, Passion, Integrity and Responsibility.

Respect

It is important for everybody, particularly a leader, to feel and show respect towards a range of factors: the needs of a situation, the local environment, wider, more global considerations and, above all, other people.

Without respect, it is hard to be an effective team member or player. That's because having respect is about being open about your limitations and recognising the scale of the challenges you face. It means you should always be looking for the help of others. Don't try to go it alone.

Many otherwise successful individuals struggle with the need to depend on other people, simply because over the years they've been taught to be confident. That is certainly important – but only once you've done all your homework, sought advice, talked to your stakeholders, read research materials and generally opened up your mind to the outside world.

Until that point, confidence is nothing more than misplaced pride.

For me, finding the balance between confidence and respect takes fine judgement. It takes recognising that you may know a great deal, but that there is still much to learn – much as Socrates said all those thousands of years ago. Taking this approach certainly helps me to judge every situation I come across with respect. And this enables me in turn to ask for help and to value the input of other people.

In France in the early 1980s, there were only a few companies that you absolutely had to work for to get a blue-chip training and maximise your personal growth opportunities.

Once I graduated from ESCP, I joined Colgate and took a position in their marketing department. At the time, some of the big focus areas among marketers were brand positioning, advertising and innovation. As a result, marketers largely ignored the fundamental importance of the trade – and consequently the sales team who actually sold to retailers.

There was a bit of arrogance around. Product managers, with great business schools behind them, really seemed to think they were set to change the world, prioritising strategy over execution.

I believed they were not talking enough to the right people – they weren't talking to those in the factories or the salespeople who were actually doing the work. Just as important, they were reading research rather than talking to consumers. So, I took a different approach.

I spent roughly a third of my time out in the field. I talked to the sales teams, gaining an understanding of how they were selling brands like Colgate and Ajax into retailers and the trade. I also spent a lot of time with consumers – I became known as the marketing manager who did most consumer interviews himself, pounding pavements and looking for answers to my questions from the people who actually bought our products.

I found this approach tremendously helpful. And it was based on the respect I had for what consumers were thinking, how the trade viewed our brands and what was the day-to-day experience of our own teams in our factories.

Certainly, whenever I wanted to launch a new product, I had the complete support of the sales team. They knew I was on their side and that I was never going to launch a new product without their input.

It was an early example of how I've always tried to lead with EQ.

Courage

The corporate world needs to be considerably stronger when it comes to courage. How many hours are wasted in pointless discussion, simply because people are not brave enough to share their opinions or to take a risk?

It's a vitally important quality. It means not just having the courage of your convictions, but also being prepared to take risks when the prize is big enough.

One of the many great leaders I worked with at Burger King was our CEO, Dennis Malamatinas. He used to simply say, 'you can't make an omelette without breaking eggs.' It's so true.

Creating a culture that values courage and risk taking is essential to drive performance and compete harder than the opposition. It has a positive impact on so many levels. This starts with an ambitious vision that will stretch your organisation and your people to perform at their best. It helps to define the boldness of the goals you and your people are prepared to go for. And it has to do with the level of creativity in your innovation processes that clearly differentiates your organisation from its competitors.

There's more. Courage is also the quality that means you can support your people when times get tough. In my view, once you've decided who is on your team, unless and until you change your mind, you should simply never let them down. You need to recognise how and when to step in to help them manage any challenges they face.

Another exceptional person from my Burger King days, Sten Magnus, the CEO of Burger King Norway, had something to say about this: 'Leadership is like helping your kids to walk. It's not about holding hands. It's about showing the way and giving them confidence to start walking on their own. If you don't help as a leader, if you don't have the courage to offer support when people are facing difficult challenges, then you're not really leading at all.'

Having courage is incredibly important too when you're trying to fully understand a problem or an opportunity. Many years ago, at business school my Marketing Professor Christian Michon taught me that if you don't get this right at the planning stage, you're unlikely ever to achieve what you're aiming for. You need to have the courage of peeling the onion several times to challenge the current views and define the problem or the opportunity properly.

Many years later, this still affects how I work every day. The principle is simple: never leave a situation or a meeting without getting everything off your chest. That's how to make sure the awareness of a problem or challenge is clear and shared. This is always the first step towards finding a solution.

This does take courage – both in being prepared to identify the true nature of a problem, and in being direct with your communication. Overall, I'm certain that raising problems early means finding solutions more quickly. That's best for everybody. So, a direct, courageous communications style with the right level of EQ is vital in helping organisations be visionary, innovative, intrepid and bold.

Passion

I define passion as the positive energy that helps drive people to achieve or exceed their goals, overcome challenges and consistently excel at everything they do. It's a quality that lends itself to communicating in a way that inspires people. It can rally and unify people behind the company's vision, motivating them to push harder and show your organisation at its very best. It can also have a huge external impact, conveying a good corporate or brand image to attract customers and encourage further communication.

Passion is important for every business. But it's mission-critical in the retail and service industries, where the quality of an offering depends so much on how employees and customers interact. The passion of front-line employees is often all that separates an exceptional customer experience from an utterly dreadful one.

To maximise passion at every level within an organisation, you need to start at the very top. Leaders must be passionate at every point where they interact with the organisation. They must be energised, they must be confident. There is no place for a public display of cynicism or lack of conviction.

This is just as true when your audience is external. Passion communicates itself. People respond to it positively. And that can be incredibly powerful – particularly if those people are in positions of seniority and influence that can help you achieve your own agenda.

During the challenges involved with restructuring Euro Disney, I knew it was important to ensure opinion leaders in Paris understood what we were trying to achieve. I used my own passion for the project to inspire their support. This was easier with Disney than with many brands. Everybody owns a little bit of Disney. It's a major part of the fabric of our childhoods, and those of our own children. Everybody is affiliated.

So, when I arrived in Paris in 2003, many opinion leaders were keen to meet with me. They wanted to see if they felt I had the passion they believed the project deserved. And no matter how busy I was, I'd make time to meet with them – journalists, academics, sportspeople, pop and movie stars, chefs – anybody, in fact, who created a buzz in Paris and who were important in building the right external support for Disney.

And, of course, politicians. I won't name names, but I would like to say that the personal support of one particular individual was immensely helpful to me. Without it, and without the doors that opened as a result, the restructuring would have taken far longer and cost much more.

Never forget, you might meet the right individual to help you at any moment. Share your passion, and it will create opportunities. Never stop showing your passion to every single stakeholder you come across – you never know what you might get in return. As a leader, it's your duty to convey your absolute belief in what you're doing. It's a vital feature of leading with EQ.

Integrity

To me, integrity means always saying what you mean and always doing what you say. It's a very tough principle to follow. And it's non-negotiable. Anybody who wishes to retain my trust and support has to act with integrity at all times.

First and foremost, it means being entirely honest with yourself. I try to apply that belief to my own actions as much as I expect others to live by it.

Day-to-day, behaving with integrity means finding a way to say what you really mean in any given situation, no matter how complex or compromised it might be. And it means taking whatever action you have promised in the best way you can think of. It's about making tough decisions when you have to.

It's also about leading by example, and not abusing your position of power and influence. It's about recognising your own mistakes, publicly accepting responsibility for them and any damage that may result – acknowledge, apologise and move on.

For a leader, integrity also means being honest and open with all your audiences about what is going on within your organisation. That means customers and employees, the markets and media, shareholders and board colleagues. So be consistent. Whoever you're talking to, always reflect the way it truly is. Never, EVER lie.

I believe that achieving this level of integrity is critical to creating trust and loyalty in an organisation. It is simply not possible to have a high-performance culture without it.

You don't have to look far to find the impact a lack of integrity can have. It's like a virus – once you've found it, you have to try to eradicate it as quickly as possible. It can be as apparently minor as fiddling travel expenses, accepting gifts from customers in contravention of company policies, or getting an assistant to undertake personal tasks for you. Or it can be as major as misrepresenting the results of research or using privileged information for personal gain.

The level of misdemeanour, however, shouldn't influence a leader's response to any breach. It's all about trust and character. And it's entirely non-negotiable. Any acceptance of wrong-doing puts the integrity of the whole organisation at risk.

Clearly, I cannot share examples publicly of times when I've had to deal with integrity issues. Typically, they end with contract termination. But I can tell you, over the years there have been many instances when I've had to move fast, as soon as the facts became available. It's the only way to remove the risk of the virus spreading.

Responsibility

The fifth value that I believe should be at the heart of every high-performance culture is responsibility. This is the factor that ensures organisations act in the right way to meet the expectations of all stakeholders, including customers and suppliers, employees and regulators, communities and shareholders.

Leadership is a true privilege and a huge responsibility. It brings with it the duty to help all stakeholders achieve their ambitions. So, in my view Leadership with Soul must reflect the grand responsibility we all have to achieve the best for society.

It doesn't matter what sort of organisation you lead – a team, department, a local subsidiary of a global company, a local restaurant, a supermarket, a hospital, a community association. But can you imagine just how much better the world could be if all leaders started working on their leadership style with a shared aim? The aim of delivering sustainable performance for all by making the work environment a better place.

Leading a company into the future is highly energising – and certainly very rewarding. But it is also our responsibility to take our organisations from A to B based on more than just a clear vision and strategy. It must also be based on the responsibility to achieve sustainable performance for all stakeholders.

Sustainability is the only way to define the successful legacy of any leader. Quite simply, sustainability equals legacy.

Lead by example to demonstrate emotional intelligence when interacting with people

Demonstrating the values I have just discussed will certainly distinguish you as an individual. They are very important behavioural assets. Possessing them will make it easier for you to become a person people will respect and respond to positively.

On their own, however, they are not enough to make you a successful leader.

That requires the ability to take people with you, to follow the way you've charted and join you on a journey. A true leader needs to be able to interact highly effectively with the organisation and the individuals within it. And that's why leaders need emotional intelligence.

Some people are born with high levels of EQ as a natural gift. But there are also many, many instances of highly successful leaders who've had to learn it, sometimes pretty much from scratch. I am an example of somebody to whom it hasn't come entirely naturally, and I've had to work at learning it.

Fortunately, in my experience at least, doing so is not especially difficult. It's all about getting your communication style right: being sensitive to the needs and interests of other people – their mindset, situation, ambitions, levels of confidence, self-esteem. In every situation, it's about always thinking of the other people involved when you want to achieve your goals.

It's also about constantly seeking feedback. This gives you the self-awareness you need to ensure you understand whether or not you're being sensitive to the other person's needs, interests, issues and points of view.

Learning from other leaders is a great opportunity as you work on your own emotional intelligence when interacting with people. Over the years, I have seen great examples of EQ and of course bad ones. I have experienced first-hand how a highly emotionally intelligent leader can create tons of energy in the workplace. Unfortunately, I have also experienced how a low EQ conversation with a leader can destroy engagement.

Get these elements of an EQ-based communication style right, combine them with that strong set of values, and you'll have a powerful set of tools capable of making you a highly effective leader.

Early on in my career, I worked for Colgate in Germany, which was a highly successful operation. The Sales Director of the Household division taught me so much about how to demonstrate emotional intelligence when interacting with people. His best performance was always the annual sales conference and his speech was always incredibly energising. After having read the written remarks prepared by his team, he would keep the microphone for longer than expected and stand in front of his people giving a second speech – the real high energy one! The second speech was truly exhilarating as he was speaking genuinely from his heart, putting his people first in everything he said. That's what leading with EQ is! Speak from your heart, putting your people first.

The self-awareness challenge

For me, the hardest aspect of developing my own EQ was that of self-awareness. It can be extremely difficult. I for one find this the single biggest challenge involved in being a leader. I'm sure I'm not alone in that.

Fortunately, there are many ways of improving your self-awareness. Over the years I have used several approaches. For example, I have found the 360° feedback tool to be pretty useful. As well as self-evaluation, this involves gathering feedback on your performance from people above you, below you and at your own level in the organisation. The feedback can be hard to accept sometimes, although I believe the hardest way can often be the best way of building self-awareness.

I have also worked with two excellent coaches during my career, Darrel Poullos and Gurnek Bains. I found this really useful straightaway. We started the process with a detailed discussion of my existing strengths and the areas that needed the most work in my leadership style. We then moved on to develop a comprehensive personal plan, including short and long-term goals for my own development.

We met regularly to adjust my personal growth plan as priorities changed, and to talk through specific situational challenges. I found this incredibly useful, as I could use real-life situations as a basis for developing new ways to improve my leadership skills.

I find the most interesting thing about coaching is how it enables you to come up with the solutions that best suit you, your style and personality. A coach is not a consultant who gives you the answers. Rather, they ask you questions and provide you with some perspective on any given situation. That really makes you think.

I am a busy person, but I have always worked hard to continue learning from challenging situations. And I always take time to reflect on what skills I need to develop further and how I can improve my impact on the organisation. Almost invariably, EQ factors are central to this thinking. I'm continuously asking for feedback and taking notes that I can use whenever I want to stop and think about my leadership style.

Have the right antennae in place to ensure you never stop sensing the pulse of the organisation

Leading an organisation, no matter its size, invariably means there are many demands on your time and your attention. As a result, once you and the leadership team have established the vision, the strategy, the policies and the processes, there's always a danger you'll lose touch with the realities of the organisation and its people.

You've done all that hard work – engaging your people in strategy development, involving them in execution, setting up two-way communications channels, creating the glo-cal organisational model and embedding values to unleash a high-performance culture.

This is a very dangerous moment. And it comes precisely when leading with EQ means you should be most aware of how the organisation is feeling. So it's essential that you have in place the 'antennae' to take the pulse of the organisation and understand its people.

It starts, of course, with those two questions I mentioned at the beginning: 'Are we focusing the company on the right priorities to deliver our goals?' And: 'Are we sure we know how our employees feel?'

Sensing the pulse

Regular engagement surveys and company events where two-way communication can take place are useful tools for taking that pulse. But, as a leader, you need to maximise the number of antennae.

One very effective way is to identify people throughout the organisation, at all levels and in all geographies, who naturally sense the pulse of the organisation. Tony George, Executive VP of HR at Intertek, and who worked previously with me at Burger King and Inchcape, is incredible at sensing the pulse of the organisation 24/7. At the time of writing, I've been working with Tony for almost 25 years. During this time, we've developed an extremely effective way of communicating: no matter where either of us is in the world, we'll talk two or three times a day. We use our regular catch-ups to exchange insights and discuss how people are feeling inside the company. It's given me great insights into the pulse of the organisation when I'm in the thick of the action, helping me to sharpen my own thinking.

Having relationships of this sort will certainly give you a great advantage in leading with EQ.

To get the full picture at its sharpest, the process needs to be first-hand. Face-to-face meetings and market visits are important to check how the business is performing. But it is informal events and chats that will get you closer to its pulse and other vital signs. This is why, in all my managerial and leadership roles since I started work in 1983, I've done my best to spend at least half my time away from my own office, talking to people.

Nothing is better than a face-to-face meeting. Sure, you'll get your share of PowerPoint presentations, but you're likely to learn far more from what's being said and by reading body language. Informal meetings on the shop floor or when visiting the trade are very important too, as they'll give you real insights into what's going on and what people are really thinking and feeling.

I also organise town-hall events whenever I visit a market, updating people on progress and giving them the chance to ask questions. And I always find informal dinners and drinks with colleagues extremely useful. People are always happier than in an office setting to let you know what they really think.

Now, I am writing this during the time of COVID-19. The pandemic has clearly put tremendous pressure on leaders across the world, who had to learn an entirely new style of leading remotely.

I was one of the lucky ones. Before COVID-19, I'd spent at least half my time travelling for many years, which means I was really well connected with everyone inside the Intertek organisation. So, when it happened that we could only communicate remotely, it was easy for me to stay connected with key colleagues and remain closely in touch with our culture and our people.

Leading remotely for almost two years, I was also able to tell how people were truly feeling by hearing their tone of voice on the phone. It's the main benefit of travelling frequently: you get to know the character, the emotions and the behaviours of your key people extremely well.

In a time of crisis, with a high proportion of people working from home, regular communication is more important than ever to maintain and strengthen a passionate, customer-focused culture. For a leader, this goes far beyond talking regularly with the senior team and regional leadership. It's also vital to reach everybody in the organisation, recognise their efforts and mark their successes. For a global business, this requires a world-class digital communication platform. Above all, it demands the commitment and will of the leader to continuously support and be in contact with every employee.

Clearly, the need for remote leadership has imposed huge changes and constraints on how we work. This need for change has been particularly intense in communication. Before the pandemic I used to make two videos each year to help people understand where we are, where we've come from and where we are going. During the first six months of COVID-19, I greatly intensified this. Every Sunday, I would record a personal message for everybody, giving them a sense of what happened during the previous week.

I think this shows that leading with EQ is something you have to reinvent continuously. You must challenge yourself, using new tools and processes to deliver more frequent and high-impact personal messages that can deliver more energy and engagement for everybody.

So, however you do it, make an effort to spend quality time with your team members. It is a huge time commitment – but for me it is the right way to truly lead with EQ. Without this effort, it would certainly be much more difficult for me to be an effective leader.

Key points from this chapter:

- If you don't put people at the heart of your growth strategy and day-to-day operations, you cannot lead with EQ. That's because EQ is all about achieving great things through people.
- To create genuine empowerment, it's vital to build a decentralised and well co-ordinated operating model that empowers people close to the customer to make decisions in line with policies set at the highest level.
- It's essential to shape a high-performance culture that embraces the values of respect, courage, passion, integrity and responsibility.
- You have to continuously demonstrate your EQ through interacting with people and leading by example.
- And you need always to have the right antennae in place and to sense the pulse of the organisation at all times.

Leadership Principle 2
Imagine the journey and paint the picture for all

Chapter content:

- Do your homework to determine the size of the prize for all stakeholders.
- Articulate a simple vision that clearly defines the destination and is both inspirational and meaningful for all stakeholders.
- Develop a well-integrated communication plan that will paint the picture for all stakeholders.
- Invest personal time to communicate the vision with passion and conviction.
- Repeat, Repeat, Repeat.

As you will have gathered by now, tapping into people's emotions has a fundamental role to play in the humanist, people-centred approach that I bring to leading organisations.

Too often, in my view, the answer to an all-important question – 'What is the direction of travel, and what is the destination of the journey for everybody?' – is delivered in an entirely rational way.

This is a shame. The start of a journey is a highly emotional moment. And the question gets right to the heart of your role as a leader. You're here primarily to take your organisation from point A to point B, ensuring that this journey and its destination benefit all stakeholders.

So, you need to bring excitement, meaning, personal conviction and some real drama to your answer to that all-important question. If you fail to inspire your stakeholders, you won't bring them all along with you. When you imagine the journey ahead, it's therefore vital that you paint it with vibrancy and energy in a way that you can communicate to everybody when you share the pictures in your mind.

And the more people you take with you, the more opportunities you will have to make the world a better place for everybody.

This is why the word 'visionary' contains such a strong element of inspiration.

And it's why formulating a vision is about so much more than merely applying a rational approach to explain the opportunities ahead. Of course, it means being really clear about where you're going. Just as important, you must ensure that everybody you want to reach is truly excited and galvanised by the opportunities ahead.

That group of people extends far beyond your immediate team to include the many other stakeholders, both inside and outside your organisation, you want to take with you – including those opinion leaders I touched on in the last chapter.

Do your homework to determine the size of the prize for all stakeholders

Anyone who has worked with me will have heard me talk about 'the size of the prize'.

Put simply, this is about doing our homework to establish the scale of the opportunity that exists to take the organisation to new heights for all its stakeholders.

Except it's not simple at all.

Understandably, there is enormous emphasis at business schools, in management books, in training courses and in global corporate research, about how having a vision for growth is a key imperative for a business to grow successfully in a sustainable way.

There is widespread agreement that the vision needs to be more than a strategic statement or an aspirational goal. It should also be based on a long-term, well-orchestrated plan that is clearly stretching yet deliverable.

But where it gets really complicated is when you look at defining the opportunity that's at the heart of the vision – identifying the growth levers that, when properly pulled, will unleash the company's true potential. That takes real commitment and effort, which can take months of concentration and analysis to get it absolutely right. This is what I mean by quantifying the size of the prize: properly identifying the opportunities before you progress to defining and vocalising the vision for your business.

This work has to be done and has to be right. Too many companies and departmental teams regularly waste time, energy and money on trying to fulfil a vision that's based on flawed research and analysis. This happens when they have miscalculated the size of the prize.

Unleashing the full potential of your business

To avoid the risk of this happening on your watch, your approach must include qualitative and quantitative elements that bring together numbers and other hard data with the views of your stakeholders. This is where the secret lies – determining the full potential of your business based on disciplined quantitative analysis alongside a rigorous and deep assessment of all stakeholder interests.

For a leader, there is no alternative to doing this yourself: only you and your leadership team can quantify the size of the prize. You are in a unique position, right in the flow of the business. Your understanding of your business is unique in its depth and its breadth. You must gather everything you need through first-hand insights based on market forces analysis and interviews with all stakeholders, because you're the one who will be developing the strategy and leading its execution.

And you must be prepared for this process to take as long as it takes. Joining the dots can take a very long time, because you'll come across multiple bends and even switchbacks in the road. Sometimes you uncover a data point or come across an insight that at first sight seems important. But how can you be sure? You must constantly question, challenge and check your facts, to peel through every layer of the onion. The stakes are too high to take anything for granted. And there will be multiple times when the easy option is not the right one to take.

When it comes to data analysis, differentiating real insights from non-essential points can be particularly difficult. In my experience, you need to find a way of gaining a clear and critical focus on external market factors such as consumer and trade channels, as well as relevant intelligence with emerging and established competitors.

To do so, I recommend talking to people – anyone with a vested interest in your ecosystem, including employees, suppliers, customers, shareholders, analysts and board members. Talking to a wide range is vital, as every group will have its own perspective and set of incentives to help you. Only in this way can you get a complete picture of the situation. And then you have to apply your own judgement.

So, what does this homework look like in practice? Here are a couple of examples.

Delivering a structural fix

When I joined Euro Disney in 2003, the tourism crisis following 9/11 and the start of the Iraq War was in full flow. This was creating a huge slowdown in European demand for short breaks, resulting in very weak trading in 2003. The tourism crisis had hit the traffic of the theme park as Euro Disney was not immune to the decline in the European short-stay market. In addition, the recently opened Walt Disney Studios – a second park created to increase length-of-stay – was not delivering on its business plan despite the investments we had made.

When announcing the restructuring, I committed to my team, to our shareholders and to myself that this was not going to be just a short-term fix. I was determined that it had to be truly structural – it couldn't just be a Band-Aid for a few months, followed by crossed fingers that attendance would grow again by magic.

This meant that whatever we did had to be structural to deliver sustainable growth. We needed to make sure that the refinancing would provide the funds necessary to invest in initiatives that would reposition Euro Disney to drive growth for many years into the future.

Although identifying the opportunity seems easy in hindsight, it wasn't at the time. When you are leading the operation day-to-day, it's all too easy to get overwhelmed by multiple discussions and viewpoints, trying to work out who's right, who's wrong and how to tell the difference between the two.

So, we had no choice. We had to roll up our sleeves and do everything possible to find a viable solution that worked.

An investment of time

Doing so took six months. That's a long time when you are facing liquidity issues and people are impatient for change, continuously asking you, 'Where are you going with this?' But we had to take our time – talking to all stakeholders was fundamental to getting it right, and there were many groups to cover. I mentioned in the last chapter how we approached the cast members through the Summer Camps, listening to 12,000+ employees on one site. Although this was critical in designing the strategy and keeping people's energy at boiling point, it was far from the only source of inspiration as we worked hard to identify the true value of the Euro Disney opportunity.

I was able to draw on the Walt Disney Company's worldwide experience, regularly consulting intensively with board members, key managers, previous Euro Disney executives and all relevant opinion leaders in Paris that I could identify. During this time, I talked to anybody who had a point of view on the situation.

There is one group of people I would really like to thank all these years later. This is a large group of heartfelt Disney fans, who as long ago as 2003 already ran their own social media platform. Members were from both inside and outside the company, and this combination of their passion and insider knowledge meant they knew more about Disney than anybody else. They gave me continuous input as I looked for the right answer.

I got a lot of ideas from engaging all relevant stakeholders. But, even with all this help, I didn't find what I was looking for – the distilled essence of the opportunities facing us.

I was initially disappointed, but I wasn't dismayed or dispirited. I knew that this might happen. And talking to people is only half the process, the qualitative element. So, I went back to one of my favourite hobbies – looking at data from every possible angle, trying to reveal trend patterns and gaining insights that would be useful to understand.

The broad-based qualitative analysis was quickly followed by an end-to-end quantitative analysis that I did with Bertrand Mallet, who was in charge of the strategy for Euro Disney and who played a major role in helping reposition Euro Disney for growth.

Peeling the onion

First of all, we looked at the competition. This included making visits to all the theme parks we were now competing with. Euro Disney had been the continent's first big theme park. By this time, however, there were major parks in Spain, Germany, the UK, the Netherlands, Italy and other countries. They had all been watching the Disney approach and had learned precisely what it took to create family entertainment.

Critically, we found that the most successful of these new competitors were all operating strategies based on product innovation, regularly launching new attractions and continuously growing visitor numbers. Disney had created the theme-park market in Europe many years previously and was focusing its sales and marketing activities largely on increasing the existing customers' length of stay.

Our second key finding was that while extending the length of stay would be beneficial, it was not the main source of growth to unleash the resort's full potential. Euro Disney was, we found, still in its market-penetration phase. Consumer awareness of the resort was extremely high, but millions of families had not actually visited it. So, there was still a vast market of potential first-timers which we were not targeting with our sales and marketing activities. We were not maximising the return on the investments we had made.

Our third finding was at least as significant: once consumers had made their first visit, the exceptionally high levels of customer satisfaction (the highest I had ever seen) meant they were likely to return several times.

The answer was clear. We had to focus the product, sales and marketing strategies on the first-timers, opportunity to truly unleash our potential and capture the huge size of the prize in the European short-stay tourism market.

Clarifying the way ahead

At last, we had clarity. When I arrived, the new Walt Disney Studios concept was being criticised internally and externally for failing to grow visitor numbers. We had shown that this was not where the problem was. Rather, the true size of the prize had not been fully identified as the main opportunity consisted in convincing the first timers to visit Euro Disney, knowing that they would come back and increase their lengths of stay given the incredibly high level of customer satisfaction.

And without doing our homework, we would never have realised this.

Now our way ahead was obvious. The Walt Disney Studios development was a great new attraction for repeat visitors and to extend the length of stay. But it wasn't what first-timers were looking for. They wanted to feel the Disney magic: the Castle, Mickey Mouse, Pirates of the Caribbean and Space Mountain. And, because the competitive environment had changed, Euro

Disney couldn't sit back and rely on established attractions. Innovation from the core was required, in ways that were directly connected to the Disney magic.

This realisation gave us the backbone of the investment programme we built capitalising on the funds we would get access to with our refinancing strategy. A multi-year 'innovation-from-the-core' programme with a focus on delivering the world's best family entertainment targeting the huge first-timers opportunity was the strategic answer on how to reposition Euro Disney for sustainable growth.

In short, we brought all our attention back to what made Disney so successful, so important to people, so magical in the first place. So the first thing we did when I was sure about the problem definition was to find a way to bring back some magic to the Disneyland Park to get additional business as quickly as possible, before finalising our refinancing.

And we had some fantastic franchises to work with. For example, I realised pretty much straightaway that there was no Lion King show in the theme park.

So, in August 2004, we launched a 20-minute Lion King experience, short enough to hold kids' attention, long enough to tell the whole story.

This was just one of many innovations we rolled out in that incredibly exciting period, with the full support and understanding of all stakeholders. It was an amazing time that laid down the strategy and vision for the success of Disneyland Resort.

Achieving clear differentiation

Not all the businesses I have led had the massive brand awareness of Disney and Burger King. As I write Leadership with Soul, I am CEO of Intertek, a London-based global company with a long and distinguished background in testing, inspection, certification and assurance. In fact, one of its founding fathers was Thomas Edison, inventor of the phonograph, motion-picture camera, the first commercially viable light bulb and many other world-changing devices.

Today, Intertek is a leading Total Quality Assurance (TQA) provider to industries worldwide. Listed on the London Stock Exchange and a constituent of the FTSE 100 index, Intertek's network of more than 1,000 laboratories and offices in more than 100 countries, delivers innovative and bespoke

Assurance, Testing, Inspection and Certification solutions for its customers' operations and supply chains. It adds value to their products and processes, making their brand stronger in the global marketplace and helping to meet end users' expectations across increasingly diverse quality, health, environmental, safety and social accountability standards in virtually any market around the world.

Intertek's history spans over 130 years, and its origins are with great pioneers in the industry. As well as Edison, these include Caleb Brett, Milton Hersey and Chas Warnock (which became 'Warnock Hersey', one of the largest testing and inspection entities in Canada). When I joined the business in 2015, research showed that Intertek, given its strengths, had the opportunity to differentiate itself from its competitors in the eyes of customers, at a time when growth was slowing in the industry. The question of differentiation occupied my thoughts, both before and after joining the company. I knew that finding the right unique selling proposition (USP) for the business, unifying everybody behind it and presenting it to our customers as a genuine advantage, would make it far easier to drive our growth agenda, given the increased quality, safety and sustainability risks inside corporations.

I'd already started work on this several months before my appointment was made public, and it was another eight months before I actually joined the company once the Board of Intertek announced I would join as the CEO of the group in May 2015. Indeed, before joining and thanks to the support of the Intertek Chairman Sir David Reid, I'd already met some 80 Intertek senior executives and 40 opinion leaders from outside the company, I'd been receiving performance reports from markets across the world, and I'd been able to think long and hard about the size of the prize.

As I was thinking, my mind kept going back to the earliest days of my career, as an auditor in West Africa. Then, I'd been struck by how much clients benefitted from the shift away from the straightforward certification of financial accounts to financial auditing: looking closely at operating procedures and management systems to ensure the end-to-end rigour and controls were in place that would assure the accuracy of all financial data.

I was keen to clearly differentiate Intertek from the competition by introducing a stronger and more differentiated value proposition. Intertek has been the pioneer of the testing, inspection and certification industry across the world for 130 years and has a proven track record of innovating and anticipating the growing needs of its clients.

We conducted a major global market research program and identified that the intensifying focus by corporations on managing risk in the supply chain had substantially increased the role of assurance in their day-to-day risk-mitigation activities.

In identifying that our customers now needed systemic and in-depth Assurance, Testing, Inspection and Certification services (ATIC), we had added a new dimension to our traditional Quality Control offering by placing Assurance at the cutting edge of our value proposition.

A vast amount of work followed, crunching the data and talking to stakeholders across the world. These efforts confirmed that the demand was there. And we became the only company on Earth to offer organisations everywhere the end-to-end value proposition of TQA, helping them operate successfully in an increasingly complex world.

Findings from the extensive research we conducted with customers around the world showed that Intertek had a significant opportunity to differentiate itself from its competitors by offering a TQA customer service focused on four key pillars:

1. Precision – a consistent approach regardless of market/auditor/lab; highly accurate data, easy-to-read reports with actionable insights and recommendations.
2. Pace – a clear, realistic time plan from the start of project, delivering work on time and as promised, with regular communication about progress.
3. Passion – a single point of contact for queries, responding quickly to requests. Regular strategic discussions, proactively recommending improvements and bespoke services tailored to clients' needs.
4. Expertise – access to corporate and individual expertise, subject matter experts and experienced account managers demonstrating that we understand our clients' businesses.

From this, we developed our new Customer Promise: 'Intertek Total Quality Assurance expertise, delivered consistently with precision, pace and passion, enabling our customers to power ahead safely'. And our strapline (or brand USP), 'Total Quality Assured' was a distillation of our Customer Promise – a powerful statement of intent.

I'd already been with the company for close to eight months when I announced the scale of the opportunity we saw to take Intertek to greater heights. People had been wondering what I was up to. But these things do take time to get absolutely right. And Intertek's performance since then has proven that taking time is the right thing to do when it comes to accurately identifying the size of the prize.

Articulate a simple vision that clearly defines the destination and is both inspirational and meaningful for all stakeholders

Once you have identified the size of the prize – once you know what you are aiming at – it is time to formulate the vision for your organisation.

Again, be prepared for a slow process. The formulation of the vision needs to ensure that everybody understands the destination of the journey the organisation is on. More than that, it must be highly motivating for all stakeholders, by capturing their views on the size of the prize and illustrating exactly what is in it for them – both individually and collectively.

Internally, a well-formulated vision is highly motivational for individual employees, as it gives them something they can personally relate to, enabling them to recognise how the organisation's direction of travel will deliver opportunities for personal growth. Of course, it must also help shareholders understand how the business will create sustainable value.

Shaping a vision that achieves these goals isn't a short or simple process. It is of course a creative process but underpinned by rigorous analysis. The choice of words is extremely important, and it can take several weeks of drafting and revision to get it right. What's more, it isn't a straightforward logical process. You have to be strategic in your thinking, forward-looking, visionary, imaginative and engaging. Take time to debate the choice of words with your closest colleagues.

The starting point for formulating the vision is a high-level summary of those key quantitative and qualitative insights you identified while establishing the precise nature of the opportunity – or, as I call it, the size of the prize. You simply cannot start the process without doing this work.

Identifying the right levers of growth

Burger King was making no money in Germany when I became country manager in September 1996. The BSE crisis had shaken the industry. But this was far from the only reason behind the company's poor performance.

Critically, the German operation was subscale – far smaller than McDonald's. Burger King had just 120 restaurants, 60 of them franchised, in Europe's largest marketplace. And, with the unification of West and East Germany gathering pace, all the investments to increase the number of restaurants were focused in East Germany as it was a real white space for Burger King.

As for many multinationals in Germany at the time, the sudden arrival of millions of new consumers, all speaking German, using the same currency and apparently aspiring to live the western lifestyle, was a massive temptation.

Burger King was actively opening new restaurants in East Germany with unsatisfactory financial results as more restaurants generated losses, given a lower than expected revenue compared to restaurants in West Germany.

As it turned out, this was a case of wrongly analysing the size of the prize. The reason it wasn't working was simple: the costs of doing business were much the same in the East as in the West but the fast food market was under-developed.

What had been missed was that East Germans were simply not used to eating burgers in quick-service restaurants.

As a result, the franchisees in East Germany were losing money, and they weren't happy about it. I spent my first three months visiting all restaurants, talking to all stakeholders and seeking the key insights that would enable us to turn the corner into profitable growth. During that time, I spoke to all the managers, franchisees and suppliers, and started to piece together a picture of where the business found itself.

This rapidly became clear. Quite simply, the existing German restaurants were not profitable enough. Until this was fixed, trying to drive growth by opening new restaurants was futile.

This was the immediate finding that resulted from crunching the data. We worked hard to identify the true potential of Burger King Germany and how we could meet the expectations of all stakeholders, Again, combining qualitative insights of all key stakeholders with end-to-end systemic and rigorous data analysis gave us the big insight we were looking for and which underpinned the profitable growth strategy we developed for Burger King in Germany.

Leveraging the drive-through experience

We found that different restaurant formats drove very different levels of profitability. And the most profitable of the lot was the drive-through. In the 1990s, German people enjoyed convenience, just as much as the Americans and the Brits – marry this up with their love of cars, and the drive-through experience was highly rated by consumers.

But this was only obvious once we'd crunched the data.

Late September in 1996, I was flying from Berlin to Munich with Pascal Le Pellec, my Marketing Director, doing what I love most while on a plane – looking at data. During the flight, I was looking at the recent restaurants' profitability numbers.

A few moments after we took off the answer was loud and clear!

The most profitable restaurants were drive-throughs in West Germany that could deliver revenues of more than 3 million Deutsche Marks (DEM) each year and achieve EBITDA margins in excess of 12%.

At the time, there were few Burger King drive-throughs in West Germany.

Once we understood the full value of this powerful consumer insight giving us the formula to operate profitable restaurants, we had the breakthrough we needed when it came to articulating the vision.

'Pascal', I said. 'You know what – 3 million DEM a year is about 10,000 a day'.

That was it.

We both immediately recognised that this was the simple message, the single thought that everybody could sign up to. And, four months after I joined Burger King Germany, we launched 'Vision 10,000' at a conference for all restaurant managers and franchisees.

Our vision was simply that 10,000 DEM could and should be the average daily turnover per restaurant across the entire network.

Psychologically, the figure had enormous resonance. First, it was ambitious, as the average Burger King restaurant in Germany was turning over less than 6,000 DEM (5,786 to be precise) each day in November 1996. Just as important, it was credible: the best-performing restaurants in the network were already hitting and exceeding the target.

So, it was stretching, and it simultaneously gave everybody hope. It was easy for everyone in the restaurants to understand. And it gave managers, franchisees and their teams the opportunity to celebrate success every single day.

Its true beauty lay in its simplicity. It aligned everybody behind the destination, providing a strong platform for all the hard work involved in delivering our growth strategy.

By the time I left Burger King in 2003, seven years after I joined, I was President of Burger King International (in charge of all Burger King restaurants in the world outside the USA). As you can imagine, the German operation was always my baby – I never stopped being involved, I never stopped communicating.

By this time, Germany was the most profitable and fastest-growing Burger King operation worldwide. Restaurant numbers had grown from 120 to 450, with drive-throughs making up a very high proportion of the new sites. And the average daily turnover of each outlet was more than 10,000 DEM.

I don't believe that we'd have achieved any of this without Vision 10,000.

Develop a well-integrated communication plan that will paint the picture for all stakeholders

Your vision will only align and inspire your people – it will only inflame their imaginations, energy and ambitions – if you support it with a rigorous, consistent and integrated internal and external communications plan.

Without rigorous attention to communications, it's impossible to ensure all stakeholders will understand the direction of travel and be convinced that this is the right journey for them.

Never underestimate just how important this is. Never fail to plan or prepare. Never be tempted to go off the cuff. Even professional broadcast journalists work with prompts and scripts – those who don't are quite exceptional. Even politicians and national leaders read carefully crafted, scripted speeches.

Those who can get away without planning and preparation are very, very rare. Most of those who try it fail. So, however tempting it may be, resist the desire to improvise.

Something else to resist is any temptation to start communicating your vision too early. It's quite understandable. You're excited by it and proud of it. But to go live before every detail has been considered, understood and addressed will dissipate your message. It will create confusion and reduce impact.

The essential principles

So, what are the key factors to consider? These are the essential principles that I follow every time, no matter how much time pressure I am under.

First, when creating your plan, think through precisely what it is you want to communicate. What are my goals? What are the 'must-airs'? Write them down, work hard on the wording and ensure total clarity.

Next, consider the audience. Who are they? What are their interests? How do they differ from group to group? Go through a rigorous process of developing an approach for every stakeholder: objectives, key messages, specific content for each group, a tailored media plan and a feedback mechanism.

When the audience is internal, communication will inevitably be closely linked to the leader, who will naturally spend a great deal of time spreading the word about the vision. But it is also important that you build the plan from day one with cascading in mind, through every level of the organisation, with country and functional leaders communicating directly and consistently with their own people.

Never forget that what is communicated internally will be automatically shared with the outside world. So, you need to ensure your 'must-airs' messages to all stakeholders are in complete alignment, while being customised to the specific interests of each audience. Getting your external communication right is critically important and takes detailed planning. Always be sure that you consider by stakeholder group the potential downside of anything that is said: what is positive for one audience may be negative for another.

Always start communicating your key messages internally, even if it is just a few moments before an external announcement. Leading with EQ is about putting your colleagues first and I have seen a lot of CEOs losing trust and respect internally when communicating important news externally before engaging with their colleagues internally.

Putting plans into action

Perhaps it's best to provide an example of all this in action. Putting together and delivering the communications plan behind the Euro Disney restructuring was difficult and complex. After more than 20 months of negotiating with our lenders, we were finally ready to go public with our plans in March 2005.

We were under a lot of pressure. Rumours were rife at the time, and everybody had their own opinions about what we should do and our chances of success. So, it was vital that our planning was absolutely first class. All these years later, I'm still extremely grateful to the very talented in-house PR team, led by Philippe Marie and Catherine Gros from Image 7, the best PR agency in Paris in my view, which had been created by Anne Méaux. This was the core team that helped everything come together on the day.

Essentially, we had a communications plan for the cast members. We had another for the analysts. We had a third for the shareholders. And so on, for audiences including journalists from France, Britain and Spain.

Importantly, we needed positive consumer stories to augment the positive financial news with some exciting marketing news to attract first-timers and repeat visitors. To do this, we had a plan to relaunch Space Mountain. This emphasised the importance of using the right innovation at the heart of Disneyland to communicate the amazing investments and innovations we were starting to implement to attract first timers to the resort. Opinion leaders from across Europe were there to see this brilliant event, which really drove home in a highly original and creative way the importance of innovation to the Park's success.

The evening before the day we kicked-off our communication plan externally, we briefed all leaders so that they could announce the news to their colleagues in the morning.

This is how the day went: I was on French TV at 7.00. Less than an hour later I was on the radio. By 8.30 I was driving back to the park to have our first 9.00 meeting with cast members. At 12.00 I talked with the analyst and financial communities. Then, at 14.00 I was doing interviews with the evening media in both France and the UK. Then I did the second cast member meeting at 15.00 and the third at 18.00. Then I went for dinner with some carefully selected opinion leaders, before heading off to launch our shareholder roadshows across France, the UK and the USA the following days.

In just one day, we shared positive messages with all our key audiences. And, thanks to the passionate support of our comms team, we got tremendous positive coverage. This was essential. We had massive reputational challenges to address. But at the same time, we were essentially relaunching Disneyland Resort Paris too. The last thing we needed was poor corporate news at the same moment we were investing in growth. It was vital that everything we did and said only supported families' decisions to book a trip to Euro Disney. And we wanted every family member to be convinced and, above all, excited about their next visit to Disneyland Resort Paris.

The outcome of that day, all the planning that preceded it and the ongoing communications effort that followed, was outstanding. It not only hit all our immediate messages of repositioning Euro Disney for growth. It also had a significant positive impact on the resort's future performance, providing the right communication platform for our growth strategy, enabling us to announce future new attractions with credible and consistent messaging.

All that preparation paid off many times over during my career. And that's exactly how I still approach every announcement today. I always go back to basics.

What are we trying to achieve? Who are the audiences? What are the 'must-airs'? Who's writing the presentations? Who does the script? What are the Q&As? How do we make sure we have a clear plan for all, day-by-day and minute-by-minute? When do we rehearse?

Typically, the process looks something like this:

1. **Objectives:** identify precisely the outcomes you're after.
2. **Audience:** define who they are, why they matter, what they need to know and who is best to tell them.
3. **Key messages:** clarify exactly what you want the audience to know, to think, to feel and to remember.
4. **Channels:** what are your communication channels? During COVID-19, digital was king. Is it still? Is it as engaging as face-to-face? What can be done to make it so?
5. **Storyboarding:** break down the entire process into its constituent steps, answering who, what, where, when and how. Create an overview of the entire event. And clarify responsibilities for presentations, scripting, Q&A, rehearsals and so on.
6. **Drafting:** what must the audience remember? Write your speech in short and punchy sentences with the right metaphors to make your points

clearly. Then build: add slides, stats, images, charts and stories. Ensure they all support the key message. And redraft, redraft, redraft.

7. **Rehearsal:** how does the **content** come out? Is it sharp, memorable, to the point? If not, redraft. Does your **storyboard** work in practice? If not, adapt and rehearse again. Are your **listeners** promoters or detractors – and is the event hitting the right **emotional tone**? Adapt accordingly. And what is your fall-back if there's a technical failure – never be without a **contingency**.

Above all, I keep telling myself, be really, really prepared. And never improvise.

Invest personal time to communicate the vision with passion and conviction

It's hard to express just how important it is that the leader takes the time required to communicate the vision in a way that ignites the emotions of every listener.

If you fail to do so, the vision will never get a grip on the organisation's collective imagination. And your plans won't ever come to fruition.

Communication has to start at the top. And that means you have to make quality time, no matter how busy you are, to consider how to personally deliver the messages that best articulate the vision. You need to be well rehearsed. You must demonstrate your personal passion and conviction in every word. Your style needs to be utterly authentic. You need to use a lot of storytelling to contextualise your messages and give them colour and drama. And you need to consider how best to tailor your approach to each of your various audiences – from employees to customers, analysts to shareholders, communities to regulators and more.

That takes careful scripting. And ideally it takes a lot of rehearsal too; working with your closest colleagues to make sure you get it absolutely right. Trust me, I've made my share of mistakes. I've gone in thinking I can improvise and have suddenly found that I don't like what I'm saying. Then the doubts really set in – 'Maybe you're losing it,' you find yourself thinking. 'Maybe you never had it in the first place.'

So, script it and rehearse it. In short, give the audience the respect they deserve for giving you the time to share your thoughts with them.

When rolling out the vision across your audiences, always recognise the primary importance of your internal audience. Minimise as far as possible any chance that team members will pick up your messages from external sources. Start with face-to-face sessions with all levels of leadership within the organisation, before progressing to deliver roadshows at key locations across the business.

All your communications must be highly personal and interactive, giving the audience the opportunity to ask questions and share their own thoughts.

Earlier in this chapter, I described some of the broad principles involved in calculating the size of the prize at Intertek. At its simplest, this is how we then communicated the TQA vision that resulted from that work:

- In January 2016, I explained the vision and its rationale to 300 colleagues at a global internal conference in Wales.
- Then we broadcast the key points to all employees across the world, using the web to ensure everybody received the same messaging at the same time.
- We briefed leaders throughout the organisation, giving them access to all the thinking and materials they needed to cascade the messaging to their own teams.
- In March, I presented the strategy and vision to our shareholders and analysts, supported by a suite of carefully prepared and rigorously polished communications materials.
- We further supported that external messaging with the content of our Annual Report and Accounts, issued in May.
- I carried on re-emphasising the messaging as it evolved to internal and external audiences across the world – and have continued to do so ever since. Before COVID-19, I spent around half my time travelling. I always aim to use this well, talking in person to as many colleagues as possible and using much of my own time to communicate the Vision.

A vital element of this is restating what really matters, time after time. That's why the fifth principle in this chapter is Repeat, Repeat, Repeat.

Repeat, Repeat, Repeat

It takes time for key messages to be properly understood and become part of the organisation's DNA. So be prepared for the fact that making the vision compelling and clear for all parts of the organisation and every external audience will take several years. For this reason, your communication plans must take a multi-year approach.

Once you are clear about the key messages and have shared the vision, you will have to repeat them again and again. Of course, some things will change. The business will evolve over time. There will be innovative thinking, new concepts to talk about, changes to the external environment – but you must always stay true to your core communication messages.

This takes focus and discipline. Repeating the same messages year after year can get boring. But you must resist the temptation to change. You must stay consistent.

This is particularly important in turbulent times. Facing challenges, internal or external, that have an impact on short-term performance can easily tempt stakeholders to call for a change in direction. But this is precisely when your messaging has to be consistent. Staying true to your vision will be highly reassuring for all, delivering a disproportionately positive impact on the confidence and the energy of everybody in the organisation.

For example, having launched our new Intertek purpose, vision, strategy and customer promise to the senior leadership team in Wales in 2016, we then augmented them further to the same team when we revealed our new brand identity in New York in 2017. We further reinforced them to the leadership team over the years ahead with the launch of 5x5 Ever Better operational plans in Dallas in 2019, emphasising them again during our sales conference in Cancun in 2020. In 2021, with the virtual launch of the Intertek-inspired community-led Build Back Ever Better movement (see chapter 10), we made the link between our purpose, vision, strategy and customer promise crystal clear, recognising that sustainability had become the movement of our time. This is what I mean by being consistent.

The challenge is to find new ways to create stories that continue to bring the vision to life year after year, engaging people afresh over and over again. So, launch new activities, encourage and reward innovation, celebrate new ideas – but remain true to your vision and purpose with consistent core messages.

Key points from this chapter:

- Do your homework to determine the size of the prize for all stakeholders, and understand the different expectations from group to group.
- Articulate a simple vision that clearly defines the journey's ultimate destination and is both inspirational and meaningful for all stakeholders.
- Develop a well-integrated communications plan that paints the picture for all and takes into account the different interests, expectations and aspirations of all different groups.
- Invest your personal time in communicating the vision in a way that will energise your audience, thanks to your own conviction and passion, based on an in-depth preparation.
- Never stop driving home the messages that matter: repeat, repeat, repeat!

Leadership Principle 3
Energise the organisation to outperform

Chapter content:

- Ensure there is total clarity on what 'outperformance' means.
- Empower the organisation with daily/weekly/monthly operating systems.
- Lead outperformance from the front with high energy, always being genuine.
- Never stop challenging the organisation with ever better ideas.
- Celebrate and recognise success every day.

The subject of this chapter is probably the leadership principle that my colleagues most associate with my leadership style.

They know that what really matters to me is energising people in a way that makes us collectively better and more successful than the competition.

In other words, igniting the organisation to grow faster than the industry and outperform the competition.

So here, we are going to look at how leaders can ensure they maximise the energy of their people to outperform their competitors every single day.

In many ways, this chapter is not so much about what many people associate most with the role of the leader – the purpose, the vision and the strategy.

Once you have formulated these, you've delivered maybe 1% of your responsibilities as a leader.

Rather it is about the CEO as 'Chief Energy Officer' – getting properly organised to inspire people, direct them, support them, challenge them and energise them. It's about the nuts and bolts of strong and effective leadership.

Employees should expect this role of their leaders. The days of the 'armchair' CEO sitting behind a desk and reading performance reports written for them by other people are gone. Instead, in our highly complex and competitive world, employees expect to see the CEO out there, investing a great deal of time in day-to-day performance management, leading from the front in a highly visible way as part of the action with her or his team.

A leader's failure to get into the thick of the action will inevitably be noticed. This can be extremely damaging. It will not only undermine the full potential of the strategy – it will also create an organisation that is critical of and cynical about the journey ahead.

People sometimes question if the CEO should get so closely involved. 'Is it because we can't be trusted to do the job ourselves?' they wonder. 'Is it micro-management?' Absolutely not. It's about being personally invested and involved in the wider team effort, inspiring, giving direction, supporting, challenging to win every day in the marketplace as a team. Said differently, it's being part of the team.

Most important of all, it's about getting the level of interaction right at every layer in the organisation to show how delivering against short-term performance goals contributes to the long-term achievement of the vision.

Ensure there is total clarity on what 'outperformance' means

To achieve outperformance, everybody needs to be completely clear about what it means – for them individually and for the organisation as a whole. Without this understanding, it is practically impossible for you to create and lead an outperforming organisation. So ensuring total clarity is one of the first things you have to get right as a leader.

We have spent a considerable amount of time at Intertek as a management team to define the key value drivers for any business area around the world. Each of the 7 value drivers we have identified is very demanding on its own and what truly defines outperformance for all of us at Intertek is delivering on these 7 value drivers every day in every operation. We measure our performance with a high bar because we know that the pursuit of excellence is the only way to outperform, monitoring rigorously our progress and always looking for a better way to outperform what we did yesterday.

- Living our culture every day, being purpose-led
- Attracting, developing and retaining the best talents
- Total quality customer experience with zero defects
- Zero-to-One and One-to-100 innovations
- Doing business the right way in every operation
- Profitable investments in high-growth and high-margin sectors
- Consistent margin-accretive revenue growth with strong cash conversion.

We looked in the last chapter at creating and communicating a well-articulated vision, which is fundamental to the successful delivery of your strategy. But the challenge still remains of how you operationalise your compelling vision to ensure that everybody does what is necessary to outperform the competition.

There is a simple reason why outperformance is important; the leaders who win do so because they have attracted and retained the best talent in the industry. We all need to drive excellent performance consistently because, if we don't, our best talent will go and work for competitors.

That's why we have to work so hard as leaders to get the organisation to a 10× level.

At its highest level, I believe it's all about competition. To enable investment in growth, today's business leaders have to compete not only for capital but also for people.

The moment you start underperforming, the moment your growth starts slowing, you run the risk of losing your best talent. That's why the corporations that write history all have the reputation of being magnets for attracting and retaining the best people. Part of their success lies in having leaders who understand the true meaning of outperformance.

What do I mean?

Delivering outperformance means outperforming every day, which requires the right balance between the short-term agenda and the long-term priorities with one principle in mind: consistently outperforming in the short term will drive outperformance in the long run.

Said simply, short-term outperformance will give the CEO licence to invest in growth and outperform in the long run.

Consistent outperformance on a daily basis will make it easier for any CEO to attract and retain the talents needed to implement his growth strategy.

The true meaning of outperformance is what Leadership with Soul is all about; putting people at the heart of your growth strategy.

I have always run complex global businesses with a portfolio of businesses – some doing well, and some not so well. Helping the underperforming businesses to fix their issues and start outperforming naturally takes an important part of my time. My colleagues will tell you that the rigour and intensity I provide to find the solutions can be surprising for some. One reason I do this, is – of course, like many – I like to win. The real reason I do this is because I know so well that an underperforming business will lose top talent and the opportunity to win in the marketplace on a sustainable basis. Outperformance is a duty for any CEO and a company cannot outperform without attracting, developing and retaining the best talent in every part of the business portfolio.

The human factor

I get my energy from being a leader because it enables me to help create a better future for people. This is a two-way street: effective leadership attracts the best people, who in turn help to drive the best possible corporate performance.

If employees see growth slow down, they will recognise there may be greater opportunities for them elsewhere. So as soon as a leader stops driving outperformance, they run the risk of losing their best people.

This is why the companies that set the standard for excellence in their industries are those with the deserved reputation for attracting and retaining the most talented and committed employees. It is the leader's duty to make it possible to achieve the performance that keeps them satisfied and offers them a better future. I feel passionate about this one. It's so important for leaders to understand the true meaning of outperformance.

Resolving a frustrating conflict

In many organisations, there can be a frustrating conflict between short- and long-term goals. When this occurs, it is often a barrier to high performance. People can ask questions that seem eminently reasonable. 'How can I drive revenue up and costs down at the same time? How do you expect me to deliver growth in profit and cash while investing in growth? How can I achieve strong returns in the early years of my capital programme when it takes time to build the infrastructure I need?'

To provide the answers, the CEO will have to create the right outperformance culture and be 100% clear about the need to deliver every single day.

In my early days as CEO of Intertek, I joined the dots between short- and long-term objectives and initiatives with a 'Track 1' and 'Track 2' concept. This aimed to ensure people were really clear about the time horizons of the day-to-day agenda.

It was based on a simple but very important mantra: our short-term performance gives us the freedom to do the right things for the long term. In other words, certain activities are critical right now – they have to be done today. Others are far more important over the long term, and that is what we are all working towards collectively.

There are clear differences between Track 1 and Track 2 initiatives. Those in Track 1 are to do with the here and now, including factors such as revenue, margin, cash, performance, customer service and all the actions that successfully motivate and energise your teams. Those in Track 2 are for the longer term, including the investments driving the strategic differentiation that helps you accelerate organisational growth on a sustainable basis.

It is down to the CEO to create an outperformance culture in which it is clear that achieving short-term goals every day is what enables and underpins the ability to meet long-term objectives. Taking your company from A to B over time and delivering your vision is about understanding how you reconcile the short- and long-term interests of all stakeholders, with one important imperative in mind: consistent short-term outperformance will give licence to the CEO to invest in growth and deliver long-term outperformance.

Building the outperformance culture

The key building blocks of any growth strategy are the organisation's value drivers, its strategic priorities and enablers, as well as its corporate goals.

To clarify these, for yourself and the organisation as a whole, you need to articulate the long-term journey around the key drivers that create and deliver long-term value for all stakeholders. Identifying these **value drivers** will involve a great deal of thinking time – they are mission critical to the organisation, as they will be a key point of focus for it to identify its strategic priorities and its enablers.

Once you have identified the value drivers and ensured that people have a clear outperformance mindset to sign up to, the next logical step is to identify **corporate goals**. This will also be testing and time-consuming. Many people will have conflicting views. But the job of the CEO is to ensure there is total clarity and alignment between all individuals and all stages of the strategic-planning process.

We have developed a comprehensive set of value drivers, strategic priorities, enablers and corporate goals for Intertek.

Our 5 × 5 differentiated growth strategy is anchored on 5 strategic priorities and 5 enablers that guide every team on how to outperform consistently.

Strategic priorities:

- Our Total Quality Assurance brand proposition
- Superior customer service
- An effective sales strategy
- Our growth- and margin-accretive portfolio
- Operational excellence, based on market-leading quality and turnaround time.

Enablers:

- Living our outperformance culture to the max
- Disciplined performance management
- Superior technology
- Energising our people
- Doing business the right way.

These in turn enable us to achieve the following **corporate goals**:

- Fully engaged employees working in a safe environment
- Superior customer service
- Margin-accretive revenue growth, based on GDP+ organic growth
- Strong cash conversion from our operations
- An accretive and disciplined capital allocation policy.

Achieving and exceeding these goals is what we mean by outperforming our competition based on the 7 value drivers we discussed earlier in this chapter.

- Living our culture every day, being purpose-led
- Attracting, developing and retaining the best talents
- Total quality customer experience with zero defects
- Zero-to-One and One-to-100 innovations
- Doing business the right way in every operation
- Consistent margin-accretive revenue growth with strong cash conversion
- Disciplined investments in high-growth and high-margin sectors.

Rising to the calibration challenge

Once you have reached this stage, you have made good progress. You have clarity on the direction of travel, your people are engaged by the compelling vision you've created, you have a strategy in place to achieve the vision based on your value drivers, your strategic priorities, enablers and corporate goals.

But one of the most challenging and potentially divisive aspects of high-performance management is still ahead of you.

This is the moment at which you have to quantify the yearly goals after having agreed the five-year corporate goals. You have to ask – and answer – how high is high? This isn't just challenging. It's also incredibly significant, as it will have very important implications for pay and bonus structures, career advancement opportunities and job satisfaction right across the organisation.

In setting and quantifying the yearly goals, the CEO is taking responsibility for raising the bar for the organisation and everybody in it. You have to ensure that the goals you set achieve three key objectives:

1. They meet the demands and expectations of stakeholders by stretching the organisation to perform at its best
2. They inspire and energise your people with the ambition to truly outperform, creating personal growth opportunities for all
3. They ensure everybody is rewarded in line with their achievements, creating the right personal wealth opportunities for everyone.

Achieving this is never easy, and many leaders feel highly conflicted at the prospect of setting the bar at the correct level. If you have a naturally generous spirit, you want your team to be able to qualify for the best possible bonus. But the answer is never to set an unrealistically low target that people can smash their way through. This is not encouraging outperformance. This is playing safe – and it is essentially dishonest.

Equally, there is no point in having yearly goals that your people are never going to achieve or even get close to.

At this point, I like to use what I call the 'mirror test'. Outperformance as a leader is to be really clear about where the competition is. About how high is high. And about giving yourself and the team goals to be proud of.

I'm not saying that goals should be unachievable. I'm saying they should be stretching, so that at the end of the year, when you look at yourself in the mirror, you can be proud of yourself for hitting or, even better, exceeding them. When setting goals with my team, I also refer to the yearly goals 'pride threshold' targets as, true to our outperformance mindset, there is no point in delivering results you are not proud of!

These are never easy conversations of course, given the understandable uncertainty when you start a new fiscal year but these are the right conversations to have.

Keep it simple...

Once the calibration work is complete, it's time to communicate what the new direction of travel means for everyone involved and what the expectations are for the organisation and every one of its people.

Just as when sharing your vision and strategy, it's important to communicate your corporate goals clearly and simply. If your messaging is too complex, people will never properly take it to heart. Only when it is straightforward and to the point will people remember what's expected of them. Only then will the messages fire their imaginations and become established as an almost instinctive part of their everyday working lives.

Simplification is the key to leading for outperformance.

The way to think about it is to break down your complex strategy into a series of bite-sized operational priorities. Yet, this takes hard work again. It is vital that you spend quality time on articulating and communicating your executional plans, and that you constantly keep your audience in mind, from your closest leadership colleagues to people working in the organisation's engine rooms.

The work I described above about joining the dots with long- and short-term activities is one example of this sort of simplification. It was an understandable and approachable concept that everybody could grasp.

In 2016, at Intertek we launched the 5×5 differentiated strategy for growth to the Intertek senior management team. A few years later, we recognised the need to deepen the understanding of the direction of travel and simplified the message by articulating our 5×5 Action Plans based on the levers that were available to each operation, no matter their location or size. We used this important simplification exercise to reinforce our outperformance culture which we call '10×'. True to our 5×5 strategy and our 10× culture, we named our action plan: 5×5 Ever Better Action Plan.

- 10× leadership
- Be uncompromising at quality, compliance and sustainability
- Accelerate our revenue growth
- Step up our margin performance
- Get smarter at cash management.

Again, these are extremely simple and easily understood. They leave people in no doubt about where their focus should lie. And, when everybody is focused collectively on the key priorities that do most to drive outperformance, then outperformance is achievable.

Getting to this point is not easy. But it is doable – and we have businesses across the world that are proving this, every single day.

Empower the organisation with daily/weekly/monthly operating systems

Once you have defined your corporate goals, based on the right value drivers, you need to spend quality time with your management team on defining the right ways of measuring and tracking performance. This involves identifying lagging (financial) and leading (non-financial) metrics that enable performance management using a clear set of definitions that are fully understood across the organisation.

These are the metrics we agreed to focus on with my senior team at Intertek when we created our 5×5 differentiated strategy for growth:

Leading & Lagging Indicators

Leading indicators (Operational Metrics)		Lagging indicators (Financial Metrics)	
Marketing Leads	Health and Safety	Revenue Growth	Pricing Power
Customer Retention	Sales Funnel	Margin	Working Capital
Customer Acquisitions	Back Log Management	ROCE	Capital Allocation
Employee Turnover	Net Promoter Score	Cash Conversion	Cost
Operational Excellence	Site Capacity Utilisation	Customer Profitability	Investments in Growth

Having defined those metrics, you need to work with the management team to develop systemic operating systems to capture data at every level of the organisation. This is the only way of ensuring there is total alignment in measuring performance and that everybody is being assessed by the same criteria.

Critically, these systems need to deliver relevant performance data on a daily, weekly and monthly basis. This needs to be extremely well organised and structured. If there are inefficiencies or instances of poor design that make them hard for people to use, they will not use them to best effect.

Visualisation for performance management

Visualisation is a very important tool – it's an excellent way of helping teams and individuals measure and manage performance. The best approach that I have come across is to use a balanced scorecard not only at corporate level but also in every regional, national and local operation across the world.

Both the IT and the Finance departments will be closely involved, ensuring the right infrastructure is available and the right metrics are featured. As leader, the CEO will also need to ensure that line management has a direct role to play when getting the metrics in place. Without this, issues around the ownership of processes or reporting tools are almost certain to emerge.

One such pitfall is that local managers could see their operation as different from the rest of the world, meaning they won't sign up to a global reporting tool. The balanced scorecard therefore needs to make perfect sense for everybody in the business, including local operators. Otherwise, there's the very real danger that the business will end up with multiple reporting tools and different systems.

At Intertek, we use our 5 × 5 scorecard in every business, no matter its size or geography. This provides a tremendous alignment on how to run the business.

Learning from Toyota

During my time as CEO of Inchcape, I was fortunate enough to work with most of the world's leading automotive manufacturers. Toyota is very impressive when it comes to visualisation. When you go into a Toyota factory, you'll see that all production lines are split into many small teams. Without the right system in place, this could make it difficult for team leaders and individuals to know where they stand in terms of performance management.

But Toyota's answer is incredibly efficient – each team leader has a precise visualisation of the metrics they need to achieve on a daily, weekly and monthly basis, all backed up with tailored action plans to ensure that what needs to be done is completed on time, every time.

This is the Kaizen approach in action, enabling people at all levels from across the organisation to work proactively on delivering continuous improvement via countless incremental steps, always anchored in the right data.

For me, Toyota's focus on daily, weekly and monthly metrics is an extremely powerful driver of the leadership that they have achieved in the automotive industry.

Data management is also very important in sport, for teams and athletes competing at the highest level.

For example, the former Sky cycling team focused on finding a continuous flow of small performance gains rather than seeking giant leaps. This approach helped the team win 327 races, including eight grand tours, between its creation in 2010 and its transformation into Team Ineos in 2019.

Similarly, the sport most associated with the value of marginal gains is Formula 1, where incremental improvements in technology and its application are key to gaining significant competitive advantage, relying on probably the most impressive performance management cockpit with data processed, of course, at incredible speed.

Getting the cadence right

In my experience, the 'daily, weekly, monthly' performance management cadence helps to foster an outperformance culture that values and rewards consistent, short-term delivery to achieve sustainable performance over the long run.

Importantly, you should not use the same indicators for your daily reports as you do for your weekly and monthly reports. There are factors you should report on once a day, others once a week and others on a monthly basis. Get these right, and you are significantly more likely to drive outperformance in your organisation. Everybody will be clear about precisely what is happening and what is expected of them. And if you're not clear on a daily basis, how can you possibly be clear over the long run?

Performance management underpins engagement

As discussed at the beginning of the book, the low level of engagement in most companies prevents these organisations to truly unleash their potential.

In my view, employee engagement is vital to the short- and long-term successes of any company. All the research done on engagement recognises that a key element of engagement for every employee is about being clear regarding what's expected of them. If they're not clear on a daily basis, how can they be engaged?

Gallup has helped companies monitor their level of engagement for many years based on 12 essential questions and it's no surprise that their first question is all about expectations: 'Do you know what is expected of you at work?'

That is why performance management with the right daily, weekly, monthly cadence plays a major role in driving engagement by clarifying first and foremost what is expected from everyone.

Self-performance management

In business as well as in sport, winning teams don't wait for their leaders to instruct them to interrogate the data. They want to be on the front foot and get access to the data as soon as it is available, enabling them straightaway to start using it to take any required corrective action. They do this because they want to win as a team – not because they want to please the boss.

There is no better illustration of this in action than a F1 racing team, with everybody focused on live data streams to see how, individually and collectively, they can optimise the performance of their cars at any moment during a race or a practice session.

This is why every team at every layer needs access to their own data and balanced scorecard on a daily, weekly and monthly basis. For this to happen, two things are essential. First, the operating systems need to be built and engineered specifically to empower every operational team.

Second, you will need to ensure that every team plans quality time on its agenda every day, every week and every month to understand what the data really means. There is huge value for leaders at every level – from a site to a department – to establish daily morning or evening sessions to ensure everybody is on the same page for the day immediately ahead. Then sessions on every Monday or Friday can be used to ensure the right weekly focus.

Equally, it's incredibly valuable for any team, at any layer of the organisation to take time every month to step back and look together as a team at all the data from across the previous period, consider progress against the previous month's action plans and determine the goals, priorities and challenges for the weeks ahead.

Driving creativity

Such sessions deliver a great opportunity to think deeply, to be creative and to come up with new ideas. What could we do differently next time? What great examples could we learn from? What has the competition done?

I could not emphasise enough the power of monthly self-performance management sessions within any team at every layer in the organisation, including the top team of any organisation. In just a few hours, it enables you to come up with a series of action points and ideas – some of which might revolutionise your performance over the days, weeks, months and years ahead. Just as important, bringing everybody together in this way is a fantastically powerful and positive team-building tool. Delivering a process to drive continuous improvement – based on Kaizen principles – actually makes self-performance management fun. It creates a spirit of outperformance and drives engagement throughout the team.

Making this sort of thinking part of the fabric of how you work means your people can relate more closely to what is expected of them, relating more closely to what's expected of them on a daily, weekly and monthly basis. That helps them continuously improve their performance. And it gives you the parameters you need to decide how to recognise and reward teams and individuals on a regular basis.

The third dimension

Finally, don't forget to benchmark your performance against what Best-in-Class performance truly is! This is a really, really important aspect of performance management.

When you're looking at data, there are three main ways of gauging performance. Two are pretty standard.

You can look at it versus last year, plus or minus; or you can look at it versus budget, plus or minus. The third dimension is the most important dimension in performance management. It's called Best-in-Class.

Driving outperformance is highly dependent on your ability to set the right and most relevant operational targets, based on what I call 'Best-in-Class' targeting.

I adopted this thinking based on the simple premise that most people – and certainly everyone I want to work with – wants to win and be the best they possibly can. Certainly, this is a way of ensuring your organisation has a culture that responds well to challenges, where people relish initiatives that properly stretch them and help them operate at their best.

It's a relatively simple process, but in my experience, it creates an incredibly important and powerful shift in mindset. One way to set Best-in-Class targets is to compare the metrics you are interested in, such as pricing, margin and customer service based on the span of performance achieved across your industry or within your organisation.

Clearly, you set the top score as the Best-in-Class measure.

Once you have done this, you can look at your performance metrics as a percentage of the Best-in-Class score. Naturally, your goal is to close the gap over time, eventually achieving the Best-in-Class mantle across as many different metrics as possible.

Managing performance in three dimensions – last year, budget and Best-in-Class – will help you and your organisation to outperform on a sustainable basis.

My Best-in-Class thinking was born when I attended a summer course called 'The Restaurant Executive Programme' in September 1998 at Cornell University. The course was developed and given by the world's academic authority on restaurant multi-site management, Chris Mueller. Chris became a friend and gave me the insight that in a restaurant business, understanding what Best-in-Class looks like is easy; you just need to look at how each restaurant is performing on one single metric. In the same country with 1,000 restaurants of a given brand, not every restaurant will perform equally and the span of performance across all 1,000 restaurants is a huge performance management opportunity. All the research I saw on the span of performance has shown that the biggest correlation between great and poor performing restaurants is due to the quality of leadership at the site level. Chris' thinking when it comes to multi-site restaurant leadership is well described in his book 'The Leader of Managers', and is totally aligned with Leadership with Soul.

Simplification

Daily, weekly, monthly rigorous performance management is all about Big Data, delivered by well-structured and automated digital operating systems.

Easier said than done, and one of the insights of data management is that you always need more data or a different type of data faster to make a decision.

That's why you never stop reinventing the type of data you process and how you visualise the trends with always looking for simplification of the daily, weekly, monthly dashboard you produce.

At Intertek, Ross McCluskey was our CFO for several years, after having been the Group Financial Controller. Together, we used to spend a lot of 'stop and think' time on how to redesign our operating dashboard, true to our 'Ever Better' mantra. I have to say that Ross's Big Data management excellence enabled us to take our performance management to the highest level I have ever seen in any corporation based on one single belief: you are more likely to outperform if you know your business cold 24/7.

Lead outperformance from the front with high energy, always being genuine

I've already said that the CEO is the Chief Energy Officer. This should always be the case for a business that targets outperformance. So the CEO needs to make a clear time commitment in the agenda, leading from the front throughout the year. The energy involved in doing this needs always to be genuine. If it is not, if it is faked in any way, others will notice. And all that leadership effort will be wasted.

Your annual strategic planning and budgeting sessions are critical moments in ensuring all business units are focused throughout the year on the right issues and opportunities. As CEO, your involvement doesn't start with attending these meetings. You will also be involved beforehand, working with functional teams to prepare for these. So when you attend, you'll already know the issues involved for every unit, you'll have identified the key issues or opportunities and you'll be able to ensure that all the right insights are debated to make each event truly successful and meaningful.

The essence is the same whether you lead a small team or a large organisation. Treat these annual meetings as the opportunity to report back on the progress the company is making and to clarify the short-term expectations that will contribute to further improvement over the year ahead. In addition, I can only recommend hosting annual events for all your employees to cascade the goals for the year and make sure everybody understands what is required, and that everyone is on the same page.

Formal performance reviews

In addition, it is essential that you attend regular performance reviews for in-depth discussion with team management throughout the year. In my experience, these work best on a monthly basis for your core business units, and quarterly for those that are non-core.

More than ever, careful preparation is vital. You will need to know in advance about all the key issues, targets and challenges. And you need to be prepared to listen carefully to the teams presenting before you ask any questions or raise any performance shortcomings or challenges.

The reason for this is simple. There is nothing more frustrating or disheartening for a team than to hear the boss ask a stupid question or raise something that has already been satisfactorily addressed. It could imply that you don't care, that you're not up to speed with reality, or that you've simply not been listening.

Promoting real ownership

The discussions that take place during these budget sessions and performance reviews are at their very best when the CEO ensures they are fact-based and that there is real ownership of the business, right around the table.

It is also important that conversations are always open about how best to resolve a situation, without anybody being made to feel defensive. It is common to see situations in which people get emotional when you ask a question that is challenging or make a comment about performance slowing down. You need to make sure people understand it's not about them. It's purely business.

All this can only happen when you have a culture where respect, courage, passion and integrity and, importantly when emotional intelligence is deeply embedded in the fabric of the organisation.

The importance of an open mind

From time to time, it will be very important for the leader to stop the flow of a meeting and call for the conversation to be reframed. We all know that it can be tough for teams totally immersed in the day-to-day action to gain that all-important perspective on a situation. It's often much easier for a leader who comes in from a few steps removed to see clearly what the trends are and how they relate to the bigger picture.

This ability of the CEO to change the focus of discussion can be really important for two reasons. First, it can bring about a shift in thinking that is really helpful to the team, sometimes helping them to break out from an unproductive rut. Second, it can demonstrate that you truly started the session with an open mind with no preconceived notions. Just as important, it shows that you're willing and able to roll up your sleeves and really help a team get to grips with a problem.

Lastly, these sessions can be memorable team events, as the team leaves the session with bold and innovative thinking to take their business forward.

Formal and informal communication

To fully connect with your teams, you have to invest time in visiting operations. No matter how good or technologically advanced your internal reporting system might be, nothing beats direct personal interaction when it comes to gathering information across the organisation. Nothing beats a market visit for helping you understand the latest consumer trends, meet your customers, read the competition and get a sense of what is really happening in the business.

As CEO, you therefore need to establish a clear plan for when to visit operations throughout the year. This is a huge time commitment, but there is no avoiding it.

I strongly advise you to plan formal forums for communicating interactively with employees during these visits. My favourite format is a one-hour 'town hall' approach, which gives you the opportunity to make a small presentation about what is going on across the business before opening the floor to questions. This is an excellent formula for connecting deeply with the audience. I have also found that a great way of closing an event with high energy is to recognise 'local heroes' with awards for particularly strong performance. Frequent recognition of this sort is vital for a leader who is authentically committed to leading from the front.

Informal communication is also an incredibly powerful way of leading from the front. Don't miss out on all those opportunities – the chat in the kitchen area, the chat over lunch, the chat in the lift. There's that moment when you and your colleagues are checking in at the hotel, and when you're sitting around over drinks in the evening. These are the places where people will let you know what's on their minds, when they'll open up and give you great insights into what's really going on across the organisation.

This sort of informal contact has strong benefits in both directions. It always amazes me to see just how strongly the presence of the CEO elevates energy levels inside an operation. Interacting directly with the CEO is a highly motivational moment for anyone in the business. Equally, it's a vital internal research opportunity for the CEO, enabling a fuller understanding of how the organisation is performing at every level. It also provides the chance to demonstrate their personal commitment to hearing the voice of the employees, actively seeking their opinions and demonstrating that you respect them. This is probably the area where emotional intelligence will have the biggest positive impact – provided it is used genuinely.

Get organised!

Being extremely well organised is another vital ingredient. In normal times, I spend around half of every year visiting operations across the world, and I often see other leaders who spend similar amounts of time on the move.

Speaking personally, having run global businesses for more than two decades, I have concluded that spending less than 50% of my time doing this is not enough, and spending more than that amount is too much.

To make a schedule like this work, you need to be extremely well organised. I have never seen a chaotic leader be successful.

No one particularly enjoys agenda management, but leaders have no choice. You've always got to be on time. You've got to be there when the team needs you. You need time in advance to think things through. And you cannot allow meetings to overrun.

This is why every year I try to be as disciplined as possible when it comes to planning how best to use my time to lead from the front. A major part of this involves developing a detailed 12-month agenda for the year ahead, which includes all recurring meetings and other events as well as those travel plans.

Trust me, being highly organised will save you a lot of stress.

Inverting the pyramid

When I arrived at Burger King in Germany, I was not a restaurant specialist. I quickly understood the importance of being really close to the restaurant teams – the important consumer facing side of the organisation. So one of my first initiatives was to make sure everybody from head office in Munich spent a day a month with an assigned 'restaurant partner'.

Of course, this extended to me. As well as the monthly visits, we were also responsible for supporting our partners remotely during the month. This was a classic case of inverting the pyramid, making sure that the functional leadership team was supporting the front of the operation. The initiative created a clear improvement to the working relationships between the head office and the restaurant teams. Personally, it helped me enormously to deeply understand the true drivers of performance at the restaurant level – this initiative is a 'must have' in any multi-unit business like Burger King.

I took as my partner our newest restaurant, on Cologne's Schildergasse, the city's oldest and most popular shopping street. I really enjoyed working with our General Manager, Anil Sundri, who made the restaurant exceptionally successful. He was so good, in fact, that by the time I left the company in 2003 he was in charge of all our company restaurants across Germany and the Netherlands.

One day, on the way to Cologne, I asked myself a question that led to the creation of the best communications event I experienced for many years. The question was this: 'Who should you, as the leader of the business, recognise with an amazing initiative that money can't buy?'

The answer was super clear. 'The heroes, the ones who are outperforming.'

Armed with this idea, I went to our head of training, Antonie Goetz-Lemke, to get her help on developing a special leadership event. We decided that every year I would take the 10 top-performing restaurant managers to the Bavarian Alps, where we would spend a couple of days climbing together, having a nice dinner, going for a hike and sharing ideas about the business.

I was amazed by how much value we got from this amazing recognition initiative. It wasn't just highly motivational for the attendees. It was also a great source of inspiration and ideas for me. These people, after all, were the top-performing 10 out of a population of 450 restaurant managers. They were ahead of the rest. They'd worked out the answers, had implemented great ideas, were leading their own teams from the front.

This event would take place in December. And for the next 12 months, almost all the best ideas we implemented across the Burger King business were given to me during those two days in the mountains.

If I have one advice, spend as much time as you can with the heroes in your business. They will get energised and you will get equally energised to take your business forward as you will hear directly from the heroes in your organisation who have always figured out how to outperform the competitors day in–day out – simple!

Never stop challenging the organisation with ever better ideas

The best leaders are paranoid about what's happening in and around their business. They can never relax. They know that the good times won't last without constant attention and effort. They know that reinventing the way they perform when they outperform their competitors is the best way to strengthen their competitive advantage and keep outperforming in the long run. They recognise that an Ever Better approach will make sure that the competitors are always in a catch up mode, a few steps behind.

Unfortunately, some CEOs, glowing in the warmth of short-term success, get too easily carried away by the joy of the moment and come to believe too much in their own stories.

When I was at business school, *Business Week* was a very popular management magazine. I'd play a kind of game. Every time a CEO was featured on the front cover, I'd lay a bet that his or her business would hit some kind of problem within a few years.

My stakes were always pretty safe. That's because I had realised then that taking the time to tell the world about your latest big success could be a sign of complacency for any CEO. Developing a PR campaign to start explaining your success is of course important but can take time and focus away from doing the day-to-day business to continue to outperform.

Celebrating and recognising outperformance within your own organisation is, of course, extremely important. But never forget that competitors will react (just as you would if the boot was on the other foot). Shifting market forces will impact on your business unless you manage to keep ahead.

So recognise achievement. Celebrate success. Focus your valuable time on what matters – and be constantly on the look-out for the next challenges and targets. Continuously seek perfection. Never stop looking for a better way to outperform.

An organisation will only ever achieve sustainable outperformance once continuous improvement is happening at every level, driven by a mindset that demands 'ever better' thinking and planning. This means that at the very moment of celebrating past successes you're already feeling the urge to set the next goals and reach for the next peak of performance.

Storytelling

We're lucky to be leaders today. We have access to enormously powerful internal communication tools that make it easy to inspire colleagues to climb that next mountain. All you need to do is tell the story of how someone, somewhere in the organisation has just achieved the seemingly impossible – having and implementing an 'ever better' idea that has smashed the competition and is accelerating the growth momentum.

With the right mindset in place, telling these stories enthuses people to achieve the same – or even more. So storytelling is vital in bringing outperformance to life by challenging people throughout the organisation to find and harness some more of that elusive magic. So be constantly on the lookout for stories to share. They are hugely energising.

Mission impossible

Delivering outperformance on a consistent basis is hard and it's totally understandable that organisations will want to celebrate their achievements and take the time to reflect on what they did right. It's totally understandable also that the risk of being complacent for a winning team is real in any organisation.

Identifying the risk of complacency is important for any CEO and once the risk has been identified, it's the role of the CEO to challenge the organisation by sometimes creating a bit of tension. That's where the concept of mission impossible comes in – giving the organisation a new challenge so seemingly insurmountable that overcoming it would be a sign of incredible ingenuity and operational excellence.

This is a technique that's very close to my heart as a means of creating positive energy and driving outperformance. It also teaches a very important lesson: it's a jungle out there. As soon as a business starts to outperform the market, competitors will drop their prices, work hard to attract your people (and consequently your customer data). There will also always be a competitor who sees an opportunity before you do – that's guaranteed. Your own organisation might believe its own story and take the eye off quality. Regulators might feel you need bringing into line. You might lose some of the sharpness of your focus on the leading indicators and fail to spot shifting trends.

So never forget to be paranoid and keep asking the question 'what if...?' There are many reasons not to be complacent. So manufacture that tension – create a larger-than-life challenge by making the impossible possible in a highly visible way.

Creating a 'mission impossible' opportunity to outperform can also be important at a time when confidence is low and you as CEO want to prove to the organisation just how good it really is.

The best example of this from my career was in 2001, when I set Burger King the challenge of building a restaurant in 24 hours.

Achieving the impossible

I'd been at Burger King for four years. We were doing very well. We'd ridden out the BSE crisis. We were delivering double-digit profit growth in Europe on the back of a strong multi-faceted relaunch including quality, service, innovation, investment in advertising and restaurant growth. And then the second wave of BSE swept across Europe.

Immediately, we were back in an incredibly tough trading environment. During the Easter break, I thought long and hard about how to resuscitate the confidence we'd lost so we could once more focus our energies on creating growth.

That's when the leadership team and I came up with the idea of what we called 'BK1'. At the time, we were building a lot of restaurants in Europe. Our revenue came from a combination of our network of existing restaurants, where it was growing at a double-digit rate, plus any new restaurants we could open.

There was a very important practical consideration behind picking this particular challenge. When we budgeted for a new restaurant, we would estimate the revenues it would generate in any given financial year based on its opening date. But anyone who has ever built a house or added an extension to their home knows that it always costs more and takes longer than the original estimate. It doesn't matter what country or continent you're in, construction is always slower and more expensive than you'd hoped.

The same applied at Burger King, meaning we were often missing our budgeted numbers when it came to openings. So could this challenging project help us come up with some workable and effective new ideas to drive down the time taken to build a new restaurant?

The challenge was immense – reducing what normally took between six and eight months to just a single day. So of course, we had to do a great deal of work in advance to make it remotely possible, and we allocated a large team to the preparations, getting a great deal of prefab concrete and other materials to the site.

All this was done in the utmost secrecy, so not the faintest whisper of the challenge ahead reached the lucky participants before the big reveal.

The day itself was fantastic fun. It centred on Rotherham in the UK. I'd just flown in from Miami. I still had jetlag as I stood up to say to the assembled throng: 'Welcome to the theatre of the impossible. Together we're going to build a restaurant in 24 hours'.

A sort of thrilled panic filled the room. Eyes started from heads. Exclamations were bitten off in mid yelp. People looked stunned.

But we did it. The restaurant was opened within 24 hours – and I think it is still operating.

More important, this success injected a huge boost of confidence into the whole organisation, strengthening morale in the face of the adversity we faced. And it has had a lasting legacy too: that day, we had ideas and developed skills that reduced average build times by more than four weeks.

For a leader, being paranoid about slipping standards, shifts in the market or growing complacency is never a bad thing. Always keep your eyes open and constantly challenge your teams to see what you see. Never stop studying the leading indicators – and from time to time, toss a lit firework into the mix in the shape of a seemingly impossible challenge.

Anyone suffering from complacency will be shocked out of it. And anyone who is low on energy and belief will receive a massive boost of enthusiasm.

Celebrate and recognise success every day

I've already mentioned Gallup's famous 12 questions. Now, I want to concentrate on just one of them – number four: 'In the last seven days, I have received recognition or praise for doing good work'.

I cannot overemphasise the extent to which I believe celebrating and recognising success every day is a fundamental driver of outperformance.

Recognition is essential to keep energy high in the organisation – and these involve much more than the yearly appraisal and bonus letters. It's down to the CEO to create an operating culture in which exceptional individual and team performance and achievements are recognised on a daily basis.

Staged presentations, where individuals and teams are congratulated publicly in front of an audience, are an important building block of a high-performance culture. It is an extremely effective way of making sure the concept of outperformance reaches a wide audience within the organisation.

As a leader, you are also well positioned to provide recognition, acknowledgement and appreciation every day, without any requirement for getting on stage. And it can be incredibly rewarding for you too – the emotional responses you sometimes get can be something you'll remember and value for the rest of your life.

Recognition again ranks at number four in Intertek's internal Twelve Principles of Engagement, which for me sum up the fundamental duties for any leader who truly wishes to engage everybody in the organisation.

1. Expectations: I check regularly to ensure that each team member is clear about the expectations on them
2. Tools: I make sure each team member has the tools/equipment to do his/her work well
3. Strengths: I give each team member the opportunity to play to their strengths
4. Recognition: I create a culture of acknowledgement/appreciation/recognition
5. Caring: I care for team members in a genuine way
6. Opinions count: I always listen to everyone's opinions with an open mind
7. Create meaning: I regularly spend time reminding each team member of why their work is so vital to the team's and the company's success
8. Work quality: I do not accept poor performance from anybody
9. Trust: I create an environment of trust, friendship and belonging
10. Development: I encourage each team member's development
11. Progress: I have regular discussions with each team member about their progress
12. Growth plans: I invest the time to enable each team member to develop meaningful growth plans and follow up regularly.

Going beyond health and safety...

I believe that the basic rule of recognition for any leader is to be mindful that the working environment can be dangerous, that problems can lie in wait for just about anybody.

For this reason, leaders need to be constantly alert and remind people that there are essential actions everybody needs to take to protect and promote their health, safety and well-being.

We also need to recognise that the pressure organisations can exert on employees can cause them to take risks. For example, I have recently seen a report on the number of car accidents that take place because people are tempted to multi-task while driving.

Addressing issues like this head-on – showing people that their well-being and safety are more important than anything else – is the ultimate recognition of their value in the eyes of the leader.

A few years ago, I visited our laboratory in Manchester and I was moved and inspired listening to the safety moment the team had prepared. The safety moment was in the form of this Chinese proverb:

Be careful of your thoughts because your thoughts become your words. Be careful of your words because your words become your actions.

Be careful of your actions because your actions become your habits. Be careful of your habits because your habits become your character.

Be careful, finally, of your character because your character becomes your destiny.

I always carry this Chinese proverb with me as it is a profound statement about the impact we have on the well-being of our colleagues every day.

Naturally, physical and mental well-being were high on our agenda at Intertek during the COVID-19 pandemic.

I don't think we did anything exceptional, but it was always risk-based, well thought through, well delivered and well received. Quite simply, we implemented a tailored COVID-19 HSE policy at the onset of the virus and issued regular updates as the situation developed, ensuring that the protections we had in place for all our people remained current and appropriate.

We also introduced a Global Wellbeing programme, 'Kindness', that our people could experience online at their leisure. Featuring six core spaces of well-being they could focus on, this was a hugely popular and successful initiative for colleagues everywhere. It continues to be well received.

Key points from this chapter:

- Make sure everybody understands with total clarity exactly what 'outperform' means for their role, their department and the organisation as a whole.
- Set up daily, weekly and monthly operating systems to empower the organisation with constant insight into comparative performance and progress against targets.
- Commit yourself and make yourself highly visible as you lead from the front with high – and highly visible – energy.
- Always be genuine and authentic as a leader, continually challenging the organisation with ideas and programmes to drive continuous improvement.
- Recognise and celebrate success every day, providing excellent role models and inspiring others to outperform.

Leadership Principle 4
Customer intimacy

Chapter content:

- Establish a 24/7 capability to deliver zero-defect quality.
- Build a truly customer-centric organisation.
- Independent Total Quality Assurance.
- Listen to the voice of the customer.
- Customer intimacy is the ultimate advantage.

Customer retention is the best test of sustainability for any business.

There is no point in investing in new product development, marketing, advertising or sales initiatives to gain new customers if you're losing the ones you already have.

If you are losing customers, it is very likely that the quality of your products or your service delivery isn't good enough. If that's the case, there is no point asking people to buy more stuff from you. You are already perceived as not delivering value.

Customer retention depends on an organisation's ability to offer and deliver a superior value proposition. That starts with zero-defect quality, which matches customers' expectations and is offered at a price that the customer is willing to pay.

Leaders have a very important role to play in ensuring every part of the organisation delivers its best-ever quality, every minute of every day with every customer.

Operational discipline, for which the Chief Energy Officer (CEO) is ultimately responsible, is all about the consistent delivery of your customer value proposition.

You hear a lot of CEOs talking about the importance of putting the customer first every day!

Here is why.

Outstanding customer satisfaction, delivered consistently with every customer, will in turn drive the sustainable growth you and your shareholders are looking for. It will also create the ultimate advantage that any company can have, customer intimacy.

Customer intimacy is what every company should target when delivering customer service. In our transparent and highly competitive world, where consumers have more brands to select from than ever before and customers can choose suppliers from across the world, you will never achieve sustainable growth if your products or services do not consistently meet or exceed expectations. The days are gone when people would stick with a supplier through lack of choice.

The meaning is clear: whatever the output of your company might be, the only way to succeed is first to know your customers well, to understand their expectations and to make sure you meet or exceed these every time you're in contact.

The concept looks simple. But nobody should underestimate the difficulty of establishing a customer-centric culture. In any organisation, no matter what it does, the risk of being internally focused is always very high.

So, what do you and your organisation have to do to become truly customer-centric and achieve customer intimacy? These are the questions I will try to answer in this chapter.

Establish a 24/7 capability to deliver zero-defect quality

The 24/7 total quality commitment is a principle that has to be part of the DNA of a company. This is non-negotiable.

A commitment to total quality 24/7 must be an essential part of any company's DNA. And responsibility for ensuring this is the case lies squarely with the CEO. He or she must use every opportunity to communicate and demonstrate emphatically why total quality is essential. In addition, leading by example is the only way to cement a commitment to total quality in any organisation.

Of course, there are temptations. You might be under huge cost pressures. But the moment the leader compromises on quality, no matter the causes, it's the beginning of the end. Not only is it wrong – but it also sets the wrong example to everybody in the organisation.

As CEO, you cannot do everything on your own. But you are ultimately responsible for making sure the organisation has the foundations on which to build the consistent delivery of total quality.

These have to be fully end-to-end across the organisation's entire ecosystem, including all suppliers at every tier of the supply chain. You need to be satisfied that the right equipment, infrastructure and technology are in place in all factories and service-delivery centres. And all operating processes, employee tools, quality metrics, information systems and training must be designed and implemented with this being front of mind.

The supplier issue is particularly important, as an organisation's quality is only as strong as its weakest link's. Do you really understand the extended organisation? Do you have deep knowledge about the quality and reputation of your suppliers, agents, your sub-contractors and other partners? Do you know about their strengths and their vulnerabilities? Are you up to speed with the risks involved in working with them?

The question of metrics

I talked quite a lot about metrics in the last chapter. Once again, these are as fundamental to ensuring zero-defect quality, 24/7 every day. It's all about capturing those leading and lagging indicators, which should be displayed in a dashboard to monitor trends and identify all risk areas on an ongoing basis.

All such metrics should be well defined, and the CEO must be personally involved as much in setting those definitions as in setting the organisation's quality standards.

First, you have to identify what the indicators are. What are the metrics that will confirm you're delivering 24/7 total quality? And which will tell you most about the risks that are getting bigger? Where are the most likely sources of mistakes that will threaten your quality capabilities?

Be sure of one thing. These risks will exist. Mistakes will be made. The need for vigilance is constant. And the need for transparency with the right metrics is mission critical. Importantly, the need to react at the speed of light when quality risks are identified should never be underestimated, no matter how busy the leadership team is.

Getting the cadence right

Some of the time, you'll be able to snuff problems out before any damage is done. At other times, you will have to act quickly to restrict the impact of something that has gone wrong. Being able to do both these things fast and emphatically depends on your ability not only to define the right quality indicators but also to track them accurately using the right cadence.

In my view, the cadence for managing quality metrics should be different from their financial equivalents, with daily cockpits in place. And if you are operating a high-throughput organisation, I would even recommend sometimes looking at metrics on an hourly basis.

Typically, the Big Data challenge for many organisations today is data overload. This can prevent you from seeing what the true trends are. The ones that really matter can be drowned out by background and foreground noise. I therefore strongly recommend that you set up a series of early-warning systems and escalation processes to alert you in case of emerging quality issues. They will be extremely useful in helping you implement a decisive response at pace.

When it comes to quality, all metrics are important, but most quality assurance issues arise when an organisation fails to pay sufficient attention to the most significant ones. Top of the pile are customer complaints. It remains a mystery to me why corporations and leaders around the world constantly fail to prioritise this area. It's a free hit – somebody has taken the time to write to you, to give you direct feedback and to ask you to do something about what went wrong.

But far too many corporations don't take complaints seriously. How disrespectful is that? And how dangerous? Here is a personal example of the penalty that can lie in wait for those companies that fail to respond to complaints.

Flying into trouble

I used to fly one particular airline a great deal when I was at Burger King, visiting our operations. One day, I had a major issue on a long flight, between Los Angeles and Sydney. I happened to have the email address of the airline's CEO, so I wrote to him and explained what had happened. I made it quite a personal letter, saying essentially: 'I am a CEO like you, and

I would certainly want to hear about anything like this happening in my organisation.'

I didn't get a reply – not even from the customer services department. So for the last 20 years I've only ever used that airline when I had absolutely no other choice. I fly a lot.

A few years later, I was flying on another airline, this time from San Francisco to London. It was fully booked – and my seat wouldn't go into the sleeping position. Again, I had the CEO's email address. Again, I wrote. And this time I got a reply, from the customer services department, asking for my understanding. But they offered me nothing in recompense, not even a small discount in recognition of the enormous number of hours I flew with them.

I have to use this airline still, but it's never with any pleasure. I wouldn't consider investing in them. I've written them off as a brand, simply because I now know they don't take customer service seriously.

It's not difficult as a CEO to take customer complaints seriously. Whenever a client has taken the time and trouble to find out my personal contact details, I will always reply in person. It's a huge opportunity to be in touch, to overturn any negative views, and sometimes to convert a critic into an evangelist. Importantly, it always gives me additional data on an area of our value proposition which is not zero defect. An invaluable data point for continuous improvement of our customer service.

Defining and benchmarking quality standards

As a leader, you have to set and demand the highest quality standards. The acid test comes when there is pressure on costs – and I have already said that the moment you start to compromise on quality is the moment that everything starts to go wrong.

There are many areas that an organisation can target to become more cost-efficient – but quality is not one of them. The moment when the CEO steps in to ensure cost-saving initiatives do not compromise quality can be a defining one, watched by everybody in the organisation. Unless you set the highest possible quality standards, people will not trust you anymore. They'll accuse you of cutting corners, of failing to live up to the Customer Promise that the organisation has signed up to.

So I will never ask anybody to reduce costs by reducing quality. I might ask for better productivity. And I will always enjoy the challenge of proving to anyone in business that you can improve quality and productivity at the same time. It's just a question of effective process management, equipment, technology, training, innovation – and, of course, leadership.

Know the competition

You must always be aware of the risk that your competition might outperform you when it comes to quality. To mitigate this, you first need to find a way of understanding just how good your competitors really are. This requires proper quality benchmarking that defines precisely the standards being attained by all existing and emerging competitors. This must be done with the right market research methodology to ensure independence and accuracy.

Failure to achieve this means that one day you will be caught by surprise when a competitor launches a new product, or is seen to offer a superior value proposition, that takes business away from you. This is not a risk you can afford to take.

Of course, no organisation is perfect. And the world is constantly finding new ways of delivering superior quality. That means there is only one way of driving sustainable customer satisfaction. This is all about creating and sustaining a culture of continuous improvement in everything the company does, challenging the organisation always to innovate and find new and better ways of delivering superior quality. No organisation can afford to cease investing in continuous improvement at every layer, in every department, function and individual operation.

Be risk aware

Recognising that no factory or service centre will ever be risk-free, in terms of quality and customer service delivery, is very healthy. In my view, the more risk aware you are, the more risk prepared you will be operating at a fast pace on a daily basis. The best companies, in terms of quality, are those that measure quality rigorously on a daily basis, accept that there are risks in their day-to-day operations, use the early-warning systems to act quickly to fix the problem identified, practice a well-structured continuous improvement process to innovate on how to drive quality, and train their teams to follow these innovative processes, making sure that customer expectations are met and exceeded. Said differently, the pursuit of zero-defect quality, while being risk aware and prepared, is an essential part of your end-to-end quality management systems.

Importantly, every operation must target the highest quality standards to exceed the expectations of its customers. In my opinion, it is by bringing this attitude to life and embedding it in every process that has made Toyota one of the best companies in the world when it comes to manufacturing.

Doing things the Toyota Way

What can we all learn from this amazing company? How does Toyota get it right? How does it get so close to perfection when it comes to quality?

On the surface, the answer is simple. It achieves all this by doing everything in just one way – the 'Toyota Way'. This is the company's manufacturing-driven philosophy. It is based on very rich, dense, intense, tough and demanding values. It's all about teamwork, precision and the constant pursuit of perfection.

One of the foundations of the Toyota Way lies in the value of empowerment. They believe in hiring the very best people, and then giving them the licence to build the best cars in the world, with the full support of the entire organisation.

The way Toyota approaches zero-defect manufacturing is first to break everything down into segments. Each segment team has a leader, and the area where they work contains a number of panels showing the key metrics that relate to them. All team members will meet three times a day: first to discuss what they are going to achieve during the hours ahead; then to reflect together on progress midday and finally, to close the loop at the end of the working day.

Ideas for improvement

During that time, they work together to come up with new ideas for continuous improvement. The signs of this are everywhere. For example, a Toyota production line can switch seamlessly to produce very different cars, one after the other – all because of innovative, precise operating procedures and a shared dedication to total quality.

There is much we can learn from Toyota's very special way of doing business and delivering quality. Empowerment – at every step during the production process – for being the best is deeply engrained in their culture. This is why, along with the automotive industry's most advanced manufacturing technology, a simple cord hangs above every production line.

This cord is very important. It enables each worker to manage his or her own quality. If you pull the cord, it means you have made a mistake. It also means you are determined not to pass that mistake on to somebody else. You are in charge of your own work. You take responsibility. You don't pass the buck.

That's because you are a Toyota person. That makes you special. And you plan to spend your life with Toyota.

How many companies achieve that level of engagement with their employees? Very, very few.

Keep the noise down

I've visited many more factories around the world than I can remember. It was in Toyota's Lexus factory in the south of Japan that I saw the single best metric for driving total quality. The Lexus brand may not be top of mind for everyone, but you should really try driving a Lexus one day. Doing so will convince you, as it did me, that it is the best luxury car in the world.

The incredible standards of the quality management systems involved in manufacturing the Lexus are apparent as soon as you see the production line. It's like ballet and opera rolled into one. There is hardly any noise. Everything flows, beautifully. I've never seen a quality management approach to match it.

After visiting the Lexus factory, I wanted to find out about how the factory manager was running such a perfect operation. To my astonishment, I was told that the factory manager uses decibels as the lead indicator in terms of zero defects, 24/7.

If there is too much noise, something must be going wrong. You cannot beat that. Very cool!

Getting back to basics

As I have said before, things were not great at the company when I first joined Burger King in 1996. It had just been through the first BSE crisis, its financial performance was poor, and people were constantly looking out for others to take the blame.

We had to turn the business around, in terms of its financial performance and its spirit. Both were toxic.

When I joined, we entered a long period of trying to analyse the causes of the problems the company faced beyond the obvious candidate of BSE. I have already mentioned the relatively small size of the company in Europe at this time, particularly in relation to McDonald's. The scale disadvantage was very clear, and with the Burger King senior management, we started to work with regarding the development of our future growth strategy to achieve the right scale on a global basis. We quickly came to the conclusion that we should focus growth on a few large markets, on which we could concentrate our efforts to scale up.

At the time, I was convinced that the company faced a set of problems that extended far beyond BSE, and our research confirmed this suspicion. We concluded that there had not been enough investment in advertising and product innovation, resulting in a weak brand image and the need for innovation in our menus.

But our most important finding was that Burger King had become complacent about quality and customer service. So we put any plans for investments in growth, advertising and new menus on the back burner while we addressed the essential fact that our number one problem was declining customer satisfaction. This was due to poor ratings for the quality of both our products and our service standards.

Until this was resolved, there was no point in investing in growing the network of restaurants and attracting customers with additional marketing investments – people were coming, and they weren't happy with what they found. A well-known mantra in retail is that you must ensure your existing outlets are performing well in terms of customer satisfaction well before you invest more in advertising to create new traffic and attract new customers. That's how you make sure existing operations are driving good like-for-like sustainable growth, which is a must before expanding your network of retail operations.

This well-known mantra in retail works in any multi-site operation of course!

Make Every Bite Right

When it came to the quality of the products we sold and the speed of our customer service, we had a great deal of work ahead of us at Burger King.

Having come in from the outside, it was clear to me where some of the problems lay. The fries were not as they should be. Teams had forgotten how to build a good Whopper. There was no focus on speed of service.

We quickly agreed that the first phase of the Burger King relaunch had to put the quality of our products and service right at the top of the agenda. This was a challenging message for our employees and franchisees, who had been expecting more advertising and new products.

But it was the right thing to do. We had to get back to basics. And this was the big idea behind 'Make Every Bite Right', the total quality programme we launched to concentrate minds and energies across the whole organisation on what really mattered.

I mentioned Vision 10,000 in Chapter 2: when launching this to our franchisees in Hamburg in late 1996, I said: 'This is all about give and take. I will get the funding to invest in growth, in new restaurants, in more advertising and new products. But first you've got to give me the quality our customers expect. I'm not going to make those investments until I'm 100 per cent happy with the quality.'

I was 36, bursting with confidence and bristling with energy. I was determined to do everything it took to turn the tide of complacency. I had no idea how long it would take – but I had plenty of ideas about how to lead by example.

I visited restaurants four days a week. And I always tried to find a way of making the point about quality. I was as challenging as I could be. I'd look in the fridges, and I'd throw buns, patties and tomatoes in the bin if they weren't in line with our freshness standards. The first time I did that, the franchisee was very unhappy.

I said, 'If you don't fix your quality issues, we will close your restaurant.'

He was really frustrated. Really angry. But word got around. The next restaurant I visited, the food was super fresh – and I changed my focus to cleaning standards. So I asked for cleaning materials and washed the floor myself to show what cleanliness was all about! Next time, it was the turn of the toilets. Then I would check that the broilers used to grill the meat were properly calibrated in terms of temperature, to satisfy our safety criteria.

Word carried on spreading about this fixated new boss. Attitudes and behaviours changed. Our products improved, so did the environment in each restaurant. We made a massive impact on speed of service too, bringing order to service times down to just three minutes in 75% of cases. And we got everybody onside with end-to-end quality management, enabling franchisees and managers everywhere to get quality absolutely right.

In time, I was able to deliver my side of the bargain. I started to invest in advertising, in product development, in expanding our presence by opening new restaurants. That was very satisfying.

The moment of truth

There is one moment in particular that I remember, because it was when I realised that we had won the quality battle. I was in a restaurant in central Stockholm, which initially had some particular challenges with discipline. The first time I visited, in fact, I found a sunbed in the basement. That didn't last long.

I used to visit this restaurant two or three times a year as it was our flagship operation in Stockholm. One day I realised that Make Every Bite Right was working in this restaurant. It was peak lunchtime and getting really busy. The restaurant was flying. I was impressed and delighted – it was doing really well.

We were hiring students at the time to help at peak hours, and I saw one young guy preparing the Whoppers perfectly, delivering our 'Make Every Bite Right' promise, with a high level of productivity and with a big smile on his face. I went up to him and started talking, with a bit of a provocative question: 'How are you getting on with your boss?' He said, 'I couldn't care less about my boss.'

I was slightly startled. 'What do you mean?' I asked. 'I don't need him,' he said. 'I'm here for a few hours a day, preparing the world's best-tasting burgers for my customers. That's enough to make me happy.'

Our operational manager for Sweden, Christiane Saüve, had a big smile on her face on the way back to the airport that day. Creating a customer-centric organisation is highly rewarding for a leader.

This kind of genuine employee engagement is amazing for a leader to watch. That sort of engagement, that commitment to delivering zero-defect quality 24/7, is very inspiring. To have a chance of hearing something similar, you need first to build a truly customer-centric organisation. Doing so involves properly inverting the pyramid, ensuring that people on the front line, like that student, are fully empowered to do the very best they can for their customers.

Build a truly customer-centric organisation

An organisation's operating model has a massive impact on its ability to create a customer-centric culture. This can only happen when customers are placed at the top of the agenda, with leadership creating a decentralised structure in which customer-facing employees are given the right resources and support to put customers first.

One of the first pitfalls emerges at the point of recruitment. It should be obvious that getting the right people to manage customer relationships is vital.

So it is vital that local operational leaders receive training and support on how to recruit customer-centric colleagues with the right skills and behaviours.

Similarly, the training and development of customer-facing colleagues must be an overriding priority for all leadership and HR teams. However, this can be enormously complicated, particularly for organisations with massive geographic areas to cover and multiple sites across countries or continents.

How can you be positive that you have people of the right quality in every role, in every site across the organisation? How, for example, does Toyota know for sure that it has the right quality in all its factories?

People management drives quality

The truth is, quality management is all about people management. Once you've recruited the right people, given them the tools they need to excel, have the right metrics in place to measure their performance and have set up the right processes, then the quality of service your customers receive depends how well you lead your teams.

Quality professionals use a common and simple saying, which I believe applies to organisations of every type: treat your employees the way you want them to treat your customers. Time and again, you see proof that the best way of driving high levels of customer satisfaction is to put maximum focus on employee engagement.

Given this, I find it incredible how so many companies fail to treat their frontline people – the most important in the organisation – with the respect their role and skills deserve. Their outstanding importance to the organisation's success means that they must be made to feel important, valued and respected. The real magic in delivering consistently outstanding product quality or customer experience comes simply from placing the people agenda at the forefront of any operational process: a simple day-to-day application of Leadership with Soul.

This is why one of the areas that I used always to check during my visit to any Burger King restaurant was the staffroom. I'd make it my last port of call in every restaurant visit. My view was straightforward – how could you expect your people to be friendly, efficient and disciplined with their customers if you weren't in turn giving them the right care? It soon became known that I would not be happy if I found that the staffroom wasn't clean, didn't have a functioning toilet or didn't provide shower facilities.

Measuring customer satisfaction is necessary to establish zero-defect quality but not sufficient. Customer satisfaction needs to be part of the reward structure to drive the right behaviours.

When it comes to customer-facing employees, it is particularly important to reward the behaviours that are important to achieving your strategy. It is best practice to make sure that bonus criteria are based on the right customer-service measurements, such as Net Promoter Score (NPS) and customer retention.

Recognising the progress your organisation makes in terms of customer service on a regular basis, using the selected metrics in place will play a disproportionate role as you try to build a customer-centric culture.

At Intertek, our yearly award ceremony, meticulously prepared by Sally Murtagh, our head of Internal Communication, is a date in the calendar that everybody looks for. Why? It's all about paying tribute to all the efforts our teams around the world have made to deliver our Customer Promise. It usually starts with a global tour around the world of Intertek, watching a hugely energising film. It's then about recognising publicly our heroes in each of our award categories and saying 'thank you' for everything they do. This yearly event is the part of my role as a CEO that I enjoy most. Saying thank you means a lot to me!

Attracting, retaining and developing the best talent in the industry is one of the key criteria that defines outperformance. Once recruitment has happened, it is important to make sure your employees can quickly see you are committed to investing in their skills and their future. Young people, particularly, are impatient for progress, so it's vital that those with the desire and potential to learn and grow can rapidly see that the organisation gives them high-quality opportunities for career and personal development.

Living the dream

Disney has the reputation of being a truly customer-centric organisation, making magic happen all the time for all guests. What is the secret behind the magic?

Recruitment is a very important moment for Disney as it's about recruiting a cast member. That is not the same as being an employee. It's a calling. It's being part of the story called Disney. It's about having the privilege of bringing your guests into a magical world that only Disney can provide.

Once you have joined Disney as a cast member, you start your career with a training programme called 'Disney Tradition'. The training programme is very powerful and revolves around just three central pillars: safety, service and storytelling.

The first two are obvious. Everybody needs to be kept safe. You also want everybody to have a great time, so they'll tell their friends and keep coming back. So you need to deliver the best possible service.

Storytelling is probably the most important aspect of the training. Cast members are expected to use their creativity, passion, knowledge and imagination to tell stories which will immerse the guests in the Disney magic. Stories about travelling to the edge of the galaxy, about Captain Jack Sparrow, about Simba's battle with Scar.

Investing time in building relationships

After Euro Disney, I had the privilege to lead Inchcape, a company that created global trade based on a passionate and customer-centric culture from day one.

How did Inchcape become a global force with a unique approach to building customer relationships?

Inchcape has a fabulous history, built on a pioneering spirit that enabled its founders in the 19th century to build trading routes between east and west across the world.

It was one of the world's first truly global organisations. It had few examples to follow – but it understood early on just how important it was to be truly decentralised, with a small head office and all the talents based in their local markets. It also had a policy of employing local people, with few expats.

However, Inchcape wanted those expats it did employ to be committed to the markets and communities where they worked. So when they appointed someone to a new territory – from Brisbane to Bahrain, Singapore to Nairobi – the initial posting would be for a minimum of five years.

With no visits back home. No holidays with the family.

This wasn't because Inchcape's leaders were mean or unwilling to spend money. They simply wanted their expat workers to spend time in their new communities, getting to know the culture and understand how business was done. In particular, they wanted them to fully connect with clients and customers and spend time building relationships.

In addition, you have to assume that the five-year rule meant that only the most committed people would want to become an Inchcape expat.

Over time, the world of Inchcape changed quite a bit, but there is one thing that will never change at Inchcape because it is part of the DNA: a decentralised and passionate customer-centric culture.

Franchising for success

The franchising model has been one of the most successful corporate expansion strategies of recent years. And it's been particularly successful for organisations that recognise franchising is about much more than just saving money and driving rapid expansion at a low cost.

Obviously, my role at Burger King meant that I spent a great deal of time studying their biggest global rival – the McDonald's Corporation. In my view, McDonald's has long recognised that its core is not about operating restaurants. Rather, it is about owning a brand, developing menus, managing supply chains and expanding the restaurant network through franchising.

Franchising is the obvious route for a business like McDonald's to take, as running a restaurant for a global brand with well-defined standards is a people business. That's because they know that if you recruit the right franchisees and focus them on local recruitment and local empowerment, they will excel at delivering the best quality. So the franchising model clearly proves the economic value in treating your people the way you want them to treat customers.

This has certainly been my experience – at PepsiCo, Burger King and to an extent also at Inchcape. Time after time, I have found that all other things being equal, franchisee's operations are usually more successful than company's operations as they put the quality of people at the top of the agenda.

This is at least partly to do with focus. The franchisee doesn't have to worry about the brand or corporate politics. They are solely concerned with their own restaurant or retail outlet. And they know that if they do a good job at recruiting and developing the best people, they will be the best at delivering high-quality customer service.

They also know that the opportunity for them is greater than just driving customer retention and growing revenue and profit in the existing restaurants. They know too that those franchisees that excel at delivering brand values through high-quality service will also be the ones who get preferential access to more franchising opportunities.

Independent Total Quality Assurance

In almost every organisation, there is an inherent tension or conflict between the commercial priority of being first to market and what it takes to deliver against the quality agenda by consistently offering the highest quality standards.

This intrinsic conflict has to be managed. It's part of your job as leader. And the only way of doing so is to ensure that you have the right level of independent Total Quality Assurance inside your organisation at all times.

In recent years, the world has changed fast for all corporations, with complexity rapidly accelerating to the point where there is a danger of it becoming overwhelming. Having multiple locations, direct and indirect production facilities, many types of products and services, sources of supply and distribution channels makes the monitoring of quality very difficult.

But it is possible. To make it happen, you as CEO will need to work with your top team on the end-to-end mapping of all your sourcing, manufacturing, distribution and delivery channels. This will enable you to fully understand the full scope of the organisation's operations and identify all risk areas in terms of both quality and safety.

Unfortunately, the growing organisational complexity I refer to makes it almost impossible for companies to perform quality-control work at every point in their supply chain.

So you have to take a risk-based approach, which starts with regular Testing, Inspection and Certification activities at those critical, higher-risk areas where physical quality control is required. Testing, Inspection and Certification are important quality monitoring activities but not sufficient, as you also need to carry out assurance activities to get a 360° evaluation of your quality, safety and sustainability standards inside your entire value chain. These will take the form of an audit of all operating procedures, management systems, skills and behaviours to help you deeply understand your end-to-end quality, safety and sustainability performance with a systemic data monitoring across your operations.

Evaluating the performance of your operations in a systemic end-to-end approach, based on rigorous Assurance, Testing, Inspection and Certification, will give you the quality-assurance peace of mind you need and enable you to build a stronger business.

Taking a systemic approach to risk-based quality assurance will ultimately present you with a clear dashboard that provides perspective over all your quality metrics, right across the organisation. It will give you accurate and timely updates on quality, safety and sustainability trends. Monitoring and calibrating these metrics is very important for all leaders. They will act as an early-warning system, giving you an indication very early of any emerging issues with your end-to-end quality assurance proposition.

Do bear in mind that monitoring these trends must take place independently of customer-facing operations – they cannot be simultaneously both the judge and jury.

When it goes wrong . . .

Companies have always been getting into trouble of one sort or another for failing to get their quality standards consistently right. Some cases of recent years have been enormously high-profile, driven by the overwhelming operating complexity that corporations face today.

Many of these give us insight into just how important Total Quality Assurance is to avoid the sort of high-profile issues that so many companies have faced, which are so often linked to the conflict between rushing to market and getting quality right on a truly sustainable basis.

Having worked with some of these companies over the years, I have observed that the lack of independent quality assurance is the most common root cause of the corporate issues that drive down company values, disenfranchise customers and cause employee-retention problems.

Listen to the voice of the customer

Many organisations that say they put their customers first do not in reality listen to the voice of the customer. While they might spend a great deal of money on customer research, they pay little attention to the best source of insight – customer feedback, including customer complaint management.

I mentioned the importance of customer complaint management at the beginning of the chapter and I believe that customer complaint management has to be a well-functioning operating system in any total quality management system.

Any customer who takes the time to write to a company about a quality issue needs to be taken seriously. The CEO therefore needs to ensure that the operating system underpinning the customer feedback procedure is set up to inform key stakeholders quickly.

Monitoring this feedback is not complicated, and many organisations focus on collecting customer data. However, it is what they actually do with it that counts, and too many companies approach its management in a vertical, siloed manner that involves only the research department and senior management.

This approach prevents complaints information from reaching people at the customer-facing front line – where it's needed most.

This is why I believe so strongly in the value of the NPS. This uses a simple calculation to come up with a score between 0 and 100. It comprises the percentage of those customers likely to recommend a company, product or service at a level of nine or ten, minus the percentage of those likely to award a rating of less than six. For example, if 70% of your customers are 'promoters', and 20% are 'detractors', your company's NPS stands at 50.

NPS gives frontline colleagues immediate information on how our customers feel, creating the right environment for leaders to engage with their teams and for those teams to engage with customers.

KitKats in the minibar ...

When I arrived at Euro Disney, I already knew that the organisation's commitment to quality was extremely strong. Even then, I was surprised by the very high-quality scores its theme parks achieved, which were the main reason for their tremendous customer loyalty.

I was particularly surprised by the incredibly sharp focus on managing customer complaints. Every park had a clear focus on both responding to the customer in each case, and then resolving the issue. This clear and visible commitment came right from the top – from Michael Eisner, Chairman and Chief Executive of the Walt Disney Company worldwide.

He was a busy man – running ABC, the studios, all the theme parks and franchises across the world. At the time, he was also working on the acquisition of Pixar.

Even with all that going on, Michael Eisner would make the time, every month, to read every single customer complaint from every theme park across the world. Every now and again I'd receive a note. 'André, the Santa Fe minibar in room 705 at 23:50 on Saturday didn't have any KitKats. Can we understand what went wrong?'

I quickly learned to get ahead of the game. 'Sure, I'm on it', I would say. It was a great learning experience for me. It's not just that customers deserve the respect for us to understand what they have to say. It's also because a complaint occurs when there is an operational breakdown at some point in the system. It's an opportunity to get better.

But NPS and listening to complaints are not the be-all-and-end-all when it comes to hearing the customer's voice. Think for a moment about those promoters – your biggest fans, the ones who know you best and who are your most loyal clients, customers and consumers. Getting the views of your most loyal customers from time to time is a hugely rewarding initiative as they will usually be very honest on what's working or not!

It's extraordinary how few companies seek these people out to understand what makes them so positive. When I was the 7Up marketing manager at PepsiCo, I worked with a very talented market research colleague, Hans Wybenga, who would always organise in-depth discussions with these 'heavy users'. The reason was simple – they knew and used our brands better and more than we did. And they were happy to share their thoughts with us on all aspects of our performance and their experience.

I strongly recommend customer research with these heavy users from time to time: it is a huge source of insight, particularly when it comes to the innovation process. And too few companies do it.

Top-to-top communication

Another area where companies could do better is when it comes to the time that leaders spend with clients. I strongly believe that CEOs and other leaders in both a business-to-consumer and a business-to-business environment should be out there more, leading by example and getting to understand deeply how their clients feel.

It's an effective route to building trusted relationships over time, and 'top-to-top' organisational wiring is a powerful best practice in truly customer-centric organisations.

At PepsiCo, for example, while we were very strong in the USA, our business across the rest of the world was surprisingly small. The implication of our sub-scale position was clear: we didn't have top-to-top relationships with major retailers across the world.

Recognising this, we developed and delivered the 'Top to Top' initiative. This proved to be a highly effective programme, in which we ensured that our most senior decision-makers gained personal access to the top management teams inside the world's largest retailers. What mattered most was that they spent quality time together, face-to-face. And it really worked, reinventing relationships at every level.

I believe that high-quality contacts at the most senior level within the organisations of your customers is key to operating as a customer-centric enterprise. I continue to apply this thinking whenever possible.

Plugging into social media

Of course, much has changed over the years I've been a CEO, and the social media revolution has certainly been the single biggest shift when it comes to managing strong customer relationships. Today, we have an unprecedented opportunity to stay properly in tune with what's happening in and around the customer base.

I would encourage any leader to ensure that they are really plugged into what their customers and competitors have to say on social media. This is how reputations get built or destroyed, and 24/7 social media monitoring is essential. You must ensure that you really know what's being said about your business on every platform, every day, every hour! Otherwise, any discussions relating to quality or safety can rapidly lead to a reputational crisis for any company. You must be in a position to respond fast and decisively.

The days when just reading the press articles was enough are long gone.

Customer intimacy is the ultimate advantage

In my experience, achieving true customer intimacy will create a unique relationship that no amount of money can buy. True, it is a long journey – but every step of the way is worth it.

It must always start with the basics. Obviously, the consistent delivery of the client's expectations is the ultimate pre-requisite for any long-lasting client relationship. For this reason, everybody in the organisation needs to be utterly paranoid about failing to serve a client by not delivering consistently on their basic expectations. That's why it's so important to monitor the right customer-satisfaction metrics.

To get to the next level, to get beyond the basics, you have to start delivering a customised offering. That involves gaining a deep understanding of what your clients truly want so you can meet the particular needs that are specific to them. So make sure you customise what you have to offer in a way that is different from your competitors, that is innovative. That way, you will achieve true differentiation, to deliver a clearly superior value proposition.

Probing for insight

When I was first considering how to kick-start my marketing career in France during the 1980s, Colgate had a reputation for being an FMCG leader in terms of innovation. This was largely thanks to its focus on real customer needs and to the fact that local management was empowered to innovate fast.

The result was that at the time it was regularly first to market with innovation ahead of rivals such as P&G and Unilever.

They had a very effective and special way of training us – they'd encourage us to go and interview consumers. Of course, they used external research agencies too, but they had the policy of sending out employees to undertake these 'probes' to help us discover new insights and validate assumptions first-hand.

I can tell you, interviewing up to 100 consumers almost every month, roaming the streets of Paris, Nice, Rennes, Strasbourg or Marseille on cold winter days, sticks in the mind – you remember what people have to tell you. I did a lot of these probes, and they were a great source of inspiration for new products.

I am confident that focusing teams on real customer insights and giving them empowerment to act quickly was what made Colgate so successful in France in the 1980s. They showed that listening to customers gives you real insights before your competitors and enables you to out-innovate them.

The ultimate step

Once you have achieved this differentiation, there is a further step beyond delivering the basics with a customised offering. You will gain the ultimate advantages of customer intimacy when you can positively surprise them by exceeding their expectations.

This will give them a memorable experience, injecting a powerful jolt of energy into your relationship and ensuring you gain the deepest trust of your clients.

There is therefore a clear formula to becoming a client's most trusted partner.

The concept is straightforward, but it takes years of hard work to implement. It is about the consistently good daily delivery of a customised product or service offering, augmented with memorable moments when you exceed expectations on a regular basis.

Recognising the moment when you have earned the long-lasting trust of your clients and you are reaping the ultimate advantage of customer intimacy is truly magic.

For instance, at Intertek, that is when a client takes you into confidence to talk through something with you before they have discussed it internally. It's when you are a client's first port of call to ask for help in fixing a problem or grasping an opportunity.

You know at that moment that you've built the kind of relationship that leaves your competitors in the shade.

Of course, there are many, many companies – strong global brands that are delivering the basics with a customised offering – that fail to get to the customer intimacy level. While successful, these companies are failing to unleash their true potential.

Exceeding expectations

Oberoi is a high-quality Indian hotel chain that really understands the importance of going beyond meeting expectations and taking the ultimate step to build customer intimacy. One night, I arrived in Delhi after a 14-hour flight. I felt – and looked – as though it had been 14 years. There was cool drinking water in the car that picked me up from the airport, as well as refreshing cold towels. So far, so good – but nothing exceptional.

Then the driver asked me if I'd like to charge my phone while we were on the move. That means really thinking about what the customer needs.

Last time I stayed, the driver asked if I'd like to order food to have in my room when we arrived at the hotel. I'll stay there whenever I can. That's what exceeding expectations with memorable moments is all about.

The magical truth . . .

'How many Mickey Mouses do you have?' A common question at Euro Disney. To answer with literal truth would have dispelled the magic. So we used always to say: 'There is only one Mickey Mouse – and he's the one that's here for you right now.'

For visitors – children, their parents and grandparents – seeing Mickey, Donald, Pluto and all the other characters walking among them was truly magical. And each of those characters was unique on that day and in that place, entirely focused on creating that magic for the visitors who were right there, right now.

Challenging the tyranny

The motor industry has a terrible reputation for customer service. When I joined Inchcape, the world's largest automotive distribution, retail and services provider, I was determined to break that mould.

This meant changing the sales culture that was endemic in the organisation – and the industry. All salespeople were on commission, and they would judge potential customers as they entered the dealership, based on how they looked.

A good suit and a Rolex – great, I can smell the money, you'll get great customer service. Scruffy jeans and trainers – not so appealing. (And so often this was the wrong conclusion – the salesman had failed to spot the Mercedes-Benz the customer had left around the corner.)

The lack of customer-centricity in the automotive industry was a tyranny. It had to be challenged – and Inchcape was well placed to do so.

I worked closely on the problem with our Group Marketing Director, Ken Lee. We wanted to make buying a car a tremendously exciting, energising experience, that befitted its importance as one of the biggest investments most people ever make. We came up with the 'Inchcape Advantage' customer value proposition, which focused on delivering 'brilliant basics' and 'magic moments' to every prospective and existing client.

Brilliant basics were all about having a clear set of processes and standards around every stage of the customer journey, from the first phone call, to how you were greeted in the car park, to the reception area, to the test drive and so on.

Licence to thrill

But magic moments were the real differentiation in terms of customer service. Quite simply, we gave our colleagues the licence to make every single customer feel special. We wanted the salespeople to think, 'How do I do this?

I've got the basics – I know the processes. But what can I find out about this customer to make them feel great?'

I would like to share two examples from the Inchcape UK operations.

One of our customers already had a Toyota, which he loved, but he wanted a new one. So our salesperson asked, 'Do you want to trade in your old car?' 'No', the customer said. 'It's a great car. I want my daughter to have it.'

The deal was done. He was told to expect the new car to arrive in about four weeks: 'We'll give you a call to invite you in for a handover'. During that call, the salesperson said: 'Would you mind dropping off your old car with us the day before the handover? And when you come to pick up your new car, could you bring your daughter with you?'

You've probably already got there. When they arrived, his daughter was presented with the old car, fully valeted and sparkling like new. And then he received the keys to his new car.

Everybody won. The man and the daughter would never for a moment consider buying a car from anywhere but that dealership. Everybody in the dealership felt great about it. And it was all achieved for the cost of doing a valet. A truly magic moment.

Another story from one of my colleagues working in a VW dealership: 'I was in my office, and this guy arrived asking for a quick chat. He told me how he and his heavily pregnant wife had been looking for a new car over the previous Weekend.'

The man had a great story to tell. 'We'd had a horrible time – nobody could be bothered with us, it was just awful. Then, on our way home, we saw an Inchcape VW dealership. We thought we'd give it one last go. The place was full and our hearts sank. But then this salesman saw us – he was busy, but he came over and asked us to sit down for a few minutes and he'd be with us.

'My wife looked at the low, soft chair – completely wrong for a pregnant woman. But the sales guy noticed. He went and got her his own chair and said, "You might find this more comfortable."'

Brilliant service. From that moment, they were going to buy a car from that dealership. It cost nothing. It was a magic moment.

Feeling the magic

When living in Munich, I was at the receiving end of a similar magic moment. I was in my mid-30s, and I had always wanted a Porsche 911. I thought the Porsche 911 was the best car you could dream of.

So one Saturday morning, I decided to visit a Porsche dealership in Munich. I drove up in my BMW 5 series, feeling incredibly nervous, not much like a Porsche customer.

But when I arrived, the salesman saw the car I was driving. He didn't ask for any identification, I didn't have to sign anything. He handed me a Porsche key. 'Here you go,' he said. 'Just come back when you're ready. Have fun!'

Magic moments like that go right back to where this book started, with emotional intelligence, with understanding what a customer is looking for and how you can help this person have a very special day.

Every company can do this, but because so many do not, those that succeed are the ones that win trust. And it's always essential that the leader sets the tone from the top.

Customer intimacy is the ultimate advantage.

Key points from this chapter:

• Ensure every part of the organisation has the capability to achieve true zero-defect quality, 24/7.

• Build a truly customer-centric organisation, in which everybody understands that the ability to meet or exceed expectations is the single most important driver of sustainable success.

• Make sure you have an independent source of Total Quality Assurance in your business that helps you manage the conflict between quality and speed to market.

• Listen to the voice of the customer, ensuring you consistently, precisely understand the challenges they face and their views on your products and service levels.

• Ensure you're getting the basics right, offering a differentiated value proposition, with memorable moments that will make the customer experience truly magical. Customer intimacy is the ultimate advantage.

Leadership Principle 5
Reinvent the future

Chapter content:

* Create a culture of continuous and vigorous innovation.
* Zero-to-One and One-to-100 growth- and margin-accretive innovations.
* Start with innovation from the core.
* Invest in innovations targeted at fast-growing adjacent markets.
* The 'Big Prize' of creating new markets with breakthrough innovations.

The fifth principle of Leadership with Soul, reinvent the future, is all about innovation. Get it right, and you've got an unstoppable source of growth for your business and an incredible source of energy for the organisation. Fail to do so, and your business will eventually join that list of gone-away brands that were so big, so successful, just a few years ago.

It is a brutal fact of life that no brand or business will remain strong and prosper forever unless it finds ways to reinvent itself with relevant innovations.

It's an essential responsibility that as leader you continually reinvent the future to sustain the success of your business during and beyond your tenure.

If you don't, I can guarantee that a competitor will do it for you and take you out of business.

Hotbeds of innovation

The speed of change is a constant refrain in business these days. If you look back over the last three or four decades, it's clear why and how the R&D activities that drive innovation have accelerated at such an incredible rate. In the 1970s, there were few places in the world that could be called hotbeds of innovation. Those that did exist were mainly urban centres such as New York, London and Paris, where education and funding were easily available.

The hotspots of today, such as the West Coast, Tel Aviv, Shenzhen, Taipei, Stockholm, Barcelona and Tokyo, were barely waking up then. There was little or no innovation coming from Africa or India.

Now, the picture is entirely different. The levels of education and skills available around the world are extraordinarily high. Bright, educated, creative people are everywhere, and funds for investing in R&D are widely available.

Look at the innovations pouring out of Africa, look at how Indian companies are leapfrogging established competitors, at the patents and IPs flooding from Israel, at the extraordinary pace of high-tech creativity in the Nordic countries.

The pace of innovation has been impressive in the last 50 years. Its key drivers have been population growth in emerging markets and increasing lifestyle aspirations both there and in more developed countries. And corporations across the world understand that innovation will continue to open up huge new growth opportunities for organisations on every continent for many years into the future.

Today, there is no industry where consumers do not have enormous choice.

The world never stands still and, in a world post-COVID, we expect companies to further accelerate the pace of innovation in the products and services they offer. COVID-19 has been a tragedy for the world but it has been a catalyst for big changes as, moving forward, everyone wants to build back a better world.

Consumers expect companies to improve the quality, safety, sustainability, value for money and convenience of their products and services, which will create an even faster pace of innovation moving forward.

Opportunities for all

Everybody has a shot at reinventing the future. But not every organisation properly understands how to innovate successfully, how to continually reinvent itself to continue driving sustainable growth in an environment where the world is changing in multiple directions at the speed of light.

The main discriminating factor is the ability of entrepreneurs and companies to read the future needs of clients and consumers ahead of their competitors.

This ability is essential but not enough, as what matters most is the agility and creativity of an organisation to be first to market and to get to scale ahead of its competitors with that new idea!

The first-mover advantage and scaling up fast will give your company an enviable position.

This chapter therefore seeks to address the question that often represents the single toughest strategic challenge facing any organisation seeking sustainable growth: what needs to be done to reinvent the future?

A stroke of genius

This is a very real and important question that needs deep and careful consideration. The right answer is hardly ever easy to find. Some lucky people might be in the shower when they're hit by a stroke of genius that will conquer the world. But that's never happened to me or to the great majority of Chief Energy Officers (CEOs) and entrepreneurs. Innovation is hard work and you need to be very demanding of your organisation.

The idea of being 'creative' is often very appealing, suggestive of the freedom that comes with blue-sky thinking and the idea of being lateral rather than linear. But no innovation can succeed unless the need for a hard commercial edge is recognised by everyone involved. Innovations are an investment in the organisation's future growth, and the primary requirement is that they have to deliver strong revenue growth with attractive margin on a sustainable basis, capitalising on the strong customer demand for a new product or service properly identified through market research.

So when you innovate, you need to do so with a very clear view of what you're looking for from an economic standpoint. Innovation, after all, requires major investments of capital, of time, and of human resources.

In this chapter, we will cover three types of innovation. First, those from the core of your business – those that it is most natural for your organisation to target, due to your existing portfolio, capability knowledge, culture and resources. Second, innovations in fast-growing segments that are adjacent, or closely related, to your existing markets and areas of expertise. And third, the 'Big Prize': creating breakthrough innovations that help you to build entirely new markets that are devoid of competition. But before you can do any of these things, you need the right culture.

Create a culture of continuous and vigorous innovation

To drive sustainable growth, every company needs to continuously reinvent itself and always be in the pursuit of perfection. That's why a high-performance culture in any business has to be based on the imperative of continuous and vigorous innovation.

For me, this means having a 'challenger' mindset, no matter how well positioned you are in your sector. It is easy to find examples of how leaders have failed to sustain their number-one market position, more often than not through complacency. In my view, the best way to remain number one is to think and act as though you are the number two.

This innovative challenger approach captures the spirit of continuous and vigorous innovation. It forces you to take necessary risks, to try harder and to work faster than your competitors when you have a new idea. In this context, trying harder is based on the simple belief that there is always a better way to deliver a solution, a way that can only be captured by taking a continuous improvement approach to everything the organisation does.

Launching a winning innovation is a big task for any team and, as I've said before, there is always a better way. That means that the moment a product or service is launched, you must immediately be thinking about how to improve it further!

Simply taking this challenger approach to innovation is an area of great competitive advantage: following a launch, very few leaders start working straightaway on determining what to reinvent and how to find a better way. Of course, they do concentrate very hard on getting a new product to market, but their immediate focus tends to be exclusively on scaling up the new product or service in the marketplace.

This is important, but it shouldn't be their only priority. The conscious decision to defer thinking about improvement until later invites the competition to get there first. However, having a commitment to continuous innovation on its own will not necessarily lead to the successful development of world-beating new products or services. What it will do is identify the areas where a company can and should innovate. But it will not create winning solutions – innovation is far tougher than that.

This is why I talk about the need for innovation that is both continuous and vigorous.

Continuous innovation – identifying an area for improvement of your value proposition – is based on the belief that there is always a better way. Vigorous innovation is the agile creative process that enables you to develop a bold and compelling new idea at a fast pace to get first-mover advantage. Continuous and vigorous innovation is essentially a rigorous approach to identify the opportunity and design the solution to seize this opportunity.

Linking continuous with vigorous

This is how they work together. Continuous innovation, based on the Kaizen principles we have considered in previous chapters, will enable you to spot the areas in which the organisation needs to be better.

Once continuous innovation has provided you with insight into the areas for improvement, a vigorous innovation approach helps you channel all your energies and focus on finding the idea, or solution that will actually deliver that improvement.

There are five essential ground rules to continuous and vigorous innovation:

Rule 1. It doesn't happen by accident

You need to put a process in place. The best model for this is the 'stage-gate' approach, enabling your team to break a process down into its essential phases and stage them with a series of decision points that determine the overall direction.

Stage Gate Process

1	2	3	4	5	6	7
Insights	Ideate	Evaluate	Develop	Pilot	Kaizen	Scale-up

Once you have decided to innovate in a precise area based on the right insights, I suggest you put a small, diverse, resilient, energetic and creative team onto the task. This high-energy team will need to invest time and effort into the process, driven by a shared belief in the power of working collaboratively, at pace and with an open mind. Perhaps above all, they'll need to be driven by a strong desire for closure – the team exists purely to find a new solution through rapid innovation.

Rule 2. Remain rooted in fact

Falling in love with a concept is absolutely fine – but take care not to get carried away. It's essential that the team's final output remains rooted in fact, and there is an overriding need to stay fact-based to evaluate the true potential of the idea. This requires using 360° analysis to continuously take account of the views of all key stakeholders in the project, including the core team and its sponsors elsewhere in the organisation. This approach ensures that any final decision will be driven purely by business needs.

Doing so will ensure everybody remains focused on the ideas that will get the support of the organisation. But there is a tricky balance to maintain here. To get the best from the team and its members, it is important that people have an emotional investment in the ideas they generate.

Everybody needs to be excited, energised and committed to giving their best.

Equally, it is important that people don't get too frustrated if their ideas don't gain the support of their colleagues. What really matters is that the company invests in the right ideas for everybody's future.

Rule 3. Manage all stakeholders

You might be surprised by how many other colleagues and departments outside the core innovation team have to be involved in preparing, authorising and delivering a new product or service launch. All too often, creatively minded people underestimate the complexity involved in bringing a new concept to market and do not understand the importance of ensuring that everybody understands exactly what is required of them.

You therefore need to identify and engage with all the various stakeholders early in the process, from the legal department if IP and regulatory issues are involved, to supply, manufacturing, sales, marketing, finance, distribution, human resources and IT.

The better you understand and consider everybody's needs, the faster, more engaged and more flexible everybody will be.

Rule 4. Be prepared to fail

Ensure that the working environment is one where it's acceptable to take risks, make mistakes and fail with innovations that ultimately don't work. As CEO, it is your responsibility to ensure that everybody understands taking risks is part of doing business.

The company that never takes a considered risk will never achieve significant success.

Rule 5. Gain sponsorship from the top

While innovation will be driven and delivered by a small, high-energy team, the team leader will need to ensure from day one that it has the support and engagement of people at the most senior levels of the company.

Never forget, innovation is a fundamental element of the company's strategy. The innovation you launch today is important not just for the next few weeks, months or even years. It is important far into the future.

Because of this, all the most successful innovations I have seen over the years are those where the ultimate business leader was closely involved from the moment of inception. This gives the team more than just the creative and strategic benefits of aligning the innovative approach with the priorities and expertise of the top team. It also gives them the licence to operate and execute the launch plans with the right investments based on quick decisions as both the innovation team and the senior management will be on the same page throughout the entire process.

In addition, innovation only makes sense if you scale it up to ensure that new products and services have the opportunity to make an impact on their markets. This is only possible with the support of the most senior management, as scaling up a new product or service will require time and financial investments from many parts of the organisation.

Steve Jobs is an obvious example of a leader who was committed to innovation. Under his leadership, Apple changed the world – not necessarily through only his own ideas, but also through the support he gave to those of other people. Jobs was a class act when it came to identifying winning ideas ahead of the competition and providing his own sponsorship during the entire stage-gate process.

Where imagination meets engineering

Glendale in California is home to Disney's R&D centre, called Imagineering – where imagination meets engineering. The people there are amazing – genius inventors with an audacious spirit. Scientists and artists, working together in tight-knit teams to reinvent the future.

They are the people who have the really big ideas that see the light of day in the company's theme parks around the world.

The centre's existence, formed in the early 1950s, illustrates Disney's commitment to innovating through teamwork. It's largely the same principle that Toyota uses, where a chief engineer runs an R&D project right from drawing board to market launch and is attending the sales presentation to present the new vehicle to distributors and dealers.

And it is the same principle that I always try to apply.

Just like at Disney, at Intertek we sponsor from the top the most significant innovation programmes – those we immediately recognise as having the potential for global reach – from the centre. In 2019, we launched a new global service, Total Sustainability Assurance (TSA), a pioneering initiative that provides an end-to-end, independent and systemic sustainability assurance from both an operational and a corporate perspective.

Until 2019, we had been providing operational sustainability solutions to most of our clients, enabling them to assess the sustainability risks in their operations. This important launch added Corporate Sustainability Certification to our service portfolio, providing a holistic assurance programme that audits and certifies the quality of corporate processes in place end-to-end in the organisation. Based on 10 Intertek proprietary standards, it enables any company to benchmark from a systemic standpoint all aspects of their corporate sustainability activities.

During the development phase, I personally led the strong team charged with delivering the project. So I was the sponsor at the top, ensuring the team had everything they needed, from our in-house experts to access to senior management at all times.

Wherever we were in the world, we were highly disciplined about catching up twice a month. While strong project management was one of the process's fundamental strengths, we also ensured that we had the agility to rapidly change direction and take new findings into account at the speed of light.

What we created, I believe, is extremely important – not just for Intertek and our clients, but also for the world as a whole. Sustainability is the movement of our time, and TSA has the power to radically change and improve the way corporations approach and resolve their sustainability challenges as they race to Net Zero.

To get their sustainability agendas right, corporations need to develop a sustainability strategy with clear milestones and targets and need to commit to transparent disclosure on the achievement of those targets, when they report externally. This is exactly what the certification programme achieves: benchmarking and auditing all processes in the organisation, end-to-end, to ensure they can report with total transparency and clarity on their sustainability journeys in their annual report.

This approach will differentiate companies as they adapt to rapidly changing disclosure requirements for their annual reports. In the future, the annual report for any company will be built around just three sections to give stakeholders everything they really need to know about a company's sustainable performance: the CEO's review; the financial report, audited independently and perhaps most important of all, the sustainability report, also audited independently.

Zero-to-One and One-to-100 growth- and margin-accretive innovations

As I have just said, I believe that major global innovation programmes should be sponsored from the top. But that is far from saying that innovation is only a senior leadership responsibility.

Indeed, too many companies, mistakenly in my view, make innovation the responsibility of just a few central departments. In the last chapter, I covered the importance of having a decentralised operating model, in which locally based, customer-facing employees are empowered to do whatever it takes to meet the needs of their customers and win their trust.

The licence to innovate at every layer in the organisation is an important element of this empowerment. Innovation is all about gaining the right insights from the market to identify growth opportunities that can be met with new solutions. This means companies need to ensure that innovations are created at the local as well as the global level. So everybody has the freedom – and should be actively encouraged – to come up with innovative concepts.

Those that arise at a local level are called '**Zero-to-One**' innovations. They tend to be based on directly observed and deeply understood customer needs, using local insights and a rigorous stage-gate innovation process to guide development from idea to live concept and ultimate launch.

Zero-to-One thinking is an enormously powerful source of innovation for a company, and the CEO needs to ensure everybody understands that they are needed to fuel organisation-wide competitiveness and success.

Said differently, the CEO needs to make sure that every local team has the licence to innovate, as a decentralised and empowered customer-centric organisation will be first to identify new opportunities in the market based on their customers' interests. It's important that the local teams know that the CEO expects them to develop, as quickly as possible, the right solution to meet the new demands of their customers.

Scale it up!

Zero-to-One innovation is the start of the journey and will open tons of opportunities. Once you have a Zero-to-One product or service that works in your country, the next step is to scale it up to 100 countries. In short, the right Zero-to-One idea might develop into a global **One-to-100** concept.

For a global business, the ability to launch winning ideas across the world is a very strong source of competitive advantage. There are two primary sources of ideas for global innovation. First, simply select those successful Zero-to-One ideas that have the potential to be scaled up across national and regional boundaries to become a One-to-100 idea. Or second, develop a One-to-100 concept from scratch, to introduce it to several markets at the same time, like the Intertek TSA approach.

Whichever approach you take, whether you have an idea at either a local or a global level, it is usually essential to act fast to exploit the full power of the first-mover advantage. Achieving speed to scale delivers a sizable competitive benefit through reaching consumers before competitors have had the chance to react. This quickly compounds into a true scale advantage, driving economic returns and delivering funds to invest in the product or service, usually in the form of advertising and other marketing support to accelerate the scale-up phase. This is a powerful virtuous cycle, which is one of the outcomes of scaling up really fast as soon as you have a winning idea.

'Zero-to-One' and 'One-to-100' innovative approaches are essential for any global business, as not every Zero-to-One idea will become a One-to-100. Also, strategic big innovations that require significant R&D and technology investments, are 'One-to-100' innovations that are developed centrally before being launched globally.

Analysing the financial profile

Whichever route you choose, you have to be prepared to make the right investments, in terms of both manpower and funding. When following the stage-gate process I mentioned earlier, your primary focus should be on the financial profile of the innovation under development. Because of the cost of development, it must have the potential to drive strong returns after launch to repay your investments many times over.

In fact, in my view the best innovations are always those that are both growth- and margin-accretive on a sustainable basis as this is the best way to define a successful innovation. It is one that can be scaled up and will be in high demand. As a result, it needs to be premium-priced, reflecting pent-up demand for its quality and will therefore also be margin accretive.

To achieve this, you need to target areas where demand is high and where revenues will grow faster than those already being experienced by the business unit developing the innovation. The reason for this is simple: there is always a risk that a new product or service will cannibalise one or more of your existing offerings. You therefore need to innovate in segments that show a stronger growth potential than your existing business or, said differently, you need innovations that are growth accretive.

The compounding effect, year after year, for a company that succeeds in bringing to market successful Zero-to-One and One-to-100 growth- and margin-accretive innovations is a key driver of sustainable value creation in any industry.

During my career, I've come across many excellent examples of Zero-to-One ideas that ultimately proved to work only in one country. Equally, I've come across many that successfully evolved into global One-to-100 concepts. Both types have merit. Successful innovation always begins with delighting local customers with new ideas and new solutions, but you cannot bank on always achieving the huge upside of developing something new that works in more than one country.

Zero-to-One ideas that worked in a single country

Colgate France, 'Genie Express' in a tube: when I was a product manager at Colgate, we identified an important insight – when going on their holidays, people don't want to carry too much luggage. They therefore need to be able to keep their clothes clean while on the go. So, in my early days at Colgate France, we developed a laundry detergent product in a tube. It's never moved out of France, but it's still on the shelves there. It's a very convenient product for keeping your laundry clean while travelling.

Burger King Germany, finger food: another product that was absolutely right for a single national market. Our research showed that Germans wanted finger food alongside their Whopper and fries. We made the concept a monthly innovation called 'King of the Month' and it was a bit hit immediately, enabling us to increase our check average per customer and importantly, offer a meal that was very differentiated versus McDonald's.

Zero-to-One ideas that became One-to-100 success stories

Burger King wraps: we developed these for the German market, but they touched a global nerve. Now, wherever you go in the world, Burger King (and McDonald's!) sells wraps.

Pepsi Max: in the early days of Diet Pepsi and Diet Coke, some consumers thought the products had an aftertaste that was unlike the original.

Pepsi started to work on a project to address the issue – to develop a product with the right taste as well as zero calories. We carried out market tests in Holland and the UK, which confirmed we had a global winner on our hands.

Pepsi Max was launched in 1992 and became a major global success.

The McD Café: created by McDonald's in Australia, implemented across the world quickly when coffee consumption on the go increased globally.

McNuggets and the Egg McMuffin: both originated in Canada, now both global brands.

Keeping in tune with the portfolio strategy

Innovation is a lot of fun indeed, provided the approach taken is rigorous, fuelled by a stage-gate process that starts with 'Zero-to-One' ideas with the potential to become 'One-to-100', or start with a 'One-to-100' idea at the global level, given the R&D and technology investments required.

A very important strategic consideration is where the innovation fits within your portfolio strategy. Typically, the portfolio strategy of a company differentiates the activities of your company in three areas: the businesses in the markets where you have scale and leadership positions; adjacent businesses in markets where you are sub-scale; and investing for growth in a new space, where you are not present at all but where you might be interested to be in the future.

A successful innovation strategy follows your portfolio strategy approach by developing new ideas and solutions in these three segments, or by acquiring businesses which will provide you with the innovative solutions you need to execute your portfolio strategy.

- The area on which first to focus your innovation activities is that where your company's experience and record of greatest success already lies – its **core**, defined by a high market share based on market-leading capabilities
- Your second priority is to focus on those high-growth and high-margin market segments that are **adjacent** to your existing business
- Third is what I call the 'white space': highly attractive markets in terms of growth, margin and potential that you would ideally like to enter – or even create – with **breakthrough ideas** that have no immediate competition.

3 Types of innovation

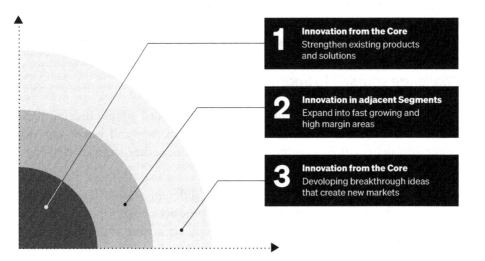

1 **Innovation from the Core**
Strengthen existing products and solutions

2 **Innovation in adjacent Segments**
Expand into fast growing and high margin areas

3 **Innovation from the Core**
Devoloping breakthrough ideas that create new markets

Start with innovation from the core

Innovating from the core is the best and most profitable way for any organisation to improve its performance in the short, medium and long term.

Many leaders find this counter-intuitive. Their preferred solution is to identify sectors where they are weak and launch new ideas in the segments where they need to improve their market share. I can see how this might make sense. But my counter-argument would be simply to say: 'The reason you're weak in that area is because you're no good at it. To become good at it will take a lot of effort, a lot of time and a lot of money. I'd strongly advise you to start by innovating from the core.'

The core is where you're already excellent at delivering a superior customer experience. But you can't afford to sit still even there. As I've already said, if you don't reinvent yourself somebody else will do it for you. So there are two reasons to innovate from the core. It's where you have already a winning position. And you cannot afford to sit still as this is where your company makes a lot of money.

Invest your human capital and shareholder funds in market segments where you have great customer understanding, an excellent reputation, a significant scale advantage and a strong capability. You've already got so many of the assets that others will struggle to build, including superior margin, brand awareness, pricing power and broad-based sales coverage. This all makes it far easier for you to leverage your investments and make the returns you're looking for.

Challenge yourself to improve

There are many examples of businesses that have failed simply because they got complacent, because they stopped looking for new and better ways to satisfy and delight their existing customers, because they stopped challenging themselves to improve.

Others, meanwhile, have failed for a subtly different reason: they found it hard to challenge the quality of an existing product or service of theirs that was market leader. Not doing so is to positively attract the attention of competitors, whose attacks will be ruthless.

Failing to reinvent your core business with the right innovation is very far from the safe option that it might appear to be on the surface. It is, in fact, a very high-risk strategy.

Step back and gain perspective

If anybody asked me for my advice on how to approach innovation from the core, I would simply say: 'Look across your business and ask yourself, which are the core products or service lines? Where are you making 70 or 80 per cent of your profits? And are you thinking enough about reinventing these core businesses over time?'

Then, focusing on these products and services, look hard at the core of your business model, start stripping everything down to the bare essentials. Look at the data, look at the NPS scores, look at customer feedback, do a deep dive into what customers really think about you and your products. And talk to your heavy users, who will tell you honestly what to improve, as they might know your products better than you do.

And get right to the heart of the matter: are there any unmet needs among your customer base on which you really need to focus to come up with innovative ideas?

Get this process right, and the rewards will be high. You will end up generating big and profitable ideas that slot right into the heart of your business model.

Innovating from the core will accelerate your revenue growth because it is 70% or 80% of your business. And it will accelerate your margin, because you have the scale and the pricing power that your competitors don't have.

I'll say it again: innovating from the core is the fastest and most profitable way of improving your market performance and profitability. It gives you a strong advantage as you leverage your insights, brand equity, market understanding, executional capability, scale and IP.

When juicier is better

At Burger King, our core was juicy, meaty burgers – not salads and desserts. When the BSE crisis was at its height, many people were saying, 'No one wants to eat beef anymore. We need to focus on salads and other healthy foods.' We never agreed with this standpoint. As we were looking at rebuilding the business following the crisis, we knew we had to strengthen our business from the core. If you're good at beef, we thought, do beef.

After all, the Burger King core proposition was about providing a bigger beef burger that was better because it was flame-grilled and freshly prepared, with fresh ingredients. This is what we had to keep in mind when we were developing new burger ideas to drive traffic back into our restaurants post BSE.

And we were proven right. No matter where you were in Europe, just six months after the first BSE crisis the best innovations to drive traffic back into our restaurants were either Whoppers or innovative double-beef burgers.

We demonstrated that juicy, cheesy, 'everything you want' beef burgers were the way to create more demand. And it worked everywhere.

In short, if you're good at beef, innovate by doing ever bigger, juicier beef burgers. Companies that have similarly innovated to respond to a changing market environment and regain their relevance include Nintendo with Pokémon Go, Polaroid by making cameras sexy again, and Adidas's move into 'athleisure' wear. All strong examples of innovation from the core.

Invest in innovations targeted at fast-growing adjacent markets

The world is not static. Ever-shifting consumer expectations continuously create opportunities for companies to enter fast-growing segments that are closely related – or 'adjacent' – to their current core business.

This has a double advantage. It enables you to target a new segment, packed with enticing growth opportunities. At the same time, it allows you to leverage your existing industry knowledge, your operational footprint, your existing brand power, your technology, your IP, your human capital and your financial firepower.

In other words, you can leverage what you're already really good at while extending your reach outside the confines of your core business.

The best of both worlds? The experience of some companies suggests this is the case. Colgate, for example, is outstanding at brand extension, as demonstrated by the ability of the Ajax brand to flourish in multiple sub-sectors. We've seen toothpaste brands extend into dental floss, pharma companies creating over-the-counter products, mainframe computer companies entering the PC market.

Mind the gap!

But success is far from guaranteed, and companies need to take great care when they consider extending themselves away from the core, no matter how closely related the new segment might appear to be.

I find the low-cost airline model particularly interesting in this context.

It is very difficult for existing airlines, no matter how big and successful, to enter the low-cost sector successfully – same planes, same routes, but an entirely different way of doing business. Many successful global and local carriers have tried and failed to launch low-cost variants in recent years.

There are lessons there for all of us. Being totally honest with how you interrogate your organisation and its capabilities massively before entering adjacent markets reduces the risk of failure.

The questions to ask

First, you must make sure that you undertake the right 'big picture' market analysis: asking a few general questions will help you decide whether or not to progress to the next stage. Do you really have the credentials to take on the specific segment you are considering? Is your IP really extendable? Has your existing operational footprint got the requisite commercial and production synergies that the new segment requires? What are the existing barriers to entry? Do you have what it takes to break them down?

Next, you need to go further and deeper in your analysis, with a deep dive into questions around the growth and margin opportunities in the segment and the levels of existing competitor strength. Crucially, you must also consider the expected levels of capacity in the segment – if too much capacity is built, this could over time dilute the opportunity to charge premium prices.

Finally, before making a 'go' or 'no go' decision, you need to consider the key practicalities involved in launching into this particular segment. Do you have the immediate operational capability that will execute a rapid and successful roll-out with a margin advantage?

If your honest answers to these questions are positive, then in my view you should be prepared to take the risks involved in adjacent innovation – for the rewards can be very high.

When research leads to reinvention

The 80s will be remembered in the drinks industry as the 'Cola Wars', which made headlines in many business press articles.

The 90s changed the landscape of the Cola industry, driven by market research-based innovation. When I was in New York, working for PepsiCo in 1988, I was the Marketing Manager of 7Up. I was actively competing with colleagues who ran stable mates such as Pepsi Cola and Mirinda, because the view was that people who drank either brand couldn't also be 7Up drinkers.

But the world was changing – multiple new beverages were gaining traction. We wanted to find out what was really happening, so we went people-watching in Central Park, one of the world's greatest market-research fields if you really want to identify the next big thing.

And we saw people drinking Evian, Arizona Tea, Snapple and many other new and emerging brands.

We realised pretty quickly that we didn't really have the insight we needed, and we asked our research department for help. PepsiCo decided to carry out a fundamental piece of research into how all these emerging new brands were being consumed. This research was a defining moment for PepsiCo.

What we found flew in the face of conventional industry wisdom. It showed that individuals actually had a repertoire of six to eight brands and generic drinks they'd turn to depending on their needs at any given time: orange juice first thing in the morning, followed of course by caffeine. Then colas or iced teas on hot days or at social events, and maybe water or sports drinks at the gym.

This was a genuine breakthrough insight, which led PepsiCo to develop a total beverage strategy that underpinned the company's reinvention. It's how the company became involved in buying sports drinks like Gatorade and juices like Tropicana, as well as developing its own water brands.

The strategy played directly to PepsiCo's scale advantage, with routes to market in more than 100 countries across the world. Today, it provides a great example of how acquiring external businesses can leverage core competencies to enter fast-growing adjacent markets. And it was all based on the company taking a planned, focused approach to its future development, built on a strong foundation of compelling customer data and insight.

Don't listen to conventional wisdom

Burger King was a challenger brand in the German market, and it was very important for us to find new ways to bring our products to consumers.

The conventional wisdom in the 1990s was that a restaurant would never succeed on the site of a gas station, given the dirty environment, the smell of petrol and the stench of diesel fumes.

But I was keen not to accept conventional wisdom when at Burger King in Germany. So after a successful trial with Total near Düsseldorf, I met the head of strategy at Aral, Jaap Schalken and managed to persuade Aral – then the country's number one gas station chain, now part of BP – to take the co-branded route.

The co-branding route was highly innovative – and it proved highly successful for us. Today, you'll see a Burger King restaurant at just about every other gas station in Germany. I'm very proud of that success – it was a truly adjacent innovation that has made a significant positive difference to the business.

Some failures in adjacent innovation:

As I said earlier, innovation in adjacent segments will not always work and here are a few examples of adjacent innovations that I was in charge of and which did not work.

* The attempt to launch Palmolive dishwashing detergent in Germany: it wasn't as adjacent as we thought it was – we didn't have the IP, the technology or the capability to outperform the local market leader owned by Benckiser.
* 7Up Ice Cola: because people love the taste of cola, we tried to launch a clear cola under the 7Up brand to offer a more refreshing cola drink. We didn't factor enough in our launch plans, the fact that people think cola has to be brown... the rest is history.

The 'Big Prize' of creating new markets with breakthrough innovations

Ask most people what innovation means to them, and they're likely to talk about big breakthrough ideas that help to access or even create an entirely new market that you can own and lead.

Certainly, just about every CEO and innovation team I've met wants to be remembered for coming up with something that changed the world for the better. It's where most people want to spend their thinking time – and it's also by far the most challenging route to innovation.

Not everybody can be a Thomas Edison, a Steve Jobs or a Walt Disney. Not every business can innovate such as Toyota or Tesla. Not every company can create a new business model such as Google or Facebook, Twitter, Amazon, Uber or Netflix.

In my own experience, and from my observation of others, I can say that hatching a successful breakthrough innovation in the identified and agreed area of the company's portfolio requires a very special set-up. Of course, it needs strong sponsorship from the top, as it will inevitably be capital intensive and require funding for a long period of time. It will also require the right human capital – a team with the full range of subject-matter expertise required to develop the new IP. And it will invariably need to follow the proven stage-gate process. Importantly, it will take time.

The space and time to think

Clearly the team must be given plenty of time, not only to gain the inspiration that's needed but also to go through multiple lengthy and costly trial and error processes as they test the viability of their ideas. There is simply no point in the CEO or anybody else pushing the team to accelerate its work. From day one, you must be aware that the process might take longer than you think. You need to give them space and time to think. Importantly, you need to give them access to the funding they need.

And you need to let them get on with it.

This is not just tough for you as a leader. It is also a high-risk moment for the organisation. This, of course, is why organisations typically pursue both organic and inorganic routes when considering which market segments they want to enter – or create – with a breakthrough idea.

Corporations can either innovate for themselves, or they can make an acquisition.

It is with the aim of being bought out by a major corporation that so many start-ups see the light of day. Start-ups therefore have a clear strategy: to prove that the business model works, that the economics make sense and that there is a market for the idea.

Having made the acquisition, your role as CEO of the buying company is to leverage your organisation's existing infrastructure and the expertise of your people to drive the innovation forward: to scale it up, to introduce it to your existing customers, to launch it into new national and regional markets. And, of course, to start that all-important work on continuous improvement.

Hybrid or full electric?

The race to develop automotive leadership in a post-fossil fuel world has been – and remains – fascinating to watch.

We've seen Toyota champion the hybrid approach, starting with the launch of the Prius in 1997. Nissan, meanwhile, put their effort and investment into creating fully electric engines.

Although Toyota has built a huge advantage over the last two decades, the all-electric vehicle's market share seems now to be in the ascendancy. This is driven by the improved battery power, which is making the range issue less significant and enabling people to make decisions based on purely environmental considerations.

Of course, the winner right now is Tesla. It has built a very powerful brand. Mercedes, BMW and VW are all making strong progress. Nissan remains formidable. Toyota just announced a multi-year investment and innovation programme to build pure electric vehicles. The race to achieve Net Zero is on and it looks like electric vehicles might outperform hybrid vehicles – until the automotive industry has found a way to make hydrogen work. Once they do make hydrogen vehicles commercially viable on a grand scale, we will all be surprised how fast the automotive industry created new spaces in such a limited period of time. Hybrid, Electric, Hydrogen.

Creating new markets

When you look at innovation in the service industry, it's hard to look beyond Amazon as the ultimate example of what is possible. Its breakthrough idea was about selling books online. And now there is almost nothing you cannot buy on Amazon.

We have all been exposed to the stressful situation of hiring a taxi to be on time for dinner in New York, Paris or Singapore because of the limited number of taxi licences available, making it impossible for the taxi companies to manage the peaks in the demand curve every day. That's why Uber is a phenomenal breakthrough idea that has found a way to put the customer first in an industry that did not have to worry too much about customer service over the years.

Consumers want more and more convenience, which has created a big and exciting new market for home delivery of products and food.

When I was at Burger King, we tested home delivery in Berlin in 1999 and I can honestly say that it was very challenging. Why? Because the only way to get it right was to build a scale operation with local drivers who could provide very fast customer service on demand. The market was not big enough at the time to build scale and we failed. Twenty years later, Uber Eats found a way to make food delivery work with a technology-based business model that meets the required scale threshold at the local level, enabling their operations to offer choice and speed of service to their clients. Simply brilliant.

We have all seen the quality of television programmes deteriorate over the years as more channels were opening up, given the low costs of entry for any TV channel. The significant increase in TV channels is offering a much bigger choice to consumer, which has of course triggered a change in the economics of the TV broadcasting market. Given that the TV market is now much more fragmented, the TV channels have lost a lot of scale in terms of audience, which has made their economics much more challenging. The fragmentation of TV demand has therefore resulted in the need for TV channels to increase the amount of advertising per programming hour. This has opened the door for advertising-free TV channels financed through subscription only creating a new space of high quality-advertising free broadcasting.

Canal Plus was one of the first subscription-based, advertising-free companies created in 1992, which became a strong success almost immediately in France but which never found a way to become a European or global player.

Netflix was founded almost at the same time – five years later in 1997 – on the West Coast and has changed the world of home entertainment globally.

At Intertek, we have recently added a breakthrough service to our portfolio with our People Assurance offering.

People Assurance was originally pioneered by Alchemy, a small, brilliant US company we acquired to scale up its concept across the world. The idea is apparently simple – to enable companies to measure how close the skills and behaviours of their people are to their Best-in-Class standards – and then help them to close the gap with industry-leading training.

Through its unique SaaS (Software as a Service) platform, Alchemy is a global leader in People Assurance, providing world-class solutions to its clients, enabling them to get their frontline employees to operate with the right skills and behaviours.

This answers some very real needs for business. Take the example of the CFO, or the marketing director, of a global corporation with teams in many cities and countries across the world. Without some form of People Assurance, they have literally no real measurement in place to quantify the span of performance across the various countries when it comes to finance or marketing capability. Nor do they have the platform to close the capability gaps identified and improve their operational excellence by reducing the capability span of performance at every layer, specifically at the frontline.

They have no real quantitative benchmark about how competent or effective their people are to deliver the expected level of operational excellence in their operations every day.

This is important because of the vast sums that corporations have invested over the years in areas such as processes, equipment, plant and factory, technology, recruitment and training. All these investments have the same ultimate goal – to help deliver operational excellence. But how can you do this if you cannot measure the gap between what you expect that excellence to be and the day-to-day reality of the skills and behaviours at large in your organisation?

People Assurance helps management first to identify the gaps between what people should do and what they really are doing, then to train them accordingly, close those gaps and monitor progress. People Assurance is the next frontier for all corporates to take operational excellence to greater heights and exceed the expectations of their customers.

So I can tell you what it feels like to have a breakthrough technology-based innovation like Alchemy on your hands. Tremendously exciting!

Key points from this chapter:

- Create a culture of continuous and vigorous innovation, meaning the moment you launch a new product you start considering how to create something better.
- Focus at local (Zero-to-One) and global (One-to-100) levels to create growth- and margin-accretive innovations.
- Start first with innovation from the core of your business, where you have scale and expertise.
- Identify and invest in fast-growing segments that are adjacent to your core business where you can capitalise on your strengths.
- Ultimately go for the Big Prize, whether organically or inorganically, achieving breakthrough innovations that open up exciting new markets.

Leadership Principle 6
Master complexity

Chapter content:

• Understand the capability/complexity equilibrium in your organisation.
• Formulate a comprehensive capability plan to deliver the vision.
• The magic of talent planning to unleash your full growth potential.
• Attracting the right talents for today, tomorrow and the day after.
• The imperative for leaders to sponsor the careers of high-potential talents.

The world is a complicated place. It's fast-moving and increasingly competitive.

Like never before, these forces are compounding the complexity felt by organisations.

As a result, leaders need to be fixated on how to build an organisational capability that's continuously ahead of the operational complexity they face.

This means continually addressing and resolving all the capability gaps that might exist across the organisation, in the key areas of capital, people, processes, technology and assets.

For this reason, it's never been more important to ask a simple question: 'How do I create the right capability in my business to deliver the growth agenda?'

It's much easier to ask this question than it is to answer it. The only answer is to formulate, develop, implement and constantly refresh a comprehensive, end-to-end capability plan that enables your organisation to achieve your short- and long-term goals.

Considering, creating and then implementing your end-to-end capability plan is what this chapter is all about. Doing so will help you master that pervasive complexity by taking an evolutionary, step-by-step approach to capability-building, providing a dynamic enabler that helps you cope over time with the growing complexity you will face as you grow your business.

Critically, this will involve looking at a number of factors that will fuel the smooth execution of your strategy for growth, but which often get overlooked in the strategic-planning process.

Planning the capability 'game'

Forecasting precisely what will add additional complexity is difficult, as there are many triggers of additional complexity for any business, which can be of course internally or externally driven. At the highest level, there are two major forces, which will have a compounding effect on the complexity you will have to address. First, it's growth of course as the bigger your business is, the more complex it is to operate. Second, of course is the level of competitive intensity you face in the marketplace as the more competitive your market is, the more complex it is to run on a day-to-day basis. The complexity compounding effect of a high-growth business operating in a very competitive environment is significant and will be overwhelming unless you have the right capability plan in place. But no matter the difficulty involved to get the right capability, you can't afford to get your facts wrong about any one of those key drivers I aforementioned: capital, people, processes, technology and assets.

In addition, these drivers are linked to a potentially infinite array of factors that are outside your control, such as a new competitor, a fundamental technology change, new regulations, a global economic crisis like the ones we faced in 2001 and 2008 – or even something as rare and unlikely as a global pandemic.

For all these reasons, getting to perfect capability is rather like getting to perfect quality: you can get close, but it's rare to go all the way. And if ever you do get there, something is certain to change, knocking you back and placing you once again on the same never-ending journey.

This can be frustrating, particularly if you are the kind of person who believes goals are there to be smashed. So maybe you should adopt a different mindset, at least when building the right capability. See goals instead as being designed to stretch – to get the very best out of you, your people and the organisation as a whole.

Understand the capability/complexity equilibrium in your organisation

The relative scale of complexity you face is directly linked to the size and capability of the organisation you run. There is a fairly straightforward conceptual model that I use to determine this, which involves understanding the equilibrium or balance between the organisation's current level of capability and its current level of complexity.

Taking revenue as a simple proxy for capability, if you have a $10 billion business your complexity too should be that of a $10 billion organisation. And as you make progress towards becoming a $20 billion business, you should ensure that the capability of your business is that of a $20 billion business.

In short, it is the leader's role to make sure that capability remains in line with your organisation's complexity. The capability–complexity equilibrium point is where they coincide, which is difficult to get to but once you get there you will sense it immediately. It is where, as an employee as much as a leader, you get very inspired by the energy you get performing at your best because you have the appropriate capability in place to support your efforts. It's when people feel right at the peak of their game, in control, able to cope with whatever demands come their way, that one could say that there is a perfect equilibrium between capability and complexity in the organisation.

But, when you're in a growth cycle, you need to be much more ambitious.

The ideal place to aim for is where your organisational capability is slightly ahead of the complexity associated with your existing scale to make sure you deliver the growth you're pursuing with operational excellence.

This is what people call investing in the future – preparing for growth for exciting times ahead. Giving yourself some additional headroom gives you the capacity you need to accelerate growth further and be ready for the next layer of complexity.

In addition, no business is immune to an external event or performance issue that would consume senior management time in crisis management or firefighting. Having that headroom gives you capacity to deal with the unforeseen and be on top of your game managing an internally driven or externally driven crisis.

A vision of the dark side

By way of contrast, the worst place to be is where your organisational capability is insufficient to handle business-as-usual – the normal, day-to-day complexity attached to running the business. Situations like this might arise in many businesses from time to time. The determining factors, of course, are how far you are behind and for how long. There are situations in which you can manage your way out of a small, short-term capability hiccup. Having the right plans in place will enable you quickly to get back into the comfort zone.

But this isn't always the case. Sometimes, what appears initially to be a minor glitch can develop into something very serious indeed.

Let's take a fictional example: El Gran Negocio, created in Bolivia, is a well-capitalised company on the stock market, enjoying a high market share and growing fast. After having started and scaled-up the company successfully to $1.8 billion revenues, the Chief Energy Officer (CEO) and founder 'Big' Buck Cannon has decided he can manage at arm's length and has moved to Miami, Florida where he can operate remotely and have a fantastic lifestyle. He's not recruited a successor because he's convinced he's simply the best.

So he watches the company grow, strategising from the poolside. He's very astute, the market potential is huge – and all of a sudden, he has a $2.5 billion business. The only trouble is, his investments haven't kept pace. Its capability is only that of a $1.8 billion business. The organisation becomes stretched. There is a risk that people will start leaving, that forecasts will be missed and that emerging risks are not well identified or mitigated.

Soon the pain already being felt in Bolivia reaches Florida. Buck is no longer quite so comfortable on that poolside. And shortly he sees the light. He flies to La Paz several times in the same quarter. He appoints a CEO and a Board. He does everything right, putting in place systems of governance and risk management. He keeps investing.

But by the time capability has reached $2.5 billion, El Gran Negocio has the complexity of a $3.5 billion organisation. If there are too many months in which any company's capability remains behind the complexity curve, cracks will start to show, impacting customer satisfaction, talent retention, supplier relationships and of course, shareholder support.

Feeling organisational pain

At this point, you will start to sense the symptoms of stress in the organisation – even if you're poolside several thousand miles away. People will start making mistakes, getting stressed or, worse, depressed. Once you see the signals, you have to respond very fast with appropriate corrective measures. Failure to do so will lead to what's called 'organisational pain': symptoms include internal chaos, performance failures, quality problems, people leaving the business, resulting ultimately in revenue reduction, profit decline and cash flow issues.

It's all very human, and we've all felt this sort of pain at some point in our careers. We therefore know how important it is to avoid having to feel it again. That's why mastering complexity is so important.

'Big' Buck Cannon ultimately found a way to catch up and create the right capability–complexity equilibrium. The period of organisational pain was difficult and long, resulting in underperformance for two to three years. The founder learnt a lot during this period and never recovered the market share he lost during this period, creating new opportunities for the competition.

First, identify the problem

Building the right organisational capability, of course, is an extremely broad-based challenging task. This makes it hard to quantify and importantly, harder to forecast precisely what is required. But there are key indicators that will suggest what is happening and what needs to be done. As a leader you need to be tuned into looking at all leading and lagging indicators.

Of course, you need to have the right antennae, sensing the mood or sentiment across the organisation. This is a key barometer to track all the time, so that you take corrective actions quickly.

In addition, you need to be fully aware of the risks you will face when there is organisational pain and, based on my experience, there are a few well-known symptoms of organisational pain:

• Customer complaints
• Quality issues
• Health and safety issues
• High employee turnover
• Excessive absenteeism

- Dysfunctional meetings
- Excessive internal politics
- Widespread anxiety and stress
- IT security glitches
- Forecast accuracy issues
- Decreased productivity
- Finance control issues
- Cash flow problems
- Compliance issues

Being paranoid about operating with the right capability–complexity equilibrium is important for any leader. You have to identify the patterns that are visible to you inside the company, and ultimately it will come down to your own insights supported by a detailed scrutiny of the available data and where the capability gaps are.

The data always relates to those five key areas: capital, people, processes, technology and assets. The best way to truly understand the capability/complexity equilibrium of your organisation is to look at each area individually and observe the behavioural patterns inside the organisation.

Above all, never stop asking how people feel. Doing so will reveal much about the organisation's position on the complexity curve and the areas where attention is needed to address emerging problems.

Experienced-based leading indicators

Fortunately, some indicators are more leading than others when looking at your potential capability issues. One of these is employee turnover. This is what I focused on when I was responsible for the performance of around 3,000 Burger King restaurants across the world. From a distance, I knew that an increase in staff turnover in any given restaurant would be a warning signal of a bigger problem – usually poor leadership by the restaurant management.

Another leading indicator is quality. When I was working with PepsiCo bottling plants in many countries, quality issues were almost invariably leading indicators of organisational pain. At one point in my career, I was based in the Middle East and I knew that if a plant in Jeddah, or Oman or Cairo was having problems maintaining its standards, then something was going on there.

In the 80s, I was an auditor for Ernst & Young in West Africa. I could clearly see that the number and frequency of financial control or compliance breaches was a clear indicator of some lack of capability in the company I was auditing.

Then there are the IT-related issues that affect companies under threat of organisational pain – again, some of the world's major airlines come to mind.

Equally, I am unsurprised by the issues around security and personal data that have been experienced at many fast-growing global technology-driven 21st-century businesses.

I am of course incredibly impressed by the way these companies have taken a breakthrough idea and scaled it up to global dominance.

This is what can happen when corporate complexity grows in a way that's out of proportion with capability.

The way to manage a capability problem in any organisation is to build and follow a comprehensive capability plan.

After all, being able to see a problem is only the starting point. What really matters is what you can do about it.

Formulate a comprehensive capability plan to deliver the vision

Creating a plan to ensure that the organisation has always the right capability in place is a powerful source of motivation for the CEO and leadership team, as this will boost their self-confidence when executing the strategy with the organisation, knowing that they have put in place the right enablers.

But almost every executive in every company has fallen into the same trap – they have underestimated the challenges involved in executing a strategy or a new idea. They think it will be easier, cheaper, faster than it turns out to be.

This is only human nature. And it's particularly prevalent among leaders, who almost by definition are forward-thinking positive thinkers.

Another common mistake is that they do not sufficiently measure how their current level of capability measures up against that all-important complexity curve. If they fail to do that, there is no way for them to challenge (and maybe rein in) their instinctive optimism, potentially resulting in organisational pain down the road and preventing them to truly unleash their full potential.

This is what makes it essential to have a comprehensive capability plan covering capital, people, processes, technology and assets. This will help ensure that the organisation has the resources required to achieve all short- and long-term objectives. This will create the base plan for regular reviews, which will be needed to refresh their comprehensive capability plans on a regular basis.

Importantly, during these reviews the capability plan will provide the right analytical platform to look at how the enablers of the company will have to evolve given the compounding effect of both continuous growth and more aggressive competition.

An effective way of identifying the organisation's capability needs is to carry out a risk-analysis session, identifying the risks linked to capability gaps under each of the five categories.

- **Capital:** cash is king, especially at times of high growth. Having the right capital structure in place is the starting point for building your capability plan, alongside rigorous processes and planning to support the company's balance sheet and financial firepower. Ensure at all times that you're highly cash-generative, that your balance sheet is strong, that you're not taking on too much debt and that your day-to-day cash management processes have the rigour to give you the capital resources you need to run your company in good and bad times as well as to invest in your business, organically and inorganically.
- **People:** every company is a people company, and it's mission critical for all organisations to have the right people capabilities in place. So you need to have an end-to-end people strategy in place, which is based on the organisational model that addresses talent, culture, development, engagement and reward. Achieving this will enable you to energise and inspire everybody involved to take the business to new heights.
- **Processes:** most people in most businesses agree that it is very important to have the right processes in place. This can have the unwelcome result of organisations creating more processes than they actually need, adding unnecessarily to internal organisational complexity. This is ironic, as processes should exist to reduce complexity.

To ensure that you have the appropriate processes to deliver your strategy and master complexity, you should regularly review and remove any that are no longer essential. Take reports, for example. Many companies produce lots of reports, simply because they have always done so. Even when these have been made obsolete by new ways of communicating, too many people carry on producing the old versions. I have a personal solution to this: stop producing your report. If no one asks for it, don't bother doing it again.

- **Technology:** I find it incredibly energising whenever I see superior technology being used to unleash new opportunities, providing smarter and better ways to overcome challenges and add value. Today, any growth strategy must be supported by robust technologies that digitises every aspect of doing business with clients, customers, suppliers, operations and functions.
- **Assets:** the operating footprint of an organisation represents an essential component of any capability plan, as this is where the company determines the best distribution of its manufacturing, operational and corporate assets to help it compete, win and deliver its vision.

Devising and delivering your asset strategy is likely to be highly complex. To help you cope, you need to gain a deep understanding of where your organisation has come from, where your industry is going and where you need to be located for maximum efficiency and competitiveness.

Right-sizing the capital capability

When I arrived at Euro Disney the capital structure was under stress as we had a lot of debt on the balance sheet. This was clearly having an impact on the overall capability of the company and causing organisational challenges in several areas.

Because the company had recently taken a lot of debt to open the Walt Disney Studios second theme park in the resort, it was difficult to find additional funds in the short term to fund innovation in the Magic Kingdom.

My responsibility was clear: to deliver a restructuring that would bring funds not just for a few months to pay debt but to allow us to invest in an innovation programme that would drive growth for many years into the future. The repositioning of Euro Disney for growth was a major undertaking and creating a comprehensive capital capability plan was central to it.

Skills to execute

PepsiCo has bottling plants in many countries, many of which are run by franchisees. As you would expect, there was a span in terms of quality and sales performance between many of these manufacturing sites. And it was obvious this performance gap was not always caused by market or competitive factors.

Pepsi Cola International was sub-scale in many of its international markets and resolving the individual capability challenges of each bottling plant was a massive task. Addressing these local bottlers' executional challenges would enable PepsiCo to capitalise on a superior-quality product and the best advertising in the industry and deliver rapid growth to every market. That's what the capability opportunity was all about.

Pepsi Cola International developed a major capability innovation called Total System Management (TSM), which had the aim of bringing all the bottling operators up to the level of the best performers. Addressing the capability gaps of bottling operators, their general managers and their wider teams, TSM was targeting comprehensive local-market capability improvement plans to make sure all franchisees were well equipped to execute the brand strategy.

TSM started with the requirement for site managers to carry out an audit of their capability gaps across a range of metrics, including quality, speed of service, channel development, sales effectiveness, financial performance, purchasing synergies, talent development and safety. This analysis enabled each site to develop a systemic diagnosis of the capability situation, get the support of PepsiCo to implement processes they could use to address their shortcomings and ultimately improve performance, step by step, over a period of years.

It was remarkably effective, particularly thanks to the way it enabled remote bottling operations to break down the complexity of their capability challenges into a series of simple steps that facilitated straightforward resolution with the strategic and operational guidance of PepsiCo, which included training in the key functional areas.

Rising to the growth capability challenge

When we took the decision to grow Burger King's network in Germany from 120 to more than 300 restaurants, we did not have enough franchisees to help us expand in all the regions where we wanted to be.

This presented us with a major capability challenge: we were seriously sub-scale, and we had to ramp up significantly our franchise capability to achieve our goals.

First and foremost, we had a massive, difficult and above all mission-critical recruitment task on our hands. A high-quality franchisee is a vitally important and very powerful brand ambassador, who you want to be aligned with your brand strategy for at least 20 years. We also wanted each one we appointed ultimately to be responsible for 5 to 10 restaurants. So we needed to be absolutely certain we were attracting, finding and appointing the right franchisees.

But when I arrived at Burger King there was no clear process in place to build our franchise capability, and nobody was responsible for franchise sales. That had to change – and fast. We recruited an outstanding leader, Andreas Klentsch, to build and lead our Franchise Sales department.

So we designed a very clear nine-step process. We brought together a tight-knit team and worked religiously on breaking down the complexity at hand into a series of bite-sized chunks. This resulted in a detailed capability plan, which reflected the strategic importance of what we were trying to achieve – to effectively triple our presence in Europe's largest consumer marketplace.

The recruitment and selection process was highly disciplined. I spent a great deal of time interviewing all candidates, with the primary aim of checking three key points. First, I had to understand the extent of their interest in the business, particularly whether or not they intended to be simply a financial investor or a highly engaged operator delivering the best burger customer experience every day. Second, I questioned them about their financial strength and their willingness to invest in the right location and team. And third, I investigated their willingness to work in a system where they would have to follow strict operational and marketing guidelines.

This approach enabled us to attract a new population of high-quality and highly motivated franchisees. At the beginning of the journey, every one of them and their teams needed to complete in-depth training before we authorised them to start trading. This caused many of them considerable stress due to their eagerness to get started, but we were highly disciplined in creating and rolling out a rigorous, end-to-end franchisee programme to make sure the company's restaurant-development programme was delivering the expected goals and milestones.

This investment of time, effort and money was a critical factor that still underpins the success of Burger King in Germany today. I would still advise any franchisor to focus above all on ensuring they recruit and build highly capable and motivated franchisees.

It certainly takes time, but its ultimate value massively exceeds the investment involved, and I firmly believe that creating a step-by-step approach to this complex capability challenge was the right route to take.

The right asset capability

When it comes to refining or redefining an asset strategy, historical factors can play a major role in how appropriate a company's operational footprint is for its current and future ambitions. For example, a business that has evolved over time might have multiple sites in a country, when today's business might be better served by just one or two much larger sites.

When you operate a region or a country, no matter what your business is, you need to take a step back and consider deeply what and where your operating assets should be. Where are the import and export streams, where is the competition, what is the productivity of every site, how does your current capability measure against the complexity curve?

In my experience, this sort of strategic analysis most often reveals that the biggest capability challenges relate to having a sub-scale operation. It's easy to see why: when an operation doesn't deal in large volumes, it's not going to be easy to deliver strong financial results, preventing the operation to have the funds to invest in growth to outperform the competition. This means the team is small, making it vulnerable to losing talent. If just one of two people leave, it can be hard to replace them with the right skills, experience and attitude.

When business activity goes down, the easy option is to cut costs. Without the required level of revenues and transactions to support the operation, this can result in there being insufficient money to actually run the business.

In short, beware of being sub-scale! In large organisations, operating a sub-scale business in a challenging market and having an effective capability plan are contradictions in terms. Unsuccessful, sub-scale operations never get the full attention and support they need over time, as there will always be bigger opportunities in the company's portfolio.

Once you have completed your mapping of the current situation, the next step is to project your analysis into the future. Where is the industry going over the next 20 years? What are the market trends and forces that will be driving it?

What is my most efficient asset strategy during that period – where do I want my sites today, and where do I want them to be in 10, 15 or 20 years' time?

This is not easy. It is very strategic. But it is essential.

The magic of talent planning to unleash your full growth potential

The single most complex capability challenge that any organisation faces is having the right people in the right place in every position. Achieving this is super-complicated, but it's incredibly rewarding too.

Putting people at the heart of your growth strategy and operational day-to-day management is what drove me to develop the Leadership with Soul model.

That's because there is nothing more exciting than promoting or recruiting a colleague and seeing that person thriving after just a few days on the job, knowing that they are just starting out on their journey and that they will get many personal growth opportunities moving forward.

Experiences of this sort are what have reconnected me with my childhood dream of being a surgeon, enabling people to unleash their full potential and make the world a better place.

This is a very real part of the magic of talent planning.

When done with discipline, when the highest of standards are set, it is in my view, the fastest way to unleash the full growth potential of any business.

The power of small steps

For just about any business, it is mission critical to get the talent-management process right. In my experience, the step-by-step approach that follows is equally applicable to every position in the organisation:

1. Clearly define accountabilities, the technical skills required and all expected leadership competencies.
2. Set up and operate a rigorous process across the entire organisation to identify where talent gaps exist relating to every position. Then take into account the organisation's future capability needs, driven by its planned growth trajectory. To ensure sound governance, this process clearly requires a considerable degree of independence, debate with colleagues, data availability, time and fairness.
3. Where talent or capability gaps exist, give incumbent colleagues regular feedback on their performance and provide all the support they need to learn and improve. This might range from basic training through to mentoring, coaching or anything else required to bring them up to the level required. That means investing in their personal capability to meet or exceed the complexity of the role.
4. Understand that this might not always be possible. Not every colleague can be helped to meet the challenges involved, and you need to ensure that milestones are in place to help you decide whether or not to replace an individual. This is a tough call for every leader, but it is simply not possible to operate your way around capability gaps forever. When this situation arises, I always aim first to close the capability gap through an internal promotion. Running a growth company however means that you will need to recruit outside to build your capability.
5. Never lose your grip on succession planning. Ensure you understand who is primed to take your own role, if not immediately then at least at some point in the years ahead. Failure to do so means there is no sustainability in the organisation's leadership, creating a potentially massive capability gap.
6. Ensure a long-term talent-planning process is in place, visualising what and where the organisation will be in five years' time and identifying the missing skills and experience you will need to develop or recruit in the intervening period.
7. Using this process as your guide, build a 'talent bench': a population of talented colleagues with further personal growth opportunities within the organisation who can take on increasing responsibility in the years ahead. This is a critical to enabling sustainable growth.

Never take your eyes off the talent

The single best piece of advice I can give you is this: spend more time on talent planning, looking at two to three layers below each of your direct reports and ensuring your direct team can look at all other layers, so that the planning process covers all layers and all positions inside the business. But as soon as you take your eye off the plan, allowing time to pass without identifying and addressing emerging needs, it can rapidly spiral out of control and result in significant capability gaps.

I spend a considerable amount of time on talent planning. We all watch movies and TV series and can immediately feel the difference between a great movie and one that's only OK. The difference between a great film and an OK film is all about the script and the casting, nothing else.

In business, it is the strategy and the talents that differentiate a great company from a merely good one. In other words, the script and the cast.

Keep a healthy risk appetite

I have said it before. Playing it safe all the time isn't real leadership. From time to time, you need to take a risk.

This is certainly part of talent management. Every now and then you'll have to trust your gut and take a risk on somebody. Too often, leaders fail in this area. A lack of risk appetite can prevent them from taking decisions, just because the candidate didn't tick all the boxes.

In my view, this defies the purpose of talent planning, which is often simply about giving a person the opportunity to develop new skills in new areas. I'm often tempted to laugh when a colleague comes up with that type of objection regarding an appointment. So what if they're not strong in a couple of areas! If the new role doesn't give them the opportunity to get better at something, why would they be excited about making a move?

So whenever I see a leader who is reluctant to take a risk on a candidate, I remind them that they're only in their position today because somebody took a risk on them in the past, whether once or several times.

Of course, there is no such thing as a 100% pass rate in talent planning, and from time to time an appointment will not work out. But if you play safe all the time, you will fail more than you succeed. I believe that playing safe in talent planning is a contradiction in terms. So take a chance on the right person: somebody whose heart is in the right place, who works hard and understands the culture, who is willing to learn. Let them show you what they can really do, given the right opportunity and the right support.

You'll often be amazed.

Balancing the micro and the macro

The challenges relating to the relaunch of Burger King Germany in 1996 were wide-ranging at the national level. Strategic issues included brand, menu, scale, profitability and of course talents. But local micro-issues prevailed at restaurant level, and it's always been important to address single-site operational capability problems as well as those affecting the entire network at the country level.

At the time, our business in the south of Germany around Munich and Nurnberg was largely successful. However, one restaurant in the centre of Nurnberg was consistently underperforming the rest of the region, and I visited it several times in an effort to understand the problem.

The manager there consistently complained to me about the level of local competition and the fact that the restaurant needed refurbishment. I felt I wasn't getting a full diagnosis from regional management either, and focused my attention on finding out what was wrong.

When I got the answer, it was very clear. Refurbishment was needed – but worse, the manager was failing to lead his team properly. So we had a double capability problem: leadership and assets.

I knew that a poorly run team would never get the best out of a newly refurbished restaurant, and I decided to fix the leadership issue first. I appointed Frau Boehm, a fantastically effective leader, to deliver the turnaround. I set her a clear challenge: fix the existing performance failure by raising the operational capability of the team. In return, I will then invest in refurbishing the restaurant to accelerate the pace of the turnaround.

She delivered very fast. I kept my promise. Soon, the restaurant was one of the top performers in the network, and Frau Boehm has gone on to have an excellent Burger King career. She showed the difference that having the right person in place can make – the power of people.

It was the same throughout the Burger King network, across all Inchcape's dealerships and Intertek's locations: same site, same customer base, same equipment. But a different site leadership can inject a massive performance boost. That's the magic that talent planning can achieve for you at any layer in the organisation, especially at the frontline of your operations where your teams are in daily contact with your customers.

No diversity, no magic

I talked previously about the importance of investing in future growth, and I made the statement 'no eggs, no omelette', which is obvious for any leadership team signing up for an exciting growth agenda. Said differently, you cannot harvest if you don't invest.

Leadership with Soul is about putting people at the heart of your growth strategy and of your day-to-day operational management.

I dedicated a significant section to the magic of talent planning as I believe that any CEO cannot succeed without the right strategy and the right talents.

There is one area of talent planning that is today not fully understood or leveraged, and this is diversity.

I really believe that a CEO cannot create magic in the business without diversity. As you can imagine, being a humanist in action, I fully believe in the power of diversity. Diversity of origins, gender, religion, education, experience and of course character.

The world continues to be extremely divided on how to make the future of mankind better, on both the global stage and in large democracies. It's fair to say that the world's governance will need to be re-thought at one point as the challenges that we all face can only be resolved together using our broad-based diversity as a source of creativity to make the world a better place.

The challenge that Mahatma Gandhi articulated for the world is very real: 'Our ability to reach unity in diversity will be the beauty and the test of our civilization.'

What Jimmy Carter said about diversity is an excellent inspiration for any leader thinking about how to make the organisation truly diverse: 'We have not become a melting pot but a beautiful mosaic. Different people, different beliefs, different yearnings, different hopes, different dreams.'

Talent planning is all about building a beautiful mosaic of diverse talents as in life or business, diversity is a real source of progress. A lot of work has been done in organisations to understand the benefits of building a diverse organisation from an educational, gender, religion, nationality, experience and character standpoint. Some of us have been exposed to the Myers-Briggs model when building our own team and we all understand that a diversity of character inside any team will make the team more effective.

Diversity in any organisation is much bigger than diversity of character and I would suggest that you design your internal talent-planning process to make sure that over time, your organisation will be a mosaic of diverse talents, using a broad based and truly diverse definition of six areas of diversity: nationality, gender, religion, education, experience and character.

No diversity – no magic!

It all starts with HR ...

I was extremely proud to join PepsiCo in the 1980s, because PepsiCo was one of the best run companies in the world, famous for recruiting the best of the best. PepsiCo was Best-in-Class at many things. It had brilliant marketers, great finance people, outstanding lawyers, tremendous manufacturing and R&D professionals and, maybe above all, the best HR specialists in any industry.

Maybe it wasn't so good at sales, but even this was fixed over time.

At PepsiCo, HR played a major role to build the capability for growth that PepsiCo targeted, especially with its talent-planning process, which was called Human Resource Planning or HRP. This was a very big deal across the company.

The company's approach to talent management extended to every level of the organisation. It was designed to continuously raise standards, whether recruiting new people or appraising existing colleagues. In addition, the commitment of senior management to the process was highly motivating for everybody in the company.

I was in the international division, where John Fulkerson was the organisational 'champion' for the talent-management process. It was amazing to see how he and his team spent not just a few hours but days at a time reviewing talent and deliberating how to improve the overall capability of the company, putting the magic of talent planning to work.

I am convinced this was a primary reason for the company's continued success – and why today you see so many former PepsiCo people in senior leadership positions in major corporations across the world. Talk to Pepsi people today, and most will agree that Pepsi was incredible at providing them new personal growth opportunities on a regular basis and they learned a great deal for the rest of their lives.

Populating the talent bench

I have already described how we started to grow our capability to build and sustain growth in the franchised operations of Burger King Germany. I have also covered in a previous chapter how we started the business turn-around programme by launching the quality back-to-basics 'Make Every Bite Right' programme. And I've talked about how we developed strategies to strengthen the brand, develop the menu and expand in the west of the country, using drive-thru restaurants as the cutting edge restaurant format to accelerate growth.

Once we started seeing the benefits of delivering the best burger experience in every restaurant, every day, it was time to turn our attention to the growth strategy for company-owned restaurants.

After a few years, we had made enough progress on improving the basics and we were ready to increase the number of company-owned restaurants at the national level.

I had to make an important leadership decision and I wanted to find some-body from among our regional managers to become the operations director for all the company restaurants.

It soon dawned on me that there was one regional leader who never said anything that wasn't right in meetings, who continually and without any fuss kept on delivering on his forecasts and results. So I went to look at his operation in detail. His name is Sandro Mura, and he ran the Hamburg market.

What I found there impressed me deeply. His restaurants looked fine, but they were not the best assets in the network. What he had was the best team in each restaurant. Not only that, within each team, he had four or five peo-ple with the capability to step up to a manager role whenever needed.

This was fantastic news for me – essentially, he had already created in each of his restaurants strong operating teams that could act as sources of new leadership talent for the new sites. The first 15 new company restaurants we opened were highly successful, not only because of their locations and the quality of our marketing, but because Sandro had been able to quickly build the best teams in each of those 15 restaurants by appointing proven opera-tors from his home market to lead these.

This was of enormous importance for me personally. I had stood in front of the board of Diageo and I had asked for capex to fund the investment required to open the new company-owned Burger King Germany. There was of course huge scrutiny on the performance of these first 15 new company-owned restaurants. And they all performed from day one because Sandro had created a talent-management system in each of his Hamburg restaurants that was remarkably similar to PepsiCo's HRP approach. He had built a talent bench.

Within Burger King Germany we quickly learnt from the success of having the right talent bench and we put a systemic process for site-based talent planning in place across the organisation. I would advise anybody who runs a multi-site operation to do exactly the same. Every month we'd go through all the company-run restaurants we had in Germany and we'd discuss individually each of the people in the leadership teams of these restaurants. 'So this person manages this company restaurant in Berlin, and this is who she has in the team. There are a couple of issues to address with this assistant-restaurant manager, but this person deserves promotion...'

It was time-consuming work, but it brought the level of intelligence about our people, and the degree of people insights, to an incredible level. Even then, though, I cannot say that we actually spent enough time on talent planning. I would say, double or triple the time you spend – it doesn't have to be formal; it could be a phone call or a quick chat with your boss, with the head of HR or with someone from one of your teams. But make it part of your working day, every day.

Right at the beginning of this book, I talked about the two questions I ask myself every day: 'Are we doing the right thing?' and 'How do people feel?' Answering these questions is what talent planning is all about. Sustainable success is about the quality of the script and the quality of the cast – it's about the strategy and the talents you have in place.

Attracting the right talents for today, tomorrow and the day after

When it comes to running a company, the importance of being committed to continuous improvement is mission critical. No matter how successful an organisation has been, it can always be better with new insights, innovations, processes and investment in new areas.

This principle also applies to talent planning, including the recruitment of people from outside at every layer of the organisation, as it is very healthy for the organisation. I have already stated that when an underperforming individual needs to be replaced, I always look to make an internal appointment, providing the opportunity for them to fulfil their ambitions and maximise their potential. That said, recruiting from the outside is also a very important part of the talent process as it is a systemic initiative that will bring a fresh perspective that in turn will drive curiosity and new thinking. Said differently, it will help you build a diverse organisation that will stay curious and ambitious for many years to come.

I would like to emphasise that external appointments need to happen at every level – there is a widespread view that it is not possible for large and successful businesses to recruit from the outside at the most senior level.

I do not agree. Remember what Socrates said: 'The only thing I know is that I don't know everything'. There is no organisation that doesn't benefit from the fresh perspective and injection of new energy that external recruits bring with them. We all know the positive experience of working with a new colleague who brings a different perspective and a different kind of creativity, based on their different experience and background. That is just as true at the top of the organisation as anywhere else.

In short, it's about balance. We need to promote from within, and we need to appoint from the outside.

Identifying industry talent

I also strongly believe that, as a leader, you need to be aware of who are the stars of the industry you operate in. You should draw up a target list of the candidates who, given the opportunity, you would like to get to join your business. When identifying these people, you should clearly focus on their track record of course. But that is only one aspect of a person's suitability. You also need to do a considerable degree of due diligence into factors including their competencies, their skills, their level of EQ, their likely cultural fit with the organisation, and importantly how they fit into your capability gaps.

Recruiting for growth

Albert Einstein said that compound growth was the eighth wonder of the world.

Einstein's comment has major implications for the importance of external recruitment in a growth company – and makes it very important for leaders to get their external recruitment right.

Take the example of a large global company. Let's say it has 100,000 employees, and that its workforce is growing by 10% year on year. That means that in five years, the same company will have 161,051 employees.

Say this company is also really good at engaging its employees, and that each year over the same five years it loses just 10% of that original 100,000 – year one (10,000), year two (9,000) and so on. That means that 40,951 of that original 100,000 will leave the company during those five years, leaving just 59,049 at the end of the period.

Within five years, less than 40% of the company's workforce was part of that original 100,000. Another five years on, and at the same growth rate, the company has close to 260,000 employees, of whom just 34,868 have been there for 10 years or more: that's only just over 13%.

In reality, these are optimistic figures. In a typical multi-site, multinational organisation, employee turnover is more like 15%, 20% or even 25%. You do the maths!

In a growth company, it is incredibly important to recruit the right people externally. For a growing business recruiting from the outside, it is 100% life defining.

The imperative for leaders to sponsor the careers of high-potential talents

Every organisation has people whose potential is much higher than the average and it is imperative that senior leadership actively sponsors the career management of these individuals.

I'm not being elitist – it is a simple fact of life that some people have the potential to learn and grow faster than others. So it is really important for leaders to recognise high-potential talents and ensure that fast-trackers receive the best possible growth opportunities to achieve their full potential.

Doing so is a fantastic investment in the future of the business. Failure runs the risk that highly talented individuals will get frustrated and take their talents to the competition.

Retaining the interest, commitment and loyalty of high-potential talents involves giving them new and ever bigger challenges on a regular basis. In my experience, giving them a new role every 18 to 24 months during their formative years is about right. When they're rising fast up the ladder, they need the chance to move on fast and learn as much as they can.

This was the approach that PepsiCo took with me. I was learning, I'd get comfortable – and here was the next challenge. I'd get comfortable with that, and here was the next one. They never stopped pushing me. Sometimes it was very demanding, but I learned a lot. Then, at Burger King, Diageo took a similar approach. Here's Germany, see how it goes. Here's Europe, good luck. Right, here's the world...

As a leader, you therefore need to spend time identifying who the high-potential talents are, working with them closely to truly understand the extent of their talent.

Of course, this is not risk free. There is the chance that you will back the wrong person for a time – but that risk is certainly not as great as failing to spot the right one.

Sponsoring the right person is highly rewarding for a leader. And no leader should ever forget that they were once spotted and sponsored by somebody else. So always remember that you have only achieved so much because somebody in the past decided you were worth taking a risk with.

It's your turn to pass on the favour.

The leader and the leadership team have to recognise the importance of providing high-potential individuals with a fast-track personal growth plan to help these individuals unleash their full potential, and who will in turn help the company to unleash its full potential.

Key points from this chapter:

- Understand the 'capability–complexity equilibrium', and appreciate the source of the organisation's energy or pain.
- Formulate a comprehensive capability plan to deliver the strategy, based on your organisation's capital strengths, its technology, assets, processes and people.
- Unleash the full potential of the organisation through the magic of talent planning.
- Ensure you attract the right talent for today, tomorrow and the day after.
- And be sure to sponsor and support the careers of those talents who demonstrate particularly high potential – just as somebody in the past has done for you.

Leadership Principle 7
Embody the strategy at the top

Chapter content:

* The leader needs a senior team that embodies the strategy.
* The top team delivers the strategy in action with one voice.
* Short-term performance provides the licence to do the right thing strategically.
* Manage pressure points with resilience and composure.
* Operate as a team in good and bad times.

Effective leaders know how to build a high-performance leadership team.

No matter whether it's at the head of a department, a division, a region or the entire organisation, the rules are the same.

The top team is highly visible in the organisation and must embody the strategy in action every hour of every day, with a collective spirit, shared goals and fully aligned messages for the wider organisation.

There is certainly no room for cynicism or negativity of any sort inside the top team. The team owns the strategy in good and bad times. It should be able to contextualise all external pressure points and approaching challenges for their people with resilience, composure and respect for all.

The team also needs to perform, creating sustainable value for all stakeholders. It needs consistently to deliver results ahead of expectations and to ensure that the need for short-term performance never undermines the company's ability to do what's right long term.

Any onlooker knows when this is not happening. They know that a visibly stressed team that struggles to deliver against forecast, month after month, will inevitably have trouble delivering the right figures for the year and well into the future.

The success of a strategy is determined by how well it is executed – and how well the company is led from the top has a major impact on strategic execution of the vision.

In this chapter, I will focus on the duty that the Chief Energy Officer (CEO) and her or his top team share for making sure the organisation is properly led.

The leader needs a senior team that embodies the strategy

Just about the most important thing I learnt when I was running Disneyland Paris was that I was on stage all the time. No matter what time of day or night it was, whether I was in the park or somewhere else, I was always the official and personal representative of the brand with all stakeholders.

That's just the way it is when you're a leader, especially in an organisation with a high public profile. At that time and in that place, I was fair game – and so were members of my team.

While most companies don't automatically endow you with the same profile as Disneyland Paris, inside any organisation the senior team is similarly on stage at all times. The CEO cannot do it alone, and it is part of his or her responsibility to ensure that the people she or he appoints to that team can cope with the scrutiny their appointment will attract.

Clearly, this is only one consideration among many. As I've already said, when building the team, the CEO needs first and foremost to select people with the right capability and diversity to develop the vision and execute the strategy. As CEO, you need to set very high standards and be rigorous in your approach, as the top team is the most visible – and scrutinised – part of the organisation.

The best top teams typically have a good blend between highly respected colleagues from inside the organisation and carefully chosen, seasoned professionals recruited externally. The single essential factor that they all must share is their individual and unified support for the vision and the strategic direction as well as an unconditional commitment to rolling up their sleeves and delivering the strategy in action.

Beware the blocker!

One key consideration when assembling the team is that it can never contain what I call a 'blocker': the kind of person who can never agree to anything and stops things happening. There is simply no room for any detractors in an organisation's top team – it never works. If you find you do have one in your midst – maybe you've inherited them from a previous leader, or perhaps you've accidentally misjudged them – you have to act fast.

Believe me, your immediate colleagues and the organisation as a whole will be far better off and more productive after her or his departure.

Selecting the team is just the first step. Most of the hard work involves making sure the members collectively think, behave, act and communicate as a unified group.

This is an ambitious goal, and all team members, including the leader, will need to invest time in working together and importantly, getting to know each other. There are many leaders who would think this does not apply to them.

They see it as more important to spend time with clients and people in their operations.

Of course, both these things are important. But my advice is still to put plenty of time into your agenda to help build effective, trust-based relationships across all members of your team, especially when you're new to the leader's role. You will be surprised by how much time it takes.

With the right senior team in place, you've got a great forum for developing and building the vision, working on strategic priorities and making sure everybody is on the same page. But you can only maximise its effectiveness in these areas if you create a rigorous modus operandi for the team – what I call the 'shared agenda'.

Creating the shared agenda

Creating a shared agenda for the top team is important and to do so, you need to answer several questions. How often should you meet? When you do so, what is the team's main role? What do you want to do at every meeting? What areas do you want to work on together? What topics do you want to discuss – and what do you not want to discuss? What type of behaviours do you want to see at the meetings – what are the key 'dos and don'ts'?

Discuss your answers to these questions as a team and use them to give your meetings structure and purpose. In doing so, you have effectively created a 'shared agenda'.

Once the team's role is clear to all, you will be able to work as a senior team to determine the size of the prize for the journey ahead, to establish your vision for the business and to agree the strategic initiatives you want to pursue as well as the enablers you will invest in to build the right capability. We have discussed these points in previous chapters, and the logical next step is to formalise how you will execute these initiatives as a team by creating a shared agenda. The shared agenda you will develop will give you the framework to put the right project management in place for the execution of those with a precise governance within the senior team. This will ensure everybody is clear about their responsibilities and accountable for them to their fellow team members, providing a strict operating discipline to monitor progress. It is always the CEO's responsibility to chair all sessions of the top team and make sure there is the right level of follow-up.

Once you have established the shared agenda, you must make sure you don't make decisions relating to it outside the team environment. If you do so, members will quite rightly start to question why they are there, damaging credibility and morale. So make sure you put all the truly systemic issues and decisions you have to make to run the company on the meeting agenda. And never go public on an important decision without a discussion within the team to get everyone's input. You'd be amazed how often that happens in many organisations.

Delivering the strategy in action as a top team by delivering on every milestone of the project management in place is very important. Mutual trust will be built on holding one another to account on everything – not just on the vision and strategy but also the individual tasks assigned to each team member.

Building that trust at the top is critical for a high-performing team. There are many ways of assessing when a team is performing well, but for me the most accurate barometer is the level of trust that exists between its members. This can manifest itself in several ways, including spending social time together.

The really telling moment within a senior team comes when you start to help one another in tough times – when you start to contribute to one another's agenda, even coaching one another based on your area of expertise.

Getting to this point always takes a great deal of time – often many years. I've seen it happen several times, and it's very powerful. But it's not an immediate goal.

Another key factor in building an effective team is enabling everybody to take the time to get to know one another. When you organise any team meeting, be sure to build in a balance of formal and informal time. It will allow everyone to learn about the real people behind the job titles they'll be seeing at every meeting.

How I identify team members

Working out who should be in the senior team isn't easy, and I have certainly made my share of mistakes over the years. These have taught me a great deal and helped me create the following structured approach to building a team.

True to my belief in the power of diversity in any organisation, of course the need for diversity is an important goal when building a top team, considering all aspects of diversity, as discussed in the previous chapter.

First, I always do my best to recruit team members who have complementary skillsets, experiences and leadership styles. I would also only ever hire people who are more knowledgeable than I am in their core area of expertise. I want a range of personality types, abilities and attitudes – there is no point in recruiting clones, as a team put together in this way will be very one-dimensional and uncreative.

I also try to get to know people in some depth before I make a decision about whether or not to appoint them. I therefore tend to have two or three meetings with them, including at least one in an informal situation away from the office.

When getting to know them, I place considerable emphasis on a candidate's academic background – I believe educational records provide a solid measure of a person's career potential. This isn't always the case, of course, and there are many people who flourish most when they leave full-time education. But I have learned over the years that as people take on increasing responsibilities, they're more likely to succeed if they have taken their education seriously, ensuring they were 'stretched' early in life.

I also pay particular attention to the first employer, as experience has shown me that this is a highly influential moment in most people's careers. The choice of sector and company says a great deal about a person's ambition and judgement in their early years. In addition, the fact that somebody has worked for a blue-chip company early on is a testament to their potential, as they will have received unbeatable training and experience.

Before I finally make up my mind, I always send the candidates to an external company I used for many years that specialises in the personal development of senior executives. When there, each person undergoes a highly demanding process that delivers an in-depth analysis of how they think, their intellectual ability and character. This independent assessment always provides a well-balanced profile of their leadership capability.

Once a candidate has made it onto the team, I immediately stress the importance of having a personal development plan upon joining. The diagnosis of their skills and potential during the recruitment process is then used to develop a personalised plan to capitalise on their strengths and address any areas identified for development. This personal growth plan typically includes a supporting onboarding plan, which I call the 3-6-12 leadership script, setting out what the would-be leader wants to achieve. The first three, six and twelve months are when the essential 'what and how' questions should be asked.

This personalised plan, and investing time in their own development, is very important for each team member and for the wider team as a whole. To be as effective as possible as a leader, I believe you need to have a high level of self-awareness – and nothing feeds this better than an ongoing personal development programme.

I typically wait for 12 months before doing a 360° feedback session with a new member of my senior team. I've been through several of these 360° assessments over the years, and I've always found them extremely useful in building my self-awareness and focusing on specific areas for improvement. It's a healthy thing to do, and I'm confident it's made me more effective as a leader.

First step

There was no local top team in place at Burger King in Germany when I arrived. So I pulled a team together, giving a considerable opportunity to several people from inside the business, and making a few external appointments too. I've already said that we had no head of franchise development – we didn't have a head of business development either.

Having established the modus operandi, one of our earliest projects as a team was to conduct the 'size of the prize' analysis that I described in Chapter 2. This was a defining moment for many team members, who were exposed to an entirely new way of thinking. Together, we took time to go step-by-step through a comprehensive strategic analysis of the situation before creating a vision of where we realistically wanted to be. It was very important that everybody had the opportunity to contribute.

Once again, taking the Kaizen-based step-by-step approach was essential. Not everyone will have the right solutions straightaway, and it's important to take time with the team and help them walk through all the arguments in favour of one direction or another.

This ensures insights are built in an iterative manner, rather than being imposed from above by the boss. And that creates collective ownership.

Our first session included an in-depth SWOT analysis to nail down our current position and formalise the areas for change. In the next session, we looked carefully at the opportunities facing us, determining how we were going to grow. Further sessions followed, and piece by piece we built the vision and strategy that led to Burger King's turnaround in Germany.

Over this period, we built real cohesion and team spirit. That went a very long way to getting the alignment we needed in terms of strategic thinking and vision while building real cohesion inside the top team.

Draft after draft

I went through a similar process close to 20 years later with my top team when I first arrived at Intertek. What I remember from that time was the sheer number of iterations of every piece of work before we were happy with our output. Just articulating our purpose, customer promise and mission took us two days. This was the only output of our first meeting.

At another heavy-duty session, we focused exclusively on the 25 non-financial metrics we would use to measure the company's progress. Time and again, we went through every definition to refine the scope of every metric and ensure beyond any doubt that everybody was on the same page.

This has to happen with every piece of work that generates a decision or a process that becomes part of the company's culture, strategy and policies. The team must be prepared to go through draft upon draft before settling on something they all agree with and can be shared with employees.

This takes time. It can be frustrating. But it's vital that you always take that time to gain deep alignment within your senior team – it will pay off countless times in the years ahead.

Coaching inside the team

Another tool that I have found useful in further strengthening trust across the team is sharing 360° feedback between members – that is, feedback on how you lead and perform from your subordinates, colleagues and superiors across the organisation. This is very easy to do – the tools are widely available on the web. But do bear in mind that doing this might generate discussions that are uncomfortable for some members.

Mutual trust already needs to exist before you take this step. But doing so can open many doors for you as leader and the wider team, creating a new dynamic and level of trust. It will also inspire team members to share their knowledge, and it will create an open platform where colleagues within the team will ask for the help of their colleagues who have the expertise they do not have. Peer to peer coaching inside a leadership team is very rare and when you have achieved that level of trust, you and the team can take on any challenge!

Be prepared!

Every time you meet with your top team, it's a major investment of the organisation's time and money. It also pulls members away from their often tough and demanding day-to-day responsibilities. So it's vital that you prepare well for every meeting. It shows respect for the organisation as well as your colleagues.

During my career I came across many leaders who are disorganised. There's no agenda. They start on one point and ramble off in another direction. The PowerPoint isn't ready. The computer doesn't work. The lunch is late. No restaurant is booked for dinner.

Of course, preparation takes a lot of time and effort. But if you think something isn't worth doing properly, don't bother doing it at all!

That's why at Intertek I spend a great deal of time building the agenda, with Tony George in charge of HR and Ken Lee in charge of marketing and communication. We don't put the senior team meeting programme together over the last couple of days before the meeting – we start working on it six or eight weeks – sometimes even three months – in advance and ensure that all participants have the time they need to get their contributions ready. It never fails to result in a creative and productive session.

Simple – but brilliant!

After some time at Burger King Germany, the top team was fully in place, delivering a perfect turnaround and mastering all the right disciplines, from marketing and finance to operations, development, to technology. We had done all the things I've been describing. There was a high level of trust, we were all sharing the same vision and were signed up to the strategy.

All the ingredients seemed to be in place for a local team to succeed where the previous global 'functionalised' global approach that I talked about earlier in the book, had not delivered for Burger King International.

Looking around the table, I could see all the members were happy to be back as part of a local team after years of frustration at being run centrally from Miami. How could a functional head based in Miami develop policies and run the operationalisation of his or her function in America, Latin America, Europe, Asia and Australia?

In the early days, we spent a great deal of time thinking through business priorities, planning the strategic journey with clear milestones and goals on a quarterly and annual basis. Then we had to ensure that each team member was ready to put the appropriate initiatives into practice within their own departments. And I had to get the strategy and investments approved by Burger King's owners at that time, Grand Metropolitan and Diageo.

When we got the green light, we were ready to go. Everybody in the team was behind the strategy. And we had a set of initiatives ready that were poised to deliver the strategy in action. One innovative approach to getting total alignment at the top of Burger King Germany really sticks in my mind, because it was highly effective and, in my experience, quite unique.

This is how it worked. Each team member had a clear plan for his or her area of responsibility, and we'd meet every month to track progress. We also had an annual convention to inform the whole company and our franchisees about our plans.

So far, so normal. The innovation came with the Burger King quarterly operational forum we developed – a two-day event where the top team would review progress in real depth across all parts of the business. The really new aspect of this was that the team members' direct reports – 30 people in total – would present to the top team, not the other way round. Every manager would present a total of two slides: one with a scorecard of the numbers achieved, with a particular focus on the last quarter as well as goals for the next three months. The other slide simply described the action plans for delivering the goals over the next quarter.

It worked incredibly well. Each manager had to present his or her results in front of a large group every three months, creating a unique sense of performance ownership and competitive spirit. Communication between all departmental teams improved dramatically, awareness of key issues and priorities skyrocketed, cross-functional ideas gestated rapidly and informal bonding flourished.

In fact, when it comes to team meetings, these Burger King quarterly operational forums were some of the best from my entire career. They were easy to organise and provided excellent opportunities outside the formal meetings to celebrate success and recognise top-performing colleagues over dinner in a nice restaurant in central Munich. Through the Burger King Germany quarterly forum, we clearly accelerated our growth momentum by making decisions better and faster and we drastically increased our competitive differentiation by launching really bold innovations. Simply the power of our diverse and aligned senior leadership team in action!

The top team delivers the strategy in action with one voice

The real test of how far the senior team embodies the strategy comes when the meetings are finished and the individual members return to their own businesses or departments.

This is the moment they clearly demonstrate their commitment to the shared agenda by rolling up their sleeves and starting to deliver the strategy in a way that's both fully aligned and mutually supportive.

This means they have to get directly involved with their own teams in all the right areas, leading from the front.

Failure to do so will fatally undermine the effectiveness of the top team and ultimately the strategy itself. But be warned: there are many potential pitfalls, and ensuring the top team delivers the strategy in action with a single unified voice can be extremely challenging.

Setting the context

One of those pitfalls is a failure to contextualise and explain the strategic messages from the top team as they are cascaded throughout each division or department. People all too often deliver the message like this: 'Right, so I've just come back from a meeting with the big boss, and she's wanting us to stop what we have been doing and do it this way from now on... This is the new agenda she's decided she wants us to work to...'

That approach is incredibly destabilising and demotivating. It makes teams feel as though they've been wasting their time and the company's money. Even more important, it breaks any connection between the local teams and the strategy at the top.

A better way goes something like this: 'Look, this is the journey we're on. This is what we are doing and where we are going. As you know, I've just come back from discussions with the big man, and we talked through some of the new insights we've been coming across. As a result, we've agreed to make a couple of changes to our approach, and we think you're in a great position to help us do it...'

My advice as a leader is, make sure that at the end of every meeting you take action to make it more likely that this second approach is the one your colleagues will use. As your final agenda point, start to set the context around the decisions reached during the meeting. You can say something like, 'OK, that was a great session, we've made some real progress. So, these were the key decisions we've agreed as a team, and this is what we're going to say when we start talking to the wider organisation...'

Connecting the dots

Each member of the top team therefore needs to 'translate' the wider company strategy in a way that's directly relevant to her or his business unit or department. Of course, it still needs to be fully consistent with the corporate agenda but contextualised to fit neatly with local priorities. It then becomes the starting point for a set of action points for the local team, which builds continuity and ultimately drives the desired results at a local and corporate level.

You frame the message. You contextualise it; you deliver the strategy in action as one member of the broader team talking to your own organisation.

Said differently, you're embodying the strategy at the top by connecting the dots between the corporate agenda and the agenda of your team.

Connecting those dots is very important. It creates clarity and alignment – and that's exactly what your job and your duty as a leader is all about. When there's a failure to do so, confusion occurs, organisations start to become dysfunctional, people start playing politics and a lot of energy is wasted. When that starts to happen, a great deal of corrective communications is called for.

Once that clear link between corporate and local or departmental strategy has been established, each team member needs to focus clearly on accountability and performance management.

A key aspect for any leader when delivering the strategy in action is their own personal commitment as a leader. They must publicly identify the areas in which they will get directly involved. This highly visible leadership is what delivering the strategy in action at the top is all about.

Importantly, each member of the top team will also need to develop an internal communications plan, capitalising on the corporate level messaging to meet the specific needs of each department.

And, just as the CEO should take advantage of any and all opportunities for informal chats with colleagues, so should top team members take every chance to talk with their people and invite candid feedback on what's going on around them.

Wearing two hats

When working together, the CEO and all members of the top team have two roles to play. One, as a member of the top team, in charge of the company's vision, strategy and policies. The other, as the holder of a specific operational or functional responsibility. I equate this to the idea of wearing different hats, depending on which role you're playing at a particular moment. The two-hat metaphor is something I highly recommend to leaders when working with their senior teams, particularly in the early days as it helps people focus their minds and time on the shared agenda rather than thinking first about what a new initiative or policy might mean for their own operation or function.

This is not a trivial issue. You might be in a situation where you want to discuss a systemic opportunity, a point of strategy or a critical risk or threat to the organisation. Clearly you want people to be wearing the team hat.

So if someone says something that you feel isn't relevant to the team dynamic, you can challenge them: 'Which hat are you wearing – team or your own?

Right now, I'm not interested in your role, we're here to discuss a much broader agenda, a systemic issue or an opportunity to take the company to new heights...'

I recognise that it can be very difficult for people to put day-to-day issues aside to look at the bigger picture. But it can also be very developmental and empowering too, allowing people to call on their experience and understanding of the business to contribute insight across a wider landscape. It forces us to break out of our comfort zone and think differently.

Wearing two hats for a member of the top team will ultimately become part of the experience base of that team member.

I have interviewed over the years many senior executives and I was always pleased to hear them talk about their contribution while running their own division or function and about the impact they had on the global strategy of their company while being part of the top team.

In these interviews, they did not use the 'two hats' metaphor but clearly I could sense how much they enjoyed and learnt wearing 'two hats'.

One message, different depth

This principle of talking with one voice applies both inside and outside the business – but exactly how you use that voice and what you say will depend to a great degree on your audience.

Team members often have to talk to many different external groups, including customers, franchisees, suppliers, regulators and even competitors.

Deciding exactly what to say externally and how to put it for each of these can be very difficult.

This is how I approach the issue – same message, different depth. While you must be sure not to share sensitive, potentially competitive information outside the organisation, you must equally say nothing that jars with the messaging being cascaded internally. The key is to be honest and never say things that you will have cause to regret.

The importance of the top team speaking with a single voice became totally clear to me when working with franchisees at both PepsiCo and Burger

King. As you can imagine, particularly in difficult times, the relationship between franchisee and the franchisor can be a pretty stressful one. This makes it very important that all members of the top team who interact with franchisees are fully aligned and consistent with the company policies. As soon as there is any inconsistency, you can be certain that franchisees will seek to use it to their advantage.

A particular situation to avoid is one where franchisees facing financial difficulties are treated on an ad hoc basis with no policy in place. Getting it wrong will only ever result in individual deals being agreed with a given franchisee, creating precedents and making it all but impossible to implement a coherent policy in future.

This is what was happening when I joined Burger King Germany. As I've already said, we quickly created a franchise department, which was responsible for putting clear processes and policies in place, including dealing with individual franchisee problems. To do this, we put in place a system of monthly top-team meetings, which focused solely on franchisee issues, ensuring we were all on the same page and could speak with one voice.

'The stronger the better . . .'

But the biggest challenge I faced in terms of internal communication while at Burger King arrived when the owners Diageo put the business up for sale.

Basically, Diageo's portfolio was too diverse and its heartland was in spirits.

The decision was made to focus on its core business and Diageo started divesting the businesses that were judged non-core such as Pillsbury, Haagen-Dazs and Burger King. By the time Burger King was put up for sale it was the last big business Diageo had to sell.

This was an unbelievably busy time. In May 2002, I flew from Europe to Miami no fewer than seven times. I'd catch a plane on Sunday, present to investors on Monday, fly back that evening. Then I'd be back again on Thursday to make another presentation. During that, I had to keep motivating the organisation to perform day-to-day, to live up to our values, to be true to our purpose and keep the vision in sight.

That was complicated and not easy!

Only one thing was on everybody's mind. Who is going to buy us? What will it look like? I, of course, did not know. I couldn't speculate, and I focused on constantly communicating the same message: 'Our role is to make Burger King stronger than ever – the stronger we are, the better it will be for everybody.'

Understandably, the sale process created a huge pressure point for my top team and we had to deal with it!

The challenge we faced was clear: we had to support the sales process organised by Diageo while simultaneously keeping motivation, focus and performance high inside Burger King.

We got out our different hats. We separated the tasks, ensuring that the business would continue to be led as normal while we put some of our time into the sales process. We told our own teams that we would keep them informed but would only make any announcements once there was really something to say. We didn't want to cause any confusion with half news or leaks.

Fortunately, we were a strong and aligned top team. We focused on our responsibilities and at no time speculated about our future ownership. Above all, I believe we never compromised our decision-making processes. This was highly appreciated by employees and franchisees alike and demonstrated the importance of maintaining a united front during an unusual time as an important corporate event had triggered a difficult situation for the top team to handle.

Taming tension

Having a united front is one thing. Having a team of yes-people is not what diversity is at the top. Clearly there will be times when there is disagreement between members. It's part of the team dynamic and in my experience, well-orchestrated discussions with the top team will create great solutions.

There might even be some dysfunctional behaviour by members – I'll come back to this at the end of this chapter. This can give rise to some real tensions, placing pressure on you as a leader not to fall into the trap of commenting and fuelling other peoples' political agenda. Remember, you are on stage. Your words are the words of the company. Saying the wrong thing can cause unnecessary anxiety or lead to problems at every level of the organisation.

So no matter how tense relations or dysfunctional behaviour might get within the team, as soon as the meeting is over everybody still needs to speak with one voice. It doesn't matter how keen other people might be to find out how the discussions went and who said what – what happens in the top team stays in the top team.

Short-term performance provides the licence to do the right thing strategically

As I examined in Chapter 1, there is a real tension in many organisations between the short-term performance agenda and the long-term vision. This can cause friction and debate, as people from time to time will use long-term investment considerations to question or even oppose short-term priorities.

The top team, of course, has a vital role to play in reconciling the short- and long-term considerations. They have to meet their responsibilities to the full range of stakeholders who expect the company to deliver today, tomorrow and the day after.

If the top team fails to do this, there is no other body inside the organisation with responsibility for doing so.

All stakeholders, of course, are ultimately looking for the same thing from a company – good sustainable performance. Any stakeholder will find it extremely difficult to believe in the long-term success of an organisation that fails to meet short-term expectations consistently. When judging a company's likely performance, they look primarily to the CEO and the leadership team to deliver the results they're looking for. Why should they trust these people to deliver future performance if they're failing to deliver performance now?

Based on my experience, there is one mantra only to follow when the top teams are trying to reconcile the short- and long-term agenda.

If you deliver short-term performance consistently, you'll earn the freedom and the licence to do the right thing strategically for the long term.

So every leadership team needs to stress to every internal audience that there will be no long-term success without short-term wins.

Succeed in doing so, and the company's short-term performance is far more likely at least to meet – and preferably exceed – the expectations of all stakeholders. This is the only way of earning their sustained trust.

And remember, meeting expectations is the minimum acceptable standard. Exceeding them is always highly recommended! More on this below...

The confidence to succeed

Another powerful reason to aim for sustainable short-term momentum is the confidence, the time and resources that it gives the leadership team to focus on long-term strategic investments and considerations. This is only natural. If you're continuously fighting short-term problems, you probably won't have the time (or energy) to think about the longer term. And if you have a reason to feel insecure about your short-term performance, you'll be less willing to take strategic risks in the future.

Importantly, the consistent delivery of short-term performance will accelerate performance in the long run – the more you achieve in the short term, the more you will excel in the long run. Delivering against expectations boosts internal morale, creating new energy that further accelerates short-term performance and makes the development and implementation of strategic initiatives more effective. This is the virtuous cycle in which short-term performance provides the licence to succeed over the long term.

Of course, an important benefit of short-term delivery is the greater freedom that all stakeholders will give the leadership team by not asking too many questions and being willing to take greater risks with bigger initiatives.

I'll say it one more time: step-by-step, day-by-day, week-by-week, month-by-month, strong short-term performance gives you the freedom to do the right thing for the long term – and it will ultimately give you the licence to succeed year after year.

Aiming to over-deliver

Delivering the goals expected by your stakeholders is a good place to be. The better place to be is, of course, to consistently exceed the expectations of your stakeholders.

So how do you get to this point of consistently over-delivering against short-term expectations?

I would primarily recommend you focus on two areas: your shared agenda and your budget.

On the shared agenda, you need to be super clear and transparent on the need for the top team to strike the right balance between your Track 1 (short-term) and Track 2 (long-term) goals and initiatives.

A lot of time and energy is wasted by organisations by not having the right executional discipline, which will be the subject of the next chapter. How the top team spends its time has a disproportionate impact on the short- and long-term performance of the company. That's why one way to exceed the expectations of stakeholders is to make sure that the resources of the company are well invested, differentiating the importance of delivering the here and now with Track 1 initiatives, versus the Track 2 imperatives that need time from a development standpoint.

Get that balance right, and you are effectively assured of success over time as the Track 1 initiatives –will deliver short-term performance, and the Track-2 initiatives will create powerful strategic differentiators that will accelerate performance in the future, building on your strong short-term momentum.

The other area to focus on to exceed expectations is how you and your team look at your budget targets. The budget of the company is all about Track 1 and it is essential to plan for success that year.

In my view, too many people focus too much on achieving only their headline budget target. Say this is $100. A typical mistake that leaders make, early in their careers, is to get obsessed by planning to hit that figure. With experience, you come to realise that a year is a long time, based on 12 laps, sometimes with unforeseen events and executional risks to your initiatives that will prevent you from achieving your target of $100.

The solution is simple: plan to exceed expectations. Aim for $120. I can quite understand people thinking, 'If it's tough to get to 100, it's going to be even tougher to get to 120. I'll never do it . . .'. But that's not how it works in reality. It's all in the mind.

The world's most successful companies and teams know this. They always plan for success – they use rigorous activity-based planning and budgeting to max out, to achieve the best possible performance. And I advise you to do the same.

Activity-based planning

The rigorous budgeting process in which managers identify all potential areas of over-performance, is bottom-up, with precise activity-based planning looking at all performance drivers – volume, price, operating cost, margin, overheads, working capital, cash, ROCE.

Simply formulated, this bottom-up activity-based planning needs to yield a financial output ahead of the budgeted target, to offset any potential risks or surprises during the year.

It's a very powerful process, closely related to the Best-in-Class thinking I covered in Chapter 3 – calibrating every aspect of the business to stretch performance to the very best you can achieve, making sure you over deliver the $100 target in your budget.

Maxing out on performance

Reckitt Benckiser is a fascinating company. I know them well. I was their competitor when I was at Colgate. And later I was on their Board for more than 10 years. I know their culture intimately: it's a truly high-performance organisation.

If you are a manager at Reckitt Benckiser, you would start the year energised about your budget targets, secure in the knowledge that you had done bottom-up activity-based planning to deliver maximum performance way ahead of your budget – and therefore get your maximum bonus, provided of course there was no unforeseen negative development during the year.

There is a powerful lesson there: whenever you start the year with your team, make absolutely sure that you are planning for the best possible performance. If there are headwinds, you'll achieve your budget no matter what.

And if things really go your way, you'll max out with your short-term figures.

Manage pressure points with resilience and composure

When executing a strategy, it's essential that the messages from the leadership team and the behaviours from all leadership team members are consistent at all times. Erratic behaviour by a top team facing short-term performance challenges or an external crisis can be devastating to the business.

That's because if the top team is stressed – if it panics in the face of a performance issue and starts acting strangely – people throughout the organisation will quickly lose confidence and start to get extremely worried. 'If my boss is acting so oddly, shouting and saying such weird things, what chance do I have of keeping my job? I'd better start putting my CV in order . . .'.

There is no doubt – the communication and management style of the top team will be seriously tested during challenging times. When everything is good, when the business is growing and you're being recognised as a great leadership team, then speaking with one voice is pretty straightforward. It gets far tougher when you hit a few rocks and start having problems.

And this will happen from time to time.

When it does, you need to stay calm. One of the most common pitfalls for a team feeling the heat from its stakeholders around strategic direction, due to poor results or underperforming investments, is to overreact immediately without thinking through the short- and long-term implications of their actions.

So, no matter how strong the pressure is around you, never overreact. Take the time to stop and think – this isn't easy when the situation and the people around you are screaming out for rapid action. But just remember this: whatever you say under pressure is going to be remembered. That's simply because people remember events more clearly when things are going badly than when they're going well.

Never forget, these things happen. No business grows consistently in a straight line all the time. When you experience a dip, don't take it personally, don't lose confidence. Be resilient, be composed, keep yourself in good shape.

Over-communicate

This chapter is about embodying the strategy from the top, and you have to do so at all points in the business cycle. An important critical success factor for any top team is how to communicate with all stakeholders.

When managing stakeholders as a top team, in good and bad times, I have one piece of advice: always over-communicate in a transparent and genuine way.

I have seen very successful teams starting to under-communicate with their stakeholders when performance is strong because they are so busy running the business or they feel that they do not need to communicate because the business is doing well.

That is wrong!

Leadership with Soul is about leading with emotional intelligence, having all stakeholders in mind.

Remember, all your stakeholders have a vested interest in your success and for a top team to explain what's happening and why the results are so good, is a simple sign of respect that will build great relationships over time.

The trust you have built when exceeding expectations in good times and the relationships you are establishing when you over-communicate will give you a strong platform to operate from when your business starts underperforming.

When things go bad, leadership teams find it difficult to explain what's happening as they take the failure to perform very personally.

In bad times, my advice is also to over-communicate in a transparent and genuine way, as you will want all of your stakeholders to be on the same page and fully understand the diagnosis of the situation while you try to improve the short-term performance.

Blip or abiding?

So how do you make sure that you exercise the right judgement in difficult times?

First and foremost, you need to work with the top team to judge whether or not a performance issue is just a blip or something more structural. If you decide yes, that it's caused by a one-off set of circumstances, stick to the strategy, and make sure you have plans in place to reverse any negative trends within six or nine months.

You might, however, collectively decide this is not a blip and that the company is facing a new structural challenge. This might be caused by a new competitor, a supply issue, new regulation, the loss of key people, issues with pricing or many other factors.

If that is your decision, the worst thing you can do is react too quickly and take a short-term tactical approach. Tactical decisions on structural challenges might create some short-term wins, but they will have a negative impact later because you have failed to correctly define the problem.

And it's all about problem definition.

When you identify a structural challenge, I believe there is only one approach you can take. Stop. Think. Work with composure, with resilience, with the right analytics. Develop a new strategic direction that takes the new circumstances into account. And explain it well to the employees and all the other stakeholders, ensuring they fully understand the pressure points the business is facing and the proposed route to address them.

So bring your team together and say something like, 'OK, this is happening and we need to talk about it. What's happening here exactly? Let's really get to the bottom of it, let's really dig into the issues and make sure we take the right course of action...'

And be prepared to take your concerns up-line, to your bosses. Often, when someone comes across what they think might be a problem, they can be reluctant to share their worries. 'It's too much of a micro issue, it's too detailed to go to the boss with', they might think. But if it's something new, meaningful and complex, share it. Your boss will remember in the tough times if the truth was not put on the table as quickly as it could have been!

Remember, over-communicate as a top team in good and bad times.

Operate as a team in good and bad times

Just as in sport, a leadership team is made up of individuals who share a vision, are following the same road map, who operate with the same set of values and embrace the same culture.

I have explained just how difficult it can be to build a truly effective team – one that embodies the strategy and operates well together in good and bad times. The concept is simple, but the practical challenges can be very testing.

This is particularly true when the going gets tough. Everything is good when things are going well, but I've seen teams become dysfunctional in response to testing times. If the team is panicking, with members shouting at one another, gossiping and playing politics, you'll find it virtually impossible to lead the business effectively.

Yet again, this is the time for the team to show resilience and composure. And to do that, they must remain unified and mutually supportive.

We've probably all seen instances of dysfunctional behaviour by some very senior people. Here are some anonymised examples from my own experience:

* The marketing director who publicly criticised the sales team for losing market share
* The sales director who regularly would tell his team: 'You're the best! Shame about the bad advertising that marketing keeps putting out . . .'
* The head of pricing who constantly blamed marketing for poor campaign yields
* The CFO who publicly criticised operators for failing to hit their cost targets
* The regional president blaming the HQ team for making the wrong policy decision.

These are very senior, highly paid people who fail to follow the basic rules of being part of a leadership team. One thing I know for sure – just like every other leader, you will face times when you have to deal with a team that's made dysfunctional by the negative contributions of people like this.

This is what I recommend you do when it does happen. Be absolutely clear with your team about the rules of the game. The expression I often use in this situation is: 'The train is moving north . . .'. The implied message is, 'with you or without you . . .'. Don't say that overtly. You don't need to. Your audience will know you're really asking, 'Are you on the train?'

So watch, sense, observe, get feedback, use those antennae. Work out who is not working as a teammate. This is vital. If you don't do so, he or she will eventually undermine your ability to lead.

Then you'll need to have a difficult conversation with that person. Maybe you have to have a second conversation at a later point. But never, ever have a third one.

Key points from this chapter:

- Create a leadership team around you that embodies the organisational strategy, and that meets your standards.
- Make sure the top team delivers the strategy in action with a single voice.
- Focus on driving short-term performance consistently, which will give you the licence to do the right things strategically.
- Always stay composed under pressure – this is a key leadership characteristic because, no matter what you may think, you're always on stage.
- Operate as a team throughout good and bad times, making the tough calls and difficult decisions when you have to.

Leadership Principle 8
Laser-focused execution

Chapter content:

* Laser focus on the core priorities to deliver the vision.
* Create a comprehensive capability game plan to ensure operational excellence.
* Meticulous planning and disciplined execution with a zero-defect culture.
* Monitor progress with 360° leading indicators.
* Be clear about which business cycle you are in.

This chapter is about a topic that many leaders unfortunately just don't like. They feel they've worked hard to get all the way up the pole, and that they've earned the right to focus on the big things. Things like the vision, the strategic thinking, the innovation, public speaking, meeting investors and giving interviews to the press.

They think it's down to everybody else to do the execution. Well, these leaders are wrong.

Laser-focused execution is a huge responsibility for every leader: the days are gone when the leader could delegate the execution of strategy to colleagues and watch on from the wings. In today's highly competitive marketplace enjoying the easy life of an armchair strategist is not an option for any leader!

The leader's personal and public commitment to deliver the vision with her or his teams is paramount to lead with soul, and we discussed this important point in the previous chapters.

The leader needs to be seen to be deeply involved in the thick of the action, rolling up her or his sleeves and driving the strategy forward, day-by-day... Said differently, living the strategy in action.

Some people in the organisation might say, 'You don't need to get deeply involved in the business. It's my job – stop micro-managing me.'

But they're wrong too – it's not micro-management. It's simply being part of the team, working with your colleagues, providing support and guidance. And it's essential. You've got to be personally involved for the strategy to work.

High performance for any company is 1% strategy and 99% execution.

The executional challenge

Never underestimate the complexity of executing a strategy to the highest possible level. It's immense – and it's immensely important.

Right around the world, right now, there are countless corporations with a brilliant vision and a brilliant strategy. But too many of them are under-valued because they've failed to get the execution right. What they haven't realised is that without a top-notch executional game plan that's based on the same level of intensity, of intellectual energy and of engagement from all that it took to develop the strategy, they haven't a hope of success in any industry anywhere in the world.

Quite simply, even if you agree with everything else I've already covered in this book – the need for a clear vision, a non-negotiable commitment to quality, the immense value of innovation, the vital role of motivation, the need for alignment and maximum energy behind the strategy inside the company and with the top team – you'll fail without truly excellent execution.

It's what I call 'zero-defect execution': consistently delivering your core strategic priorities on a daily basis with excellence. It's the only way to drive high performance on a sustainable basis and to truly unleash the full potential of your growth strategy.

It takes a great deal of focus and organisational discipline to deliver the consistent earnings growth that leaders are expected to achieve. This requires laser focus on the core drivers of the strategy, rigorous monitoring of the leading indicators and transparent reporting of daily, weekly and monthly results. In addition, you need comprehensive planning, a zero-defect philosophy and an honest assessment of performance, all underpinned by a commitment to continuous improvement.

Laser focus on the core priorities to deliver the vision

Once you've got the vision and the strategy right, the time has come for the leader and the top team to work together on identifying the priorities that are central to delivering the strategy.

This is really important. Most senior teams will get the vision and the strategy right but might fail because they did not show a laser-focused approach when defining priorities. Selecting the wrong priorities or initiatives will assuredly result in failure.

Coming up with several initiatives that appear to fit the strategy is not difficult. Selecting the ones with the greatest potential and then identifying the core priorities that will enable you to deliver the vision is far more testing. It is essential to spend time evaluating the true potential of all initiatives and identifying the core priorities to deliver the vision.

I've said this before, but I'll say it again. Leaders are positive people who aim high. As a result, they often over-estimate their organisations' executional capabilities and have a tendency to generate too many initiatives and over-load the organisation.

This is why it's so important to prioritise initiatives, to ensure the organisation is laser-focused from an executional standpoint only on those that will make a real positive difference. In fact, I remember when working with McKinsey on our plans for Burger King Germany that at least 75% of the growth ideas we put forward were never implemented. We prioritised, and those ideas we came to first were so powerful and time-consuming to take to market that we never got around to the rest of them.

So you need to select and phase initiatives with absolute clarity. As your immediate priority, make sure you start first with those ideas you can afford and which will have the biggest and most immediate positive impact.

I think of them as 'major' and 'back burner' initiatives. Prioritise the major ones, those that are going to be really powerful in making a difference and earmark them for immediate action. Hang on to those that are important but unlikely to have the same impact or immediate value for money and put them on the backburner.

Get this stage right, and you automatically rule out those attractive big ideas that, for one reason or another, cannot be executed or will never deliver returns. This is how you do it.

First, you have to rate the initiatives in terms of several important factors: competitive advantage and differentiation; the investment required; operational delivery and long- and short-term financial impacts.

Ask yourself, what sort of advantage will this initiative bring us? Does it give us a customer service advantage? Or does it deliver a pricing advantage?

Second, will any of these advantages be sustainable? There is no point in throwing organisational effort and energy at an initiative that's only going to deliver a short-term boost. And for me, price discounting always falls into this category – it's simply never a sustainable strategy.

As for the investment required, it's true that you might lead your industry in having the biggest and best ideas to change the world. But the sad truth is that the necessary investment may prove to be too big, forcing you to turn your back on what looks like an incredibly attractive idea. You have to prioritise, admitting to yourself that you want to do it but are not going to do so. When this happens, do so without regret. By rejecting it, you have saved yourself and your organisation a world of pain.

Go through a similar process with operational delivery. Do you fully understand what it will take to deliver the initiative? If you don't have the operational capability in place, is it something you can build? If it's too complex and costly today, is it worth putting the idea to one side now with the intention of returning to it in two or three years' time? Or is it another great idea that's simply too tough to deliver?

Before making a final decision, you need to look at the likely financial impact of the initiative. Is it going to deliver for the business over the short, medium or long term? Do the potential returns make the likely executional risk worthwhile?

This can be a difficult process for everybody. We see the opportunity, we're in a hurry to make things great, but we cannot afford to overload the organisation. So planning for success is about balance: we want to aim high, but we have to prioritise to ensure we are laser-focused on the right initiatives based on several considerations from an organisational standpoint.

This is about execution, not about strategic planning or brainstorming. It defines what everybody in the organisation has to do. It involves the clear selection and phasing of initiatives to make sure you go first with those that have the greatest and most immediate positive impact. It ensures that you take the time required to pursue those ideas that will take resources and investments to provide good returns. This approach rules out those big ideas that cannot be executed or which will never deliver value.

Getting the organisation onside

So you've looked at every angle, you've precisely identified your priorities and have selected those initiatives you're confident will work best. The next step is to inform the organisation about them and get everyone energised about them. We've already looked at the critical importance of engagement when implementing a strategy. Here, a vital part of the communication effort will be to contextualise why these initiatives are so important to the strategic delivery, engaging people and ensuring that everybody is on the same page.

So to do this, you need to contextualise your thinking. You need to explain how and why you have identified the ideas, what makes them important, why you dropped some that you started to look at, why you are starting a new concept from scratch. Be totally transparent in the way you speak – discuss the risk of failures along the way, explain how your thinking worked and share your excitement about the potential wins for everyone. Being open and genuine is very important. It will help to inspire your team and galvanise the organisation.

You also need to be very precise about the goals for each initiative, describing in detail what success will look like for each one. It's dangerous not to be clear and precise. I've seen so many leaders, department heads, managers, trying to get across the ideas they've come up with. They sometimes try shooting from the hip: 'We're going to do this, and this and this and this,' they say. But they fail to precisely describe the direction of travel or said differently, what success looks like. They don't properly communicate the reasons for and purpose of the initiative. They don't show how it fits into the bigger picture. People get confused and big ideas never happen!

If you confuse your colleagues, they won't follow you. Being precise about where you're going is an absolute necessity for any leader. People will follow you if they like the look of the destination you're leading them to. So tell them in words – and show them in pictures. In other words, use visualisation to explain exactly what it is you want your people to do for you.

I typically use a striking visual, illustrated on one slide, which clearly links the key initiative you're launching with the vision and the purpose in a way that leaves no room for doubt. I always find this takes a great deal of thinking through.

You need to distil everything down to its simplest possible essence, making it really bite-sized and memorable. The power of summarising the USP of an initiative cannot be underestimated.

Link action and objectives

When you have developed and formulated an initiative, and energised the organisation about its power, ensure it is reflected in the objectives of your teams throughout the organisation.

It might seem obvious to mention, but I believe too many companies do not do this. It is a failure to follow one of the basic principles of performance management and appraisal: ensuring there is a clear architecture linking activities and goals throughout the whole organisation, from the top, right the way through to the customer interface.

Another important learning I have gathered over the years is that the execution of a strategy is always more complex than anticipated. Hence the need to allocate quality time to think with your team how you will execute your strategy with zero-defect. When you look at your agenda-planning for the year, make sure you spend plenty of time working out how you will get deeply involved in the execution of your core priorities, living the strategy in action.

For example, if you're planning to expand in the Kazakh market, you'll need to spend plenty of time researching the opportunity. And if you're going to invest in a plant in Chile, you need to gain first-hand experience of all the practical challenges involved in the country.

Here are a few examples from my own experience about what laser focus really means on a global and on a local level.

Focus on building scale

In 1996, the Grand Metropolitan board was worried about McDonald's much faster growth rate, so it hired McKinsey to answer a simple question: 'Does Burger King outside the US have any potential to create value?'

At the time, almost 100% of Burger King profits came from North America. McKinsey looked at the issues and reported back that the problems stemmed from the fact that the business was sub-scale in too many markets scattered across the world. I could sympathise from my time at Pepsi Cola International: that company too was very strong in the USA. Like many companies trying to build a global footprint, Burger King had made the mistake of trying to expand in too many countries at the same time, without building scale in a few critical international markets first.

This didn't chime with established thinking about global portfolio management, which tells us that when you're running a global portfolio, it is really important to be tightly focused on the key countries where you can build scale, with the goal over time to be number one or two in each of the markets you operate in.

It doesn't matter what industry you're in: unless you hold one of those two positions, you're never going to be strong enough to thrive. That's because scale gives you amazing advantages: economies of scale of course, the ability to attract the best people, the funds to invest in processes and technology, the resources to drive innovation and expansion in the most attractive growth areas, to ultimately grow faster than your competitors, and provide strong personal growth opportunities for your colleagues, which I discussed earlier, is critical to retaining your best talents.

In 1995, the BSE crisis was hitting Burger King harder than its main competitors in countries across Europe, simply because the company had not achieved critical scale there. So, following McKinsey's input, two essential decisions were made.

First, we should concentrate on growing and getting to scale in 10 international markets: the UK, Germany, Spain, Turkey, Australia, New Zealand, Korea, Mexico, Puerto Rico and Canada.

Second, management needed to focus on those countries where we could execute with a zero-defect approach. We should pull out altogether from countries where we had no critical mass nor strong fundamentals. It seems incredible now that these included France, one of the largest countries in Europe. But it made perfect sense. We were a distant number three there, far behind McDonald's and Quick. We had one amazing and very profitable flagship site on Les Champs-Elysées, but the rest of the portfolio was very weak.

In 1997, Burger King appointed Dennis Malamatinas as CEO (Chief Energy Officer), formerly the Head of Grand Met Asia and the architect of the brilliant global brand repositioning of Smirnoff Vodka. Like me, he's previously worked at Pepsi, so he knew all about the pitfalls of having an international division without critical mass in key markets. So, under Dennis, we were laser-focused on the countries where we could excel.

A further major implication of this decision was that we should not be looking at countries that at the time identified as 'emerging markets', countries and regions such as Russia and Eastern Europe, India, China and Brazil. This was because there was so much potential elsewhere – and management needed to focus on those countries where it could execute with a zero-defect approach.

Even by the time I left the business in 2003, when I was in charge of Burger King International, entering the likes of China, Russia or Brazil was not on my agenda. So while I nominally had 57 countries in my global portfolio, in reality, I had just 10 to focus on in my day-to-day agenda – and those 10 represented 77% of the business.

I tell this story to illustrate my point that focusing your resources on what will deliver the greatest returns, not falling into the trap of trying to do too much with your team, can be incredibly effective. You want to aim high, but you have to accept the fact that you cannot execute everything. In fact, in this case we quickly realised that even concentrating on just 10 markets would be too much for our resources, so we went to the next level of focus – at a country level.

I have already written about the difference between driving the growth of your restaurant portfolio in a given country through the company's own capex investments and working with franchise partners. For any country manager, the capex route is the fastest way to expand. But when it's the company's money, it's all about your own P&L, your own cash and the return on investments expected by your shareholders. Running a portfolio of company restaurants is executionally complex. At the time, our international business was losing money, so we knew there was no room for error in how we allocated and used our capital resources.

We decided to tighten our focus yet more stringently. We concentrated our capex investments to expand our portfolio of company restaurants in just five markets – those where we had the right capability to establish scale with corporate restaurants, rapidly and with precision. These were Australia, Spain, Germany, Mexico and the UK. And we focused even more closely on selected regions within those countries, with an obsessive determination to drive executional excellence.

In the other five countries we concentrated on recruiting the right franchisees, giving them the right tools and operating systems, monitoring them and inspiring them to achieve continuous improvement.

The effects of this laser-sharp focus were stunning. In the seven years I was there, the number of Burger King outlets more than doubled, from 1,400 to 3,000, with 88% of growth coming from those 10 markets. And this tight focus on our top 10 growth markets delivered against our profitability targets too. By 2003, Burger King International was delivering more than 40% of Burger King's profits worldwide.

Three areas of focus for portfolio strength

Just after I joined Intertek, as part of developing the 5 × 5 differentiated strategy for growth we covered earlier in the book, we developed and implemented a portfolio strategy that has proved over the years to be highly effective at delivering sustainable portfolio growth with high returns. Our portfolio opportunity is based on a three-tier portfolio strategy to prioritise our organic and inorganic investments. This is how the three tiers work:

1. Investing in the core

The first priority is to strengthen the core. I have already written about innovating from the core, and the same principle applies to portfolio management: building on what we're good at to make our strong business even stronger. This is not as intuitive as you might expect. I've seen CEOs who think, 'It's OK, we're already strong enough here – let's instead focus on improving the things where we are weak and grow our market share.'

Big mistake. In my view, you're most likely to be weak because you're not very good at it. If that's the case, getting better at it is probably going to be complicated. It's going to require investment and innovation. And it's likely that you haven't got the executional ability either.

To be strategically focused where you are weak is not the right choice. Growing and further strengthening those elements where you are ahead of the market is where you will find the most profitable wins from a portfolio standpoint, as you will capitalise on your scale, expertise and IP.

That's why my primary focus is always on ever strengthening the parts of the business that are doing really well, that are already generating the lion's share of our income and profits. If you continue to strengthen your core business, month after month, you will exceed your targets.

That's why I always spend so much time working with our largest businesses, where we are #1 or #2. There are two reasons for that: unless you get sustainable progress in your core business, you are not likely to deliver sustainable performance for your entire business; and once you've found a way to strengthen your core business, you will deliver great returns for your stakeholders.

2. Investing in high-growth and high-margin markets

The second priority in portfolio management is to leverage your core competencies and to invest in high-growth and high-margin areas where you have expertise and capability.

Every business has such opportunities. Every company has areas where it has capability and expertise but where the company has not maximised its growth potential.

So identify those markets with the highest growth and highest margin opportunities where you have strength and expertise but haven't yet fulfilled your potential – and go for growth.

3. Fixing your underperforming businesses

The third point of focus is on those areas where turnaround is required or where management action could clearly result in performance improvement. In a global business, this might be an individual operation, a division, a country and even entire continents.

There is no perfect portfolio and there are always parts of your portfolio that will require special attention. Once you have identified these businesses that need special focus, the critical success factor is to understand the root cause of the problem. That can be complicated, especially if it is a remote location that you don't know so well, if the management in charge of the business has not done a proper diagnosis, or is in denial, saying 'it was a difficult few quarters but everything is fine.'

Based on my experience, there are several explanations or hypotheses that cause a business to start underperforming.

It could be driven by an ineffective sales and marketing strategy.

Sometimes it has to do with a sudden pricing issue in the market, as your competitors are using price to take share from your business. It can be a cost overspend or a lack of focus on cash. Quality issues or customer service problems are also usually a cause for underperformance.

A staff retention issue resulting in a lot of departures, or several changes in the leadership team, can reduce the overall capability of the team and impact performance.

There is another reason, which I am always paranoid about and which is always difficult for the local team to assess: there are moments in the growth cycle of any industry where the structural drivers are changing and undermining your value proposition.

In simple terms, the market is moving around your business and your team does not see it clearly.

My advice: always be paranoid about a structural demand change in your market!

The potential root causes for underperformance I just described are of course not mutually exclusive and most of the time a proper diagnosis will identify 2 to 3 key issues to fix.

Whatever the reason for underperformance, identifying and removing the obstacles that are preventing a high-potential business from achieving its potential will strengthen the overall returns of your portfolio.

Virtuous economics

I would like to emphasise the benefits of delivering margin-accretive revenue growth with strong cash generation and making disciplined capital investments in high-growth and high-margin areas when implementing the three-tier portfolio strategy we just discussed.

Quite simply, you will create industry-leading returns for your stakeholders benefiting from what I call the 'virtuous economics'.

When you are a quality market leader, with a world-class portfolio, you should command a premium price. The moment you reduce what you charge, you've become a tactical operator. Then price becomes your primary competitive weapon – and you'll quickly be outmaneuvered, because there will always be somebody better than you at price.

It's simply not a differentiator.

Your main goal of course is to increase your revenues faster than your competition because you want to gain market share. To do this, you need to be smart with your volume, price and mix management. Always target the highest growth opportunities in markets where you can command a good price. This approach will create a good mix effect and deliver good revenue management.

In doing so, you also need to target the right margin areas, enabling you to drive gross margin accretion, provided you manage your variable costs with a disciplined productivity approach.

The next element of virtuous economics is cash generation. Collecting money is critically important – the more cash we get, the more we can invest. Putting the right cash management discipline in place to make sure that clients pay on time and that you do the same with suppliers is critical.

So far, so good! You have created the right foundation to fully benefit from the virtuous economics of your earnings model, provided you are disciplined on how you invest to drive further growth.

You now need to reinvest the cash you generated in high-growth and high-margin areas, which will further accelerate your revenue and take your margin performance to new heights.

This is what the virtuous economics model based on a three-tiered portfolio strategy is all about.

You grow faster than your competition organically. You deliver industry-leading margins.

Your cash conversion is Best-in-Class.

You have a strong firepower with more funds to invest than your competitors.

You invest your capital in high-growth and high-margin areas.

Your growth in revenue and margin will then accelerate, giving your company an incredible growth and margin advantage.

The compounding effect of delivering year after year margin-accretive revenue growth with strong cash generation, while investing in growth based on a disciplined capital allocation, will strengthen your competitive position, and drive strong returns.

This is what the virtuous economic model is all about. Simply beautiful!

Create a comprehensive capability game plan to ensure operational excellence

Any new strategy will raise the bar for the entire organisation, forcing everybody in it to focus rigorously on delivering your core priorities with zero defects. That means asking people to do more. As the leader, you need to ensure that everybody, you included, is totally clear about how the core priorities are going to be delivered. So, working closely with your leadership team, you'll need to develop a comprehensive capability plan.

Each plan should comprise five main sections, each covering one of the core priorities:

1. Talents: ensure you have a clear picture of both the numbers and the types of talent that will be needed
2. Skills: include a clear evaluation of any skills gaps, plus the right training programmes to address them
3. Tools and equipment: a certain amount of capex may be required to ensure you have everything you need
4. Process: a new initiative may change the way that business is done, meaning a set of new standard operating procedures will need to be developed and put in place
5. Technology and information systems: these will be required to make sure operational data can be processed and managed to track performance and measure progress.

I will now share a few examples from my own career that show how a capability plan structured in this way applies to just about any kind of growth initiative.

When ambience really matters . . .

When I first arrived at Burger King, the customer experience for anybody visiting one of our restaurants was inferior to McDonald's, despite the fact that our product was superior.

It had to do with service of course, and I've already described the Make Every Bite Right programme. But this 'back to basics' program didn't address the fact that our restaurants were old-fashioned and did not really demonstrate what the USP was.

Everybody in the hospitality business knows that it's about far more than the product you actually eat, as consumers really value 'the restaurant experience'.

Essentially, it's about how you feel as you're eating it, based on the product quality, the quality of service, the overall ambience.

At the time, I was a big fan of Howard Schultz and his visionary work to create a brand new 'coffee society' at Starbucks. It was the first properly themed retail environment on the high street, and I found it very inspiring.

So inspiring, in fact, that we decided to attempt something similar. This is how the thinking went.

At the time in Germany, America was very aspirational. People were excited by American brands. Of course, burgers were invented in America, a real marketing opportunity for Burger King.

The Whopper is the signature burger of Burger King and, capitalising on the USP of the Whopper, we invented Americana.

Unless you're doing your own BBQ at home, the Whopper is the best burger you can get. It's flame grilled, it's fresh, it's cooked the moment you order it.

Our big marketing idea was simply: 'The Whopper you eat at Burger King is the best-tasting burger, because it's real, it's authentic – it's part of the American dream.'

To get this across, we decided to change the décor as well as the look and feel of our restaurants. We went in a big way for Americana. Pictures of James Dean, big American cars, everything you'd expect.

We were going full throttle for the best burger experience created in America, and this meant the best from a product standpoint, a service standpoint and an ambience standpoint. That gave us a unique value proposition – something that nobody else had.

Our differentiated value proposition was simply the best burger experience in every Burger King in Germany.

We launched the Americana concept in a restaurant in Cologne's main entertainment district, the Hohenzollernring. It was very successful. We had a winner on our hands – if only we could get the new décor and branding into 120 restaurants around the country. This was an extraordinarily complex task.

It was an example of a strategic initiative – 'Change the décor of my restaurants' – that initially sounds simple, but quickly proves to be anything but.

How do you get 120 restaurants rebranded? How do you ensure all new restaurants are built and decorated accordingly? And how do you ensure that your new décor is going to last?

We were fortunate enough to have a fantastic head of Development, Heinz Peter Dickes, an industry veteran with a background at McDonald's. And we had a brilliant architect, Musa Cifti, who created the concept. We made a terrific team, and together we rebranded Burger King in Germany in just a few years.

It was super-complicated. It took an enormous amount of planning. We had to be incredibly clear on specifications. We had to vet and approve all suppliers – there were very few who could supply Americana equipment to all the restaurants in our network. We had to recruit a specific team to ensure every restaurant had access to the customised designs and would be completed on time. Only a proper capability plan would enable all this to happen – on time and within budget.

Americana was a big idea and was an integral part of the Burger King Germany success formula, which repositioned the business for sustainable growth.

Without a comprehensive capability game plan however, Americana would have stayed a big idea on paper only!

The driving power of the drive-thru

I've already mentioned the Burger King restaurant portfolio strategy to create a national network of drive-thru restaurants. This wasn't just about décor – it was about the kind of restaurants we were building.

Again, extremely detailed planning was vital.

First, we had to identify those areas of Germany that we believed presented the greatest commercial potential for the new restaurants. That took in-depth market planning.

Then we had to identify the key metrics involved at every potential site: a drive-thru on a road with 10,000 cars a day simply doesn't present the same potential as one on a road with 60,000 vehicles. So Heinz Peter Dickes and I started counting cars. Counting one street once wasn't enough. We had to measure traffic flows at multiple times during the week. Between us, we always observed the traffic flow at every site where we were considering building a drive-thru several times before making a decision.

It wasn't exciting work, but it was worthwhile. We concluded that our market share of the traffic on any given street was about 3.5% if we were alone. However, if we were up against McDonald's, that fell to around 2.5%.

For all the time I was Managing Director of Germany, I would personally approve every site. This wasn't because I was keen to micro-manage. It was because the decisions about where we'd operate were absolutely central to the success of our strategy. It therefore had to be the leader's responsibility, and I took it very seriously. Sometimes I would go and see sites at lunchtime, in the evening and at weekends, just to be sure we'd selected the right place.

When it comes to retail expansion, the experts will tell you that the mantra to have in mind when growing a network is 'site, site, site...' It simply means that the only way to build a successful branded retail network is by ensuring site-selection comes first every time.

As the pace of development picked up, we appointed teams to do this work at scale. We built a development team, staffed by development managers with their own territories. They became responsible for mapping sites, identifying landowners, gaining construction permits and all the rest of the details involved.

But I would still personally approve every site.

So it takes a lot of work to deliver an initiative that originally sounds as simple as 'Let's build drive-thrus across Germany'.

But the success was incredible. Around 95% of the restaurants were quickly exceeding or at the very least on target with their business plans. When we launched our first drive-thru in Düsseldorf, we had calls from the police complaining about the traffic jams we were causing. We had several TV stars having a Whopper at one of our Americana restaurants and telling their audiences all about it. It was amazing.

The German consumers had waited such a long time in many cities in Germany to taste the real Whopper and sometimes it felt that their dream of having a Whopper was coming true. Really incredible!

Meticulous planning and disciplined execution with a zero-defect culture

Everybody probably agrees that planning is essential to make any initiative successful. But in reality, the quality of planning differs considerably from organisation to organisation and team to team. Not everybody has the granular focus that's required to develop and deliver rigorous and effective project management.

That's why getting an initiative off the ground works best with meticulous planning based on a very clear and robust project-management framework.

In my view, projects succeed best when that meticulous planning is underpinned by a highly detailed, step-by-step analysis of what needs to be done, with a clear articulation of what success will look like.

To build this framework, you first agree what the project is – an example might be a major rebranding exercise for a global company. If there are sensitivities to the project that you don't want the outside world to know about, consider using a code name. For example, when Intertek carried out its global rebranding in 2016, we called it 'Project Cerello'.

Next, of course, establish exactly who you want to have on your team. This selection will be fundamental to driving the success of the project.

Third, and most important of all, define the workstreams involved and create project plans for each one. This means breaking down the project as a whole into a set of bite-sized component parts that together will help you plan, oversee and deliver your project. For each of these, define the goals and milestones that need to be achieved, and by whom. This is the most critical area of meticulous planning and is the point at which the success or failure of most project management is determined.

It doesn't matter how many workstreams there are or how many components there are in each, provided you have the capability to manage and deliver them. To assure this is the case, the next important requirement is accountability – determining precisely who is responsible for what, what their specific targets are and the levels of support they have, to enable them to deliver.

This is clearly a complex undertaking. You have multiple workstreams, with multiple action plans, moving in parallel but at different speeds. The only way to master this complexity is to ensure the workstream plans are regularly reviewed and updated, at least every month and possibly every week, depending on the speed of the project.

Visualising the initiative in a project-management tool is essential to ensure disciplined execution by explaining the scope of what needs to be done and portraying accountabilities and existing or new processes.

I also find it extremely useful to ensure team members complete a scorecard on a weekly or monthly basis to show green, yellow or red colour coding, indicating the progress made on every milestone in every workstream. This helps me quickly understand progress and see through the complexity of even the largest and most important projects. This in turn allows me to take action and correct the course if I see issues emerging.

I've used this approach to project management for many years – for example, when creating and launching Total Sustainability Assurance at Intertek, rolling out SAP at Inchcape, delivering Euro Disney's multi-year innovation plan and Americana at Burger King. I've used it over and over again, simply because it works.

A question of culture

You can achieve a great deal with a laser focus on your strategic priorities and performance-management processes, enabling you to drive growth with zero-defect execution. But you'll find it hard to achieve this on a sustainable basis without the right zero-defect culture across the organisation, with integrity at its heart.

This is hard to achieve, but I can illustrate how it works in practice. This is another story from my time with Burger King in Germany. I've already described various elements of our turnaround plan, including our Vision 10,000, the drive-thru expansion in the west of the country, our back-to-basics operational programme, our Americana restaurant restyling, our menu development and our exciting brand-building activities.

But without a zero-defect culture, we realised none of this would deliver the short- and long-term benefits we were targeting. In a restaurant business, it's vital that day-to-day operations drive repeat business – in other words, that the in-store experience encourages people to come back. This needs the customer-service proposition to be executed with zero defects.

We came up with a very simple way of communicating what had to be done to create a zero-defect culture. We made it clear that to achieve Vision 10,000, we had to give every customer the best experience, every day in every restaurant. We used a pyramid design to visualise this message – the

Best Experience Pyramid – which contained all elements of the turnaround plan: best restaurant, best product, best service, best value, best people and best communication.

This allowed every single employee or franchisee to relate to his or her role in the strategy. And that in turn enabled us to make every single person responsible for the quality of execution. There is no doubt that the Best Experience strategy helped to create a zero-defect culture and philosophy across the entire organisation. And this in turn ensured that the strategic priorities for the business were implemented with a high level of executional excellence.

This was soon reflected in our business performance. At the end of 1996, Burger King Germany's 120 restaurants collectively lost money. Between 1997 and 2003, it was the country's fastest-growing system restaurant, delivering double-digit like-for-like growth each year, taking share from McDonald's and winning multiple industry awards. By 2003, Burger King had more than 400 restaurants in Germany. And Germany was the company's most profitable international market.

I talked earlier in the book about the importance for any leader to never compromise on quality and I used several examples in different industries. I also gave two examples of airlines, which disappointed me with their customer service. Running an airline is complex and I admit that creating a zero-defect culture in any industry is a big challenge for any leader. The best company I ever came across at creating a zero-defect culture is an airline and it is Singapore Airlines. I have flown with Singapore Airlines for more than 35 years and I have never experienced a flight that was not zero-defect from the moment I check in, to the moment I disembarked.

Singapore Airlines is truly remarkable at everything they do because they are laser-focused on their customer promise, which they consistently exceed.

Together, they believe in having a comprehensive capability plan in place, they are meticulous in their planning, they operate with a zero-defect culture and they never stop monitoring progress with 360° leading indicators, giving them the insights they need to innovate on a regular basis.

Monitoring progress with 360° leading indicators

If the successful delivery of a strategy depends on a laser focus with zero-defect execution, this gives rise to an extremely important question. How do we monitor every aspect – from a 360° perspective– of the progress being made from the core initiatives?

This is a critically important part of the strategic-planning process, as a strategy can never be initiated without agreeing on the right goals and measuring progress based on the right metrics.

Many companies focus on financial indicators as the only means of measurement. In my view, these are necessary – but they're not enough on their own.

That's because they are lagging indicators – they need to be complemented with leading operational indicators, which are what really identify the value drivers inside a company. It takes time for a leadership team to identify the leading indicators in the business. But this is time well spent as part of the strategic-planning process.

It is also best practice to ensure that every team and every layer within the organisation operates with the same scorecard of leading and lagging indicators. That way, you can be confident that everybody is laser-focused on the same core priorities.

Then, with all indicators identified and agreed, the leadership team needs to define what success looks like by setting the organisation's short- and medium-term goals.

It takes time to implement a new strategy with a laser focus execution of the core initiatives. The core initiatives will only be maximised when every team regularly works together to review progress made against their goals using 360° leading indicators. Once they have a 360° view on the results of the strategy implementation, they can develop their action plans to optimise their approach with a focus on continuous improvement.

Monitoring progress

Monitoring the progress of an initiative's execution isn't about project management alone. It's also about performance management.

That's what I want to look at now. Specifically, how to devise and use an operating system that drives self-performance management – creating and enabling systemic behaviours in your organisation based on the right data.

In essence, performance management isn't complicated. It's about having clear goals and standard operating procedures in place, then looking at outputs, diagnosing them and planning the way ahead with new or revised goals.

Companies benefit hugely from having operating systems in place that enable their people to use data and technology to do this on a systemic basis. So, in my view a good operating system should empower your team to look at data in multiple dimensions, enabling them to consider all leading and lagging indicators when assessing how well the strategy is being executed.

An operating system doesn't need to be complex. At Burger King, for example, one we devised and delivered was simply a restaurant-opening plan that worked on a monthly basis, helping teams to track their leading indicators and open their restaurants on time and on budget. It was incredibly helpful and simplified the massive complexity of what we were trying to do.

Another example of a really good operating system was the one we had at Disney to schedule the working requirements for our Cast Members. In an operation of that scale, unforeseen events could make this a complex task. On any given day, we may have 30,000 guests. On another, we might have up to 90,000. When you have that many people coming for a great day out, you'd better know what's about to happen in plenty of time to get organised, hence the importance of what we call the scheduling of your workforce.

So we devised an operating system to help us plan how many Cast Members we needed for the restaurants, the hotels and the various attractions in the park every day. This was based firstly on the reservations we had in our hotels, and then on our best daily estimates for what we believed demand would be from the local market. It was a very important tool for ensuring we had the right capability from day to day. Without the proper employee scheduling, we could not deliver the right level of guest satisfaction.

At Intertek, every team leader is expected to spend quality time once a month with her or his direct reports, looking at data, looking at the action plans that were agreed the previous month, revisiting goals, creating initiatives and planning for the month ahead using our Cockpit operating system.

The benefits of the Cockpit operating system are numerous at Intertek.

First, it ensures our teams are aligned when looking at the data analytics and when looking at opportunities that their focus is on the right ones. Next, it clarifies the direction of travel for everybody, an enormously powerful means of engaging people at every level. It creates teamwork, energising people and enthusing them about working together. It drives innovation, as people spark off one another to come up with new ideas. And it's fun as well, creating opportunities to measure, celebrate and reward success. Finally, it gives top performing teams the energy to thrive, as one should never underestimate the thrill of winning together as a team, in sport and business!

Be clear about which business cycle you are in

An important truth I've learned over the years is that you need to flex your approach to executing your strategy depending on which business cycle you are in.

By this, I do not mean economic cycle – rather, I mean the type of cycle you are in as a business.

In my view, there are four basic types of business cycle:

* Start-up: building a business from scratch
* Turnaround: when you are having to address key performance issues
* Corporate activity: carrying out some fundamental change to the business, maybe including acquisition, divestment, financial restructuring or merger
* Good to great: when a company is on a good growth trajectory and the leadership team needs to take the company from good to great.

1. Start-up

Clearly, a start-up situation is when you are very small, and you have to build your presence from scratch. The critical question in a start-up situation is simple: how much time is it going to take to scale up the business?

That's because being small isn't good. All sorts of benefits come with size: market presence, economies of scale, opportunities and that all-important headroom to navigate when times get tough.

Getting through those early stages can be very demanding. You have to do a lot of basic things, and you don't have much in the way of management or capital resources to do them. But that's no reason not to be laser-focused on what it will take to scale up. This is overwhelmingly your most important responsibility. Critically, the team needs to identify the size of the ultimate opportunity and understand how and when it's going to reach the milestones on the way. Otherwise, it's not going to happen.

So when I'm looking at a new business with, say, a $1 billion opportunity, my first question will always be the same. 'How long will it take you to get to revenues of $100 million?' The team has to have a clear plan of how they're going to achieve that first landmark. Without one, there's no chance of ever becoming a $1 billion operation.

In my experience having a tight geographic focus, within either a country or a region, helps a start-up build that all-important critical mass quickly. That's where the magic really happens. Rapidly scaling within your selected geography and customer base has to be your number one goal, as this will deliver the economies of scale that create the platform for profitable growth.

2. The turnaround

In terms of execution, the toughest business cycle is the turnaround.

When you're running a turnaround, I strongly recommend that your key focus is on what I call the turnaround triangle, which is based on three elements: the problem opportunity definition; the bite-size initiatives and the energy plan.

The problem opportunity definition: when something bad is happening in your business, you have to spend time with your team to properly understand the reasons why you are in a turnaround situation. I've known situations when it has taken many sessions for somebody suddenly to say, 'You know what? I think I know what the problem is...' Getting there can be really difficult and challenging. Some people will be defensive and find it hard to accept any responsibility for underperformance.

The bite-size initiatives: once again, the real trick with turnaround management is to do with execution – focus on just a few initiatives, no more than three to five. But make sure these are the ones with maximum impact: ensure they are delivered extremely well, with precision, pace and passion.

The energy plan: turnaround management is challenging for any organisation. Morale is low, people are tired, they might be struggling to concentrate. You need to get their minds off their worries. And importantly, it will take time for everybody to see light at the end of the tunnel as turnaround management is hard work.

Something I have found useful is putting in place what I call the 'energy plan'. Making sure that you develop a comprehensive energy plan that you, as a leader, personally deliver. That's because the success of a turnaround lies 20% in problem definition, 30% in operational focus and 50% in energy. Again, be highly visible. Ooze energy. Communicate the diagnosis loudly and clearly. And connect with the business to look at the data on a weekly or daily basis. Report progress frequently during large team meetings to build confidence and recognise the quick wins which will boost the morale and the energy of your colleagues.

If you're leading a turnaround at a large site, I suggest you hold a monthly town hall with all site staff. Tell them, 'This is what we talked about last month, this is where we are today, this is where we're going next month'.

Ensure there is plenty of recognition for people – it's vital in helping raise morale and urging people to work even harder. Meet with your senior team at least once a week to define, agree and review weekly priorities. Last but not least, roll-up your sleeves to help at any time.

If you are leading a turnaround in a multi-site business, I suggest you visit sites on a regular basis to have face-to-face sessions several times during the year. We all have learned the power of virtual communication during COVID-19, and I recommend you over-communicate virtually with your teams when you cannot meet face-to-face.

Turnaround management is hard work!

3. Corporate activity

Whatever type of corporate restructuring your business is involved in – acquisition, divestment, restructuring programme or merger – make sure you have a separate, focused team working on it. That way, you can ensure that it's business as usual for the rest of the organisation.

During the restructuring at Euro Disney in 2003, I had two teams: the day-to-day operations, and the restructuring team. Only I and my CFO were involved in both.

The reason for this is simple. A corporate activity can be very distracting. It can take people's focus away from their own day-to-day responsibilities and create unnecessary concerns. Having a dedicated team means that the main organisation doesn't get derailed.

So create a separate, focused team, packed with the specialist expertise required, that operates next to the core of the business using its own modus operandi.

4. Good to great

Taking a successful business to the next level is the most fun and rewarding challenge a leader can face. The sky's the limit.

It's also the most complex strategic and operational challenge.

When you're in a start-up or a turnaround, you're standing on a burning platform. Stay in one place for too long, and you'll really suffer for it. You've no choice, you've got to do something about it. That's not the case with a good business. People say, 'But you're doing so well! Why change anything? Why do anything different? Why take the risk?'

It is important to understand, however, that a good to great journey isn't about changing everything. It's about identifying those areas that will give you the biggest inflections and do most to boost your future growth. Once you have found these, you are at the start of developing your new strategy. But getting to this point is not always easy, and it may take a considerable amount of time to find those inflection points.

In his book, *Good to Great*, author Jim Collins explains what he calls the 'Hedgehog model'. He explains that greatness becomes possible when you find your intrinsic strength and when you capitalise on it to create your competitive advantage. It's about identifying the intrinsic strength that lies at the intersection of your company's passion, its ambition and its economic engine.

Ask yourselves, Collins says, these three questions:

* What are you deeply passionate about?
* What can you be best in the world at?
* What drives your economic engine?

Where the three circles meet provides the inflection point on which you might wish to base the future growth of your business.

This is what Collins called the Hedgehog concept – the single-minded competitive advantage that differentiates you from everyone else, named after the hedgehog's consistent excellence at rolling into a ball to outwit the fox that wants to eat it. The organisation can then focus obsessively on this hedgehog differentiation to outgrow its competitors. Once you've found it, it's very powerful, because it's here to last.

Of course, identifying the next inflection is only half the challenge involved in delivering a good to great strategy. The other half lies in taking the organisation with you and ensuring that the changes you intend to bring will not interrupt ongoing performance over the short term.

In short, rising to the good to great challenge is about using the Hedgehog concept to identify one big strategic change of direction. Then, lead that change with EQ and maximum respect for the organisation and its people.

For Intertek, this is our Total Quality Assurance Customer promise. We **are** passionate about it, we **can** be the best at it, and it **will** drive our economic engine for the years ahead.

Total Quality. Assured.

"Intertek Total Quality Assurance expertise, delivered consistently with precision, pace and passion, enabling our customers to power ahead safely."

Key points from this chapter:

• Identify the core priorities on which the organisation needs to be laser focused to implement the strategy and deliver the vision.
• Make sure you have a capability plan covering each of these priorities.
• Carry out meticulous planning to ensure a disciplined execution with zero-defect.
• Monitor progress with 360° leading indicators, ensuring you use the right data and operating systems.
• Be certain which part of the business cycle you're in – start-up, business turnaround, corporate activity and good to great journey – as this will influence how you lead the business.

Leadership Principle 9
Ever-better branding glo-cally

Chapter content:

* Winning brands have a differentiated, motivating and honest USP.
* Seize the growth opportunity with ever-better branding.
* Glo-cal communication, congruent on all consumer touch points.
* Great advertising – but not by committee please!
* Inside-out branding – living the brand from within.

Everybody loves branding and advertising, and it's one of the subjects that leaders, just like everyone else, enjoy a lot. That's because all businesses are branded in the eyes of customers and consumers! For any company, building a trusted brand is paramount to delivering truly sustainable performance.

Your brand, quite simply, is who you are in the marketplace – and it is incredibly valuable. Strong and successful brands are built on a very simple USP that is differentiated, motivating and honest. It doesn't work any other way. Getting it wrong or acting in a way that is not consistent with your brand will damage who you are and what you stand for in the eyes of your target group.

So, owning an iconic brand is a priceless asset. But it can never be taken for granted. It will only achieve value when the brand promise is delivered and lived inside the organisation every day. Nothing stands still – the world is changing fast, and you have to continuously innovate and invest in your brand, nourishing and strengthening it through product and service improvements, ever-better communication, and the right advertising investments across all channels, to take it to greater heights and attract new customers every day.

The glo-cal dimension

All brand communication must be glo-cal in its nature and execution: that simply means, it must balance global trends with local customer insights, using specific messages that are fully congruent across all consumer touch points.

Never get the idea that developing an effective communication plan is easy. It's not. It's a lot of hard work. At its heart, there has to be a unique creative idea, sometimes in the form of a metaphor, that will augment and magnify your USP to increase the resonance of your brand promise with your target audience. It must build powerful empathy with your audience and create a strong desire to buy among your prospects.

In addition, in today's digital world, your planning needs to support interactivity between your brand and its customers. If your business owns a brand in today's 24/7 interactive digital world, never forget that you co-own it with your customers: they are part of your brand proposition. It's part of their lives, they love to talk about it on social media or face-to-face with their friends and enjoy the glow they get from it.

As I have already described, I saw this most strongly first-hand at Euro Disney in 2003. Social media was not very strong at the time, but the Disney fan club already 'owned' the brand, using their unofficial website to express their point of view, which they would discuss internally with cast members or externally with opinion leaders, the media and of course, our customers.

Winning brands have a differentiated, motivating and honest USP

So, let's begin at the beginning. How do you start with branding?

Say you are launching a business from scratch and you need to develop the brand. In my mind, there are seven distinct steps.

1. You have to be clear that your brand is about addressing a need that's currently unmet in any market – unmet until now because you are the first to spot the opportunity. It's what brands do – create a niche new market that has the potential to be scaled-up. You need to ensure that the market opportunity you spot is based on an insight or concept that has widespread appeal. There is little point in creating a brand if the potential market is not big enough to support a viable business as you build your brand and scale up.

2. Ensure that you develop your product or service capability in a way that delivers a true competitive advantage in meeting the need you've identified. This will give you a strong differentiation in the marketplace, where the first-mover advantage often delivers the highest chances of success, provided you rapidly scale up your business before any competitor can copy your proposition.

3. You must be 100% clear about the core benefits you are planning to deliver. Be completely honest here: never be tempted to oversell. Brands that fail to deliver on what they promise will disappear simply because their customers will not repeat the purchase of a product or service that under-delivers.

4. Be granular in identifying and understanding your target market. Make absolutely sure that they desire the benefits of your brand proposition and are motivated to take interest and quickly purchase your brand. Understanding your target audience will require a quantitative analysis of who they are, how they live, what they purchase and what is their current repertoire of products and services in the category in which you are planning to launch your brand.

5. When you come to brand your product or service proposition, it's about identifying and capturing a simple, universal USP in a way that is differentiated, motivating and honest that can be expressed in a simple phrase: for example, BMW's 'Ultimate Driving Machine'. Or from my own experience, 'The Choice of a New Generation' (Pepsi Cola), 'Have it your way' (Burger King), 'It's Cool to be Clear' (7UP) and 'Intertek Total Quality Assured'. In every case, lines of this power express precisely what it is that the brand stands for. Indeed, strong brands have to be built on a high-quality USP. Think of Esso ('Put a tiger in your tank'), Nike ('Just do it'), Amex ('Don't leave home without it'), Heinz Ketchup ('Pour Perfectly') and Apple ('Think Different').

Literal or lateral?

I am often asked the question about the appropriate process on how to create a brand. When it comes to choosing a brand name, there are no hard rules.

There is the literal approach: Burger King founder James McLamore went with the name simply because he aimed to be the king of the burger world. When Stelios Haji-Ioannou created EasyJet, he wanted to enable people to travel easily.

But other brands have nothing to do with the product proposition. Pepsi originally had no clear link with Cola. 7UP had nothing to do with lemon and lime. Those linkages have developed as people have come to know these brands and make associations.

So, there are many ways to actually create a brand. Many of those that we all know – and maybe even love – have been created by visionary leaders who have spotted and leveraged an opportunity to take ownership of something unique with their brands. Starbucks was based on the concept of the 'Coffee Society', Google was about universal and immediate help for everyone and Amazon was about pushing the boundaries of e-commerce.

Although the choice of brand is an important part of your marketing strategy, what will make your brand iconic and powerful, is of course the strength of your USP. The sharper you are at identifying a niche new market poised for explosive growth and the fastest you are at seizing this market opportunity with a unique product or service, the stronger your brand will be over time.

When I was at Disney, we have predicted the arrival of entertainment on demand many years ago. It's taken Netflix to make it universal and achieve ownership in a triumph of brand development.

When I was in the automotive industry, we have debated the potential of pure electric cars, given the limited size of batteries and, therefore, the relatively small driving range. Tesla found a way to resolve this issue, turning the brand into a highly valued company.

We have all been complaining about the lack of connectivity between the various medical supports we get in life and we all hope that the digital revolution will change that rapidly, to make our own medical ecosystem an easy and safe space to manage. It's taken a non-profit organisation based on the West Coast in the USA called Kaiser to give each of its members a simple and secure way to manage their health by being connected digitally to the Kaiser medical support services. Kaiser is a powerful brand with a revenue in 2020 that was close to $90 billion, making it one of the top 100 largest companies in the world.

Seize the growth opportunity with ever-better branding

When a company wants to expand and pursue exciting growth opportunities, the leadership team will look at launching new products or services, expanding its distribution channels, increasing its sales effort and evolving its marketing strategy.

The marketing strategy of a company evolves naturally around branding; seizing new growth opportunities with a stronger branding and higher media investments is indeed highly recommended.

However, when doing so, the leadership team has to be mindful of the brand they operate, understanding that a brand is fragile and a lot of damage can be created with undue attention during a rebranding exercise.

Managing the brand, and tracking and steering the evolution of its performance, is usually under the immediate control of the marketing department, with a direct line of communication to the Chief Energy Officer (CEO). This is because the brand is one of the company's most valuable assets – brand goodwill is a very important asset on any organisation's balance sheet.

As with everything else on the balance sheet, continuous improvement is the overriding approach to seizing the great opportunities ahead with ever-better branding. The marketing department, therefore, needs continuously to track and diagnose consumer insights as well as identify the right growth opportunities as the basis for evolving the brand. There are five types of brand-diagnosis outcomes that will tell you what sort of action is required to shift the brand positioning in order to accelerate growth:

1. The ideal situation is when the performance of the business and the brand image are both moving in the right direction. Staying with the winning strategy is therefore important: don't make any unnecessary changes. But it's also vital that you reflect deeply on market penetration: what it will take to win new customers – appealing to those who have yet to experience your brand while staying relevant and attractive to your existing customer base.
2. The second scenario is when the benefits of your product are understood and well received, you're well differentiated and you might even be leading your sector. But the impact of your brand communication is declining. This might be because of changes in the category where you're operating, or maybe your advertising has become over-exposed or is being

copied by the competition. You must take action – and that means changing your advertising. Just a refresh, nothing radical: you must stay relevant with your target group and consistent with your brand essence.

3. The third scenario is a more serious case – this is when your brand is losing its appeal. It is less differentiated. Your competitors are catching up. Maybe you're being out-innovated, or you have emerging quality issues. You have no choice. You have to strengthen your brand, with a clear improvement to the product or service value proposition and a new communication plan to stress your improved quality and the additional new benefits for your customers. When the brand owner innovates with a new product or service, it's all about innovation from the core, as described in Chapter 8.

4. The fourth scenario is even more serious, and usually happens when a brand under scenario three has not been fast enough to react to competitors outperforming, resulting in a rapid decline in customers. This is when a proactive and innovative competitor is leading your market through massive change and your brand is being outmaneuvered. Failing to change could result in your brand being forced out of the market forever. You have to reinvent your brand, radically changing your value proposition and communicating with a powerful campaign to reposition yourself for growth. A brand relaunch or repositioning isn't easy. It can take a great deal of time and money.

It's also laden with risk. Your customer base has been buying your product or service for many years, and even though it's sliding, there is still a great deal of loyalty out there. You can't damage your base, so you've got to find a way of repositioning with the right innovation in a way that keeps existing users happy, brings leavers back to you and appeals to new customers. Many companies get this wrong. They're in too much of a hurry, they rush their research and draw the wrong conclusions. Then they either have to admit to failure or start all over again. More time, more money and more risk. So, take the time to get it right.

5. The fifth category is innovation in high-growth and high-margin segments, capitalising on and leveraging the strength of your brand. You decide to leverage your brand equity in markets or segments adjacent to your own, but that differ in terms of category or product formulation. This way of enlarging your addressable market is called brand stretching or extension – done properly, it can work brilliantly. Not done so well, it's incredibly dangerous – if the activities involved don't respect the brand equity, it can dilute your overall brand image.

A shining example of success is Apple, making the shift from manufacturing PCs to finding new ways of using technology to make our lives easier and more fun. Disney, too, has brilliantly executed its brand extension from movies to theme parks to stores.

The pitfalls of brand management

With a great brand, you have something unique and iconic in your hands that has tremendous value on your organisation's balance sheet. When you take it forward, you, therefore, have to take it carefully, step-by-step. Along the way, bear in mind what I think of as the five biggest pitfalls lying in wait.

First, the indicators of brand equity and image move pretty slowly. This is one of the reasons why it takes time to build a successful brand. So, you've got to take your time to understand what the indicators are really telling you. In short, don't overreact to what might turn out to be short-term trends.

Second, don't forget about the intrinsic risk of ultra-ambitious managers. They don't get their buzz from managing brands – that's not where the fun lies. They get their kicks from changing brands. As leader, it's your duty to make sure that before anything is done, all the right checks and balances are in place, meaning that any changes to the brand are based on rigorous diagnosis.

Third, it's all too common that there is no real shared understanding of the brand essence throughout the organisation. In a global company, if just one country doesn't respect the brand essence in its local marketing activities, the overall damage can be immense. The same is true in a service organisation if employees fail to act in line with the brand essence every day when serving their customers. It's non-negotiable – everybody in the organisation has to live the brand. Failure to do so lands companies in deep trouble all the time.

Another major risk is when people in the communications department decide that it's a great idea to use third-party endorsement. For me, the risk is just too great. First, it means that the personality your brand is expressing is not actually yours. It's borrowed. And second, there is the ever-present danger that your chosen brand ambassador might start acting in the real world in a way that's not in line with your brand values.

The final pitfall can happen when the personalisation of the company is overly associated with the CEO. It is rare for a CEO to feature in advertising, although there have been instances of this. One example of the dangers of this final approach involves Wendy Hamburgers, whose founder and CEO Dave Thomas fronted more than 800 TV commercials for the brand – the most by any CEO in history. When he died in 2002, the company had a difficult marketing challenge that they took some years to resolve.

CEO involvement is more common when a high-profile leader, regularly in the media, is inextricably linked with the company's or its products' profile and personality. This is fine while the company is doing well and the CEO has the profile of a celebrity CEO, leading the world and inspiring confidence and success.

It's not so fine when the company's performance starts to slide downhill or there is a governance issue. In such cases, the media will start to report negatively on the CEO, and gradually her or his loss of reputation will have an impact on the perception of the brand.

Reinventing a brand: 7UP

PepsiCo acquired 7UP in 1987. I have joined as the marketing manager in charge of 7UP in 1988, working with Stuart Hangen and John Hetterick, two world-class leaders with an exceptional track record in brand reinvention. The company wanted to relaunch the brand in 1989 with one clear objective: to accelerate growth on a global basis.

My responsibility was for marketing to the world outside the USA, and when I arrived, the brand diagnosis had already taken place with the first tranche of communication development underway. The analysis was extremely simple. 7UP was a very well-known brand across the world, and it was performing very well in product testing.

But there was a problem. Essentially the advertising supporting the brand was functional and focused solely on refreshment: if you're really thirsty, 7UP will deliver superior refreshment based on a lemon–lime flavour.

As far as it went, the advertising was excellent. It communicated everything it was designed to do.

The problem was that in the late 1980s, soft-drink consumers were no longer simply after functional benefits like quenching their thirst. If that's what they wanted, they could simply drink a glass of water. What the primarily teenage core target group wanted was to make a statement about themselves – a badge that told the world about their lifestyle. It's that moment in your life when the clothes you wear, the movies you see, the music you listen to and the drinks you drink, all say something about who you are.

PepsiCo knew this – nobody knew better. The Pepsi brand was doing this really well, with its highly successful 'The Choice of a New Generation' campaign. This effectively positioned Pepsi as the edgier, more innovative challenger to Coke, which had a long-established role in the 'Americana' way of life.

So, we clearly had to reposition 7UP in a way that gave its drinkers the opportunity to make a positive statement about themselves. We had to give it an emotional badge that augmented its pure refreshment quality, and that would differentiate it from both Pepsi and Coke.

We did a lot of research and a lot of thinking. We found that people used 7UP as a kind of 'change of pace' from the two big dark colas. People drank it when they were tired of Pepsi and Coke. So, our way ahead was clear – we had to find a way to make 7UP a first choice, directly in the same league as Coke and Pepsi.

Our idea was this: if you're a 7UP drinker, you've decided to go for a clear drink, not a brown one. This makes you different, a bit of a maverick, not following the crowd who go for the 'social acceptance' offered by Coke and Pepsi. In short, although the two big brands were focusing on Pepsi and Coke drinkers being accepted by their peer group, we have decided to play the individuality card to make the 7UP drinker stand out and be proud of their different way of thinking about life.

The tagline was 'It's cool to be clear'. The joy of it was that we kept the original 7UP refreshment seeker onside as well as appealing to those who felt it was cool to be different. (Remember, this was the 1980s...)

In other words, we had found a way of linking the brand's functional and emotional benefits in a single line. This made the new positioning both authentic and credible – and the brand repositioning was an immediate success.

Incidentally, our agency had two completely different creative routes in mind. One involving a very aspirational celebrity, who had just finished a movie in which his character had a clear fit with the 7UP brand essence. The other was to use a cartoon character called Fido Dido. We chose Fido. We thought that he'd have more impact with the target audience and that 7UP would truly own the Fido campaign.

As it happens, the Fido Dido campaign was the only one that I ever ran on a truly global scale. The simplicity of the character made it appealing across the planet. It worked for us on many levels.

Reinventing Burger King Americana

I've already told some of the story here – about how we used the Americana décor to help reposition Burger King in Germany. Our Americana burger experience was ultimately about reinventing the brand as the only place to experience authentic American burgers, flame-grilled like those from your own barbeque.

The Americana element was a creative idea or metaphor to augment and dramatize Burger King's superior taste and make it really meaningful in the eyes of the consumer. It worked because this was a brand reinvention from the core, fully consistent with the established brand DNA. As a result, it was accepted immediately.

This gave us a significant competitive advantage: because we had many fewer restaurants in Germany than McDonald's at the time, they could not compete with the time it took us to refurbish all the existing units. This meant that the entire German Burger King network quickly had a superior, aspirational image, which was precisely in line with the major insights from all our research and validated what was happening in other categories. In branded retail locations, consumers were interested in a total brand experience that included the product, the service, the decor, the ambience and the energy in the store and restaurant – and we offered Americana, the best burger experience you could get in Germany.

This was particularly important at the time when brands like TGI Fridays and the Hard Rock Café were teaching consumers to expect fast-casual outlets to deliver much more than just a good American meal. I've already said how my thinking was influenced by Starbucks, and I was also impressed by the public reaction in the USA to the themed brand experience being pioneered in fashion by companies like Banana Republic.

This megabrand reinvention helped us raise the bar in the quick service industry, giving us a tangible advantage. The Americana décor redefined standards in our category and was quickly exported from Germany into most international markets across the world.

More recently, there have been some outstanding examples of brand re-invention. BMW's re-imagination of that phenomenal 1960s icon of swinging London, the Mini, was brilliant. We can all learn from how BMW used superior technology and new features to build on an existing heritage.

The way in which the iconic Adidas and Puma brands have reinvented themselves is also inspirational. Burberry's reinvention over the last 30 years has been simply magnificent.

But before you get the idea that brand management is easy, never forget that consumers can be very, very tough on brands. Over the years, we have seen several well-known brands face major issues and considerable criticism.

Whether these are to do with quality problems, ethical issues, financial issues, marketing errors or other causes, consumers often hold the ultimate judgement. In the days of social media and influencers, consumers are co-owners of the brand. They can be very vocal when things go wrong at a global or a local level, making it difficult for the brand managers and CEO to keep things under control.

Glo-cal communication, congruent on all consumer touch points

Being clear on your brand positioning or brand essence is one thing. Driving successful communications to build demand for your products or services is quite another.

Naturally, the brand communication will be established across many countries and many channels within a country, which means that when launching a global communication campaign, all touch points with the end consumer need to be congruent. Said differently, no matter where a brand meets a consumer, every consumer should get the brand message the same way. That's the only way to build a consistent, differentiated brand proposition in the glo-cal marketplace.

During my career, I've been lucky enough to work for many exciting brands on both a global and a local basis. The fact that I've worked across so many categories – detergents to toothpaste, drinks to burgers and entertainment to cars to business services – has helped me identify patterns that can be translated across categories and across borders.

What is clear to me is on the surface very simple – that you need to get your communication right end-to-end across all communication channels. All touch points with the consumer have to be congruent. In other words, if you are the consumer, you should be able to see that all communications on behalf of a brand are from the same source. It doesn't matter whether that brand is Colgate, Ajax, 7UP, Pepsi, Burger King, Disney or BMW. What is important is that each channel communicate in a way that is recognisably from that brand.

In doing so, there is always a tension between what is a local communication and what is a global communication. I wrote in Chapter 1 about the importance of building a glo-cal organisational model to ensure that employees are empowered always to do the right thing in their markets, based on their local understanding of their consumers. For me, product innovation and communication are two glo-cal models. Brands have to have a universal appeal – but to achieve this, they first and foremost need to appeal to local tastes from a product formulation standpoint and to the local culture from a communication standpoint.

This thinking might fly in the face of the accepted wisdom that calls our society a 'global village', where people understand the same things, watch the same programmes, consume the same trends, use the same apps, drive the same cars and so on. Many would conclude from this that more and more consumers expect the same communication around the world. But, at the same time, people also want to be recognised as individuals and expect customised solutions. The world might be very global, but people value their own village, their clan, their own way of doing things and more and more, their community.

When you start developing advertising, you must take this into consideration. Although you certainly have to identify global trends with precision, you equally need to understand how to motivate consumers in your local market to buy your products and services with the local cultural nuances.

Said simply, consumers certainly want to live in the fast lane and be part of the global village – but they expect to be treated as individuals and want brand owners to recognise their particular needs. So, in my view, the approach has to be glo-cal from a product formulation and advertising standpoint.

This is the essential reason why truly global campaigns that use the same ads in every market are rarely successful. When developing products and advertising, you have to identify how to motivate consumers, combining global trends and insights with local differences in tastes and culture. Another important factor is that when categories get mature, fragmentation into niche offerings is the next way of developing the category. We can see this happening in many markets, including beauty, fashion, drinks, food and more.

I am not saying that global product specifications and global ad campaigns will never be successful – it would be wrong to suggest that. But you should never assume that global advertising will work anywhere. Successful global campaigns are the exception, not the rule. Having worked across many categories around the world, I can say that the level of local market customisation for products and services is quite high.

Equally, don't fall for the 'not invented here' syndrome that sees organisations automatically reject the value of using global advertising or product formulation. It might actually be right for your local market.

But unless you do the research, you'll never know for sure. You must gain that local market understanding to ensure that your communication is successful and your product is well accepted.

The shifting landscape

The days when communication was just about getting a great ad on TV are gone. The rise of digital has created a highly fragmented media environment, where being consistent across every media channel is fundamental. So, your communication plan has, above all, to ensure a real congruence of messaging, wherever and however it appears.

In the old days, when I was a marketer, it was mainly about getting your TV work congruent with radio and press. It's a great deal more complex today, and you need to develop a comprehensive, integrated communications plan that takes into account not only all media channels, but also sales and publicity channels.

Your plan needs to cover not just TV, press and radio, but also consumer, trade and corporate PR, billboards, print, point of sale, cinema, airports, elevators and more. And then, of course, online in all its forms, including social media.

Integration across all media and channels to ensure the congruence of your brand messaging is absolutely fundamental to effectively building your brand's USP. Once you've decided the actual content of your campaign, you will be competing with many other brands to gain share or voice and grab the consumer's attention. Your resources are never unlimited, and you will have far more impact if your brand is always clear and consistent.

Many companies recognise the importance of raising brand awareness, growing its stature and confidence by investing in high-impact publicity efforts and corporate PR.

Keeping the messaging congruent with your other communication activities here is particularly challenging, given the editorial content of the articles published will have been through the 'filter' of journalists. For that reason, you also need to be entirely clear about your messaging with the press, as well as totally consistent with the visual materials you give them.

'The best ideas will always win!'

When we launched the Fido Dido 7UP campaign, the character was pretty much unknown outside the Village in New York, where artists Joanna Ferone and Sue Rose created him in 1985.

So, it was the 7UP campaign that introduced him to the world. The execution was stunning: different, highly creative and very, very impactful. It was also directly in line with our strategy, making 7UP an aspirational badge for anybody who wasn't afraid of making a bold choice – spot on the emerging individuality trends.

I was very excited and proud of the opportunities that Fido Dido presented. But I'm the first to admit that not everybody inside Pepsi Cola International was an immediate fan. This was because there was a particularly interesting challenge associated with Fido: the character was very different from the normal way of advertising soft drinks, and some of Fido's detractors were worried about the fact that Fido was too 'different'. This caused some disagreement internally at Pepsi Cola International, with some colleagues feeling he was not an appropriate brand ambassador.

When we presented the advertising to our PepsiCo colleagues at our global conference in Phoenix, Arizona, in the spring of 1989, it split the audience down the middle. Our European and Asian colleagues loved it – and adopted it. Those from Canada and Latin America chose to stick with their local campaigns, more in line with traditional soft drinks advertising.

This was fine by me – I've never believed in going global for the sake of it. In my view, if a market wants to use a particular piece of advertising, let them do so, provided it's on strategy and it works.

By the time the next conference came around, I was not confident that we had resolved the issue dividing our international markets and was prepared to go with a choice between Fido and a more conventional ad treatment. I was surprised – and incredibly proud – when all the global marketing directors went with Fido. The figures spoke for themselves.

Roger Enrico, the CEO of PepsiCo, was right. He was always saying, 'The best ideas will always win.'

And I like to explain what we really meant by it – selecting a campaign has to be based on its merit, not on a policy statement. It's tempting for the leaders of a global organisation to force ideas upon people in local markets. But it hardly ever works.

Best practice, no mandate

When I was at Burger King International, we had a clear set of brand values for our global communication – but I never issued a mandate requiring all markets to use global advertising. Local markets were totally empowered to develop the communications campaigns that were right for them, provided these stayed true to the Burger King brand essence. In my view, this was an important reason behind our success as we had the best tasting burgers and the most convincing advertising in every local market.

What we did do centrally was give local teams easy access to best practices in terms of campaigns, promotions and new creative ideas. But it was entirely up to them which ideas to actually implement, based solely on their merits. I found it amazing just how far and how fast best practice travels, just how much impact it can have, when it's made available but not imposed or mandated.

We did, of course, have a very strictly defined brand essence and guidelines. These had to be respected when developing advertising, to build a strong and congruent global brand. We were also very demanding when it came to ensuring our advertising delivered cut-through, was likeable and drove sales.

These guidelines were a key element of our glo-cal modus operandi, which ensured global consistency and successful brand communication at a local level.

In a glo-cal operating model, the global principles underpinning the strategy are not negotiable. The ideas for implementing the strategy can be developed and implemented locally, provided they are customised to exceed customers' needs. This glo-cal approach works in advertising too.

Great advertising – but not by committee please!

Developing great advertising is mission critical when implementing a marketing strategy, as the external communication efforts will have a huge impact on how fast consumers will change their behaviours and start buying your product or service.

Developing great advertising is a creativity-based process that is very close to producing a piece of art – it takes time to get it right. And importantly, it cannot be done by committee.

In my experience, the strategic and creative processes involved work best when you bring together a tight team of highly experienced marketing people and ad agency executives who really understand the brand essence and are committed to taking the brand to the next level for many years.

The actual process begins with the copy strategy. That is, the script that formulates what you want the campaign to represent, the communications strategy that you want to follow in terms of objectives, messaging, tone and more.

Next comes the story-boarding process. It's really important that this has at its heart a strong creative idea that magnifies, augments and dramatizes the message with a memorable metaphor to make your brand and your campaign distinctive. It's the springboard that enables you to really get across the benefit the brand is talking about. Companies that don't attempt this miss a big opportunity. They're reduced to simply saying 'We're great' without attempting to find an intriguing, exciting way of expressing their advantage.

Fido is a good example of a creative idea that acted as a springboard. The character said something entirely unique about not being one of the herds; that lifted the message. People understood it. And it differentiated the brand.

Thirdly, your communications approach needs to deliver the 'cut-through' or impact needed to make your advertising stand out in a crowded media scene. If no one notices your advertising, what's the point in creating it in the first place? You'd be wasting your time and money. Achieving cut-through is vital for placing your brand front-of-mind for your target consumers.

The fourth critical area to get right is the 'likeability' of your campaign. You achieve this by understanding how to connect with your consumer, which usually involves telling a fun story that also projects an aspirational image by finding a mechanism that will enable your consumers to escape from their day-to-day activities and dream of a better, more enjoyable world. For many consumers, advertising represents a route to help them make their dreams come true. They project themselves into a different world, and you want to connect with them on both a rational and an emotional level.

The final area that you have to get right – and it's one that's steeped in controversy for many marketers – is the selling or convincing power of your advertising. That is, its ability to make the target consumer actually do something – preferably, to change their behaviour and select your brand. This can be achieved by a strong call to action.

The reason this element is controversial is that many marketers believe that building the brand image takes pure brand-image advertising – that is, advertising with the primary goal of creating the right brand image that will, over time, make the brand attractive to its target consumers. As a result, many marketing 'purists' think the only way to build a brand is by running purely thematic campaigns.

I disagree. My view is that unless you have a strong call to action, you are missing an opportunity.

It's not tactical. It's about creating an urge for your product or service by presenting tangible benefits that create immediate interest in your brand. The call to action can take many forms: it can be based on a new benefit, limited features or promotional activities. But I'm sure of one thing – whenever you see an ad without a call to action, it's never going to reach its full potential.

What's the point in developing a fantastic new product or service if the communication campaign does not create the urge for the consumer to buy and try your product or service.

The Pepsi magic

When I joined PepsiCo in 1988, I was thrilled because, from my perspective, Pepsi was the advertising authority in the world!

A lot of this was to do with a very talented advertising senior executive called Alan Pottasch, the genius behind the Pepsi 'New Generation' campaign, who was in charge globally of all advertising developed by Pepsi Cola. For me, it was an amazing honour and privilege to work alongside Alan. I was very young. He was very experienced. He knew how to create magical advertising. This is how he did it – I learnt so much from him.

Alan wouldn't allow many people into the inner circle where the advertising was created. He knew that if you let in too many people, you'll end up with the lowest common denominator driving your creative process.

His way of working became legendary in PepsiCo. So much so that every year, Alan presenting the advertising programmes for Pepsi and 7UP was the central point of the company's gala evening – in a tuxedo, standing in front of all the bosses and their spouses. Everyone came, just to see the Pepsi advertising magician in action and watch the latest ads for the year.

Alan's genius made headlines every year and gave Pepsi the status of an acclaimed megabrand.

I wanna be elected!

Another really fun moment in advertising came a few years later at Burger King in Germany. It still shows the kinds of risk you can take if you're confident in your brand.

We had done all the work I've already described, upgrading our operational standards, refurbishing our restaurants and improving our menus. We were already growing fast – and now, it was time to properly relaunch our brand, with a very clear aim: to make it much more famous and attractive.

We have worked with a highly creative Munich-based agency, called .Start, led by Gregor Woeltje, an outstanding advertiser. We'd set up a protective environment around our work together, much like the one Alan operated at PepsiCo. We too were a small team – and we too knew the brand inside-out.

At the time, Germany was headed for a general election with the electorate being asked to choose between the existing Chancellor Helmut Kohl and challenger Gerhard Schröder. We came up with a political concept of our own. We created our own party, the BKD (Burger King für Deutschland) and launched a campaign asking German consumers to vote for whether the Whopper or the Big Mac should be the president, true to our irreverent attitude, being the challenger of the burger industry in Germany.

We ran it just like an election campaign. People could join our party. We put up grassroots posters, we ran TV ads and we were very active online. It wasn't just Germany's first ever comparative campaign – it was also fantastic fun. More than that, it was relevant locally, it was innovative and it was highly congruent with the brand we had built.

In terms of hitting a nerve, comparing ourselves to the real election going on around us was a huge statement of confidence. That alone raised the brand's stature enormously. We have received a great deal of press coverage, and this in turn stimulated word of mouth, particularly among young people.

We have announced the result of our election three hours before the result of the political one was known. So, everybody knew that the Whopper was the president before they knew Gerhard Schröder had been voted in as Chancellor. The Whopper wasn't the only winner. Our ad agency .Start won several awards on the back of the campaign. And Burger King won a new following across Germany.

Inside-out branding – living the brand from within

There's much more to a brand than its USP and essence, or the means you use to communicate it externally. Every iconic brand has also values that are lived internally by everybody in the organisation.

It doesn't matter whether it's a B2B or B2C business: if you build the brand from within, the brand will be stronger externally because employees of every type of organisation talk with clients, competitors, opinion leaders, friends, family members and other groups including regulators.

In any branded organisation, the way employees talk about the brand externally is impacted and shaped by the way they live the brand internally.

Ensuring every leader and employee represents the brand correctly does not happen automatically. Internal communication and training are extremely important in making employees feel part of the brand, ensuring that it is lived by the entire organisation.

Just as important, in my experience involving employees in the meaning and delivery of the brand makes their affiliation to the business much stronger. So, when an employee joins a company, it has to be about more than just a job, a salary and a career structure. For real motivation, it has also to be about a strong brand – and making every employee part of that brand from day one is an essential part of the employee experience.

Gurnek Bains described the power of living the brand from within in his book *Meaning Inc.* – "People who work for organisations whose purpose they believe in are more likely to go the extra mile to achieve that purpose and deliver high performance."

Cast members living the magic every day

One of the key reasons behind the extraordinary levels of customer satisfaction at Disney's theme parks is the way in which cast members live the brand every day. The critical importance of this is expressed by the fact they're called 'cast members' in the first place.

It's because they are part of the story. They are there to do more than provide services and ensure safety. Their primary role is to tell stories about the experiences the guests are sharing, to make the guest experience truly immersive.

I've already written about how the people who are attracted to becoming cast members are already massive Disney fans and evangelists. But they're not all necessarily born with a deep understanding of the brand and the ability to weave stories around it.

That's where training comes in – in particular, the 'Disney Tradition'. This is an exceptional programme and I've never seen anything like it anywhere else. Maybe more companies should try it.

Say you're joining Disney on Monday, January 2. At 9.00 am precisely, you'll be welcomed into the Disney Tradition. It happens to everyone without fail, no matter your role: it happened to me when I joined as CEO. I did nothing else that day. It makes everybody equal. It's a big statement.

During that day, you get a solid grounding in the importance of safety and service. But you get more. You also get a complete understanding of the importance of storytelling. You're taught how to develop your own stories, using your own creativity and your passion for the Disney brand to make the experience of the guests immersive.

It's world-class practice, in my view, to hold an event of this sort. The Disney Tradition is seen as a really magical and memorable event by everyone who has ever been through it. It's more than just training. It's a true celebration of joining the company, immersing you and your colleagues in the brand essence and vocabulary of the company you've just joined, and importantly giving you the keys, the empowerment, and the confidence to live the brand from within the next day, interacting with your customers and colleagues.

And it's a very clear illustration of how living the brand from within is the best way of making the brand successful in the outside world. It doesn't get better than that!

Reinventing the Intertek brand from within

We have redefined our Value Proposition at Intertek to broaden the appeal of our Intertek brand and accelerate growth.

Once our 5x5 differentiated strategy for growth was clear for all of our colleagues, we started to live our new value proposition by first talking to our customers about the depth and breadth of our ATIC offering to make their own brands and businesses stronger in terms of quality, safety and sustainability.

We had to get started of course with our external rebranding programme and I wanted to make sure that our brand reinvention would be from within.

I asked Martin Lindstrom to lead the brand reinvention with our team as, having worked with Martin in the past, I deeply valued his world-class marketing expertise, his strong insights and of course his out-of-the-box creativity.

Martin and his team quickly understood the size of the opportunity and worked with all of our leaders to reinvent our Intertek brand.

Reinventing your brand from within is the first step to living your brand from within!

Key points from this chapter:

- Ensure that your brands have a differentiated, authentic and winning USP.
- Seize growth opportunities by continuing to build and strengthen your brands, step-by-step: this is the road to continuous improvement.
- Realise the global, universal appeal of your business, but ensure that you connect the dots with the local desires and aspirations of your customers.
- When developing your advertising, use a very small, focused and highly creative team that deeply understands the brand and the customer.
- Take risks, be creative – to open people's minds, you need to be Impactful.
- Ensure that you live the brand values internally to build a strong brand externally.

Leadership Principle 10
Sustainable performance for all

Chapter content:

- Sustainability commitment anchored in the purpose and strategy.
- Understanding the sustainability agenda of each stakeholder.
- Operationalise the strategy with sustainability excellence.
- Lead the company sustainably, end-to-end.
- Empowering teams with self-sustainability management.

We are at an inflection point.

Leaders everywhere are asking a very important question; how do we ensure we can deliver sustainable performance for all?

The truth is that there is a great deal we can do.

Everybody, across all sections of society, has recognised the unfortunate consequences of the vibrant globalisation of the economy we've been witnessing in recent decades.

The rapid economic and consumption growth in every country, every city, has improved the quality of life for many citizens but has created extreme challenges for all of us moving forward.

I am amazed by the lack of pace and ownership in all parts of society to save our planet for good.

The data on the need to reduce green emissions fast is compelling.

Yet despite years of excessive CO_2 emissions, the world has not found a way to fix what is essentially a time bomb.

I cannot understand why so much energy is wasted at night with far too much lighting in all cities around the world.

We know that old cars, old trucks and old planes drive a disproportionate amount of CO_2 emissions but unfortunately, this issue has not been addressed systematically by the regulators.

Curbing gas emissions quickly will only be possible if all governments and regulatory bodies work together to put the right controls in place for all.

I am shocked by the fact that Glasgow, like Paris, achieved so little in making sure that there is a clear plan to get to Net Zero.

We all understand the need to pursue the right energy transition, moving quickly and safely from fossil fuels to renewables.

I am surprised to see how little transparency and planning there is inside all major economies on how to get there safely and quickly.

There is no question that green financing will be the ultimate accelerator to make sure that the funding for future corporate growth is granted with the planet in mind.

I am surprised to see how little banks and investors really know about the true sustainable performance of the companies they invest in!

Sustainability is the movement of our time.

It is long overdue and the way in which young people are advocating change is humbling. They might be less than 20 per cent of the human population today. But they are 100 per cent of the future, and that's why their voices are so important.

Everyone has a big role to play in society and there is no question that leaders in any type of organisation have to lead by example as they can make a significant contribution to the sustainability challenge the world faces by anchoring sustainability in their purpose and strategy.

We leaders of organisations, large or small, local or global, profit or non-profit, can influence the world we are in charge of – our world.

I really believe that all leaders in the corporate world can make the world a better place. Corporations have massive weight in the world economy, and their impact on all aspects of society is immense.

We have covered 9 principles of Leadership with Soul and the 10th principle, 'Sustainable performance for all' is fundamental for any organisation.

We can be a force for good.

If every leader makes his or her workplace an ecosystem where sustainable performance is delivered for all stakeholders, then ultimately the world will be a much better place from a sustainability standpoint.

Critically, I know that corporations understand the importance of improving their sustainability agenda as the awareness growing among the younger generation filters through to business leaders.

Most companies are investing more in their ESG (Environmental, Social, Governance) activities however, I believe there is a danger that they believe this is all they need to be doing.

ESG is necessary, of course, but it is not sufficient on its own when you want to lead with a comprehensive sustainable agenda.

The complexity of the ecosystems in which we operate, and the sheer number of stakeholders to whom we owe a responsibility, mean corporate leaders have to consider and respond to multiple factors before they can consider themselves and their organisations to be acting sustainably.

The Environmental, Social and Governance focus areas are of course important considerations within the sustainability agenda, but these are not enough.

What I mean by sustainable performance is the end-to-end application of sustainable thinking.

Acting sustainably means understanding and responding positively to the expectations of your consumers, your suppliers, your employees, your regulators, your national governments, your prospective employees, your communities – and, of course, your shareholders.

Achieving this is very, very difficult. But it's very, very important too. To have a chance of success, there must be a driven commitment from the very top of the organisation to lead the sustainability agenda based on the expectations of all stakeholders, with clear goals, precise action plans, transparent reporting and a genuine, authentic voice when reporting either internally or externally.

When the leadership team is genuinely passionate about putting sustainability at the top of the agenda, it will help create a culture in which everybody is empowered and encouraged to think and act sustainably.

We are at a tipping point when it comes to saving our planet.

Sustainability is the movement of our time!

Leaders can make a big difference by delivering sustainable performance for all.

Sustainability commitment anchored in the purpose and strategy

Back in Chapter 2, I discussed the importance of imagining the journey and painting the picture when developing the strategic plan with your senior team.

Of course, developing the strategy that unleashes the full potential of the company is both highly important and highly energising.

More than that though, when you're talking about the purpose, the vision, and the strategy, it is also the right moment for you and the team to think deeply about what sustainability really means for you.

That's because these are critical statements that will be anchored in stone – statements that not only articulate the meaning of the company for everybody, but which also define its destination. You therefore must ensure that sustainability is right at their heart.

At Intertek, our commitment to sustainability is central to our purpose. Within our vision, trust is what underpins truly sustainable relationships with our partners.

The Intertek purpose: To bring quality, safety and sustainability to life

The Intertek vision: To become the world's most trusted partner for Quality Assurance

The next main area to consider is how you want the organisation, and the people who form it, to behave as they deliver the strategy. Clearly, this is all about the company's values. Getting them right is a key step in shaping its culture, so ensuring sustainability is at the core will be a fundamental building block of the behaviours you expect to see in the organisation.

All our values at Intertek were written with sustainability in mind, from diversity and doing business the right way, to mutual trust, empowerment, and a commitment to sustainable growth.

The Intertek values

• We are a global family that values diversity
• We always do the right thing. With precision, pace and passion
• We trust each other and have fun winning together
• We own and shape our future
• We create sustainable growth. For all

Third come the corporate goals: these exist to clarify the organisation's direction of travel for all stakeholders.

Different goals might therefore apply primarily to different stakeholder audiences, but again the need to drive sustainable performance must be central to formalising them.

That's the way we have identified our corporate goals at Intertek.

Intertek corporate goals

• Fully engaged employees working in a safe environment
• Superior customer service in Assurance, Testing, Inspection and Certification
• Margin-accretive revenue growth based on GDP+ organic growth
• Strong cash conversion
• Accretive, disciplined allocation policy

The final step is to ensure that sustainability is an integral part of the thinking when developing the company's strategic priorities and enablers.

This is critically important, as these are what create the platform on which sustainability initiatives and sustainable activities are operationalised – brought to life to make a difference.

Within our 5x5 differentiated growth strategy at Intertek, we have clearly identified five strategic priorities and five enablers to take our company from good to great, with sustainability in mind in everything we do.

Intertek's five strategic priorities

• Total Quality Assurance brand proposition
• Superior ATIC customer service
• Effective ATIC sales strategy
• Growth and margin-accretive portfolio
• Operational excellence

Intertek's five enablers

* Live our 10x culture to the max
* Disciplined performance management
* Superior technology
* Energising our people
* Doing business the right way

These are the factors that, working together, enable the organisation to bring the sustainability agenda to life.

Companies that anchor sustainability in their purpose, vision, values, strategic priorities and enablers, will create a better future for all their stakeholders and contribute to a global movement that will make a huge positive difference for everyone on the planet.

We discussed the importance of living the brand from within in the previous chapter and there is no question that sustainable thinking, behaviours and actions have to be part of the way you live your brand internally and deliver your brand externally.

At Intertek, we truly believe that doing business the right way is the only way!

That's why we start our meetings with a 'sustainability moment', which enables us to share a powerful story that illustrates how passionate our colleagues are about sustainability and importantly, how much progress we have made on our own sustainability agenda.

Understanding the sustainability agenda of each stakeholder

Once you have anchored sustainability in what you are seeking to do with the company's purpose, vision, values, and strategy, and communicated it to ensure that everybody in the business is on the same page, then you need to understand the sustainability agenda of each stakeholder. This is the most difficult part of all.

I believe that the world is in the state it's in because it has been led and governed by public institutions and companies that have failed to address the interests of all stakeholders.

So much does not make sense.

It has to change!

There is no way that economic growth should be achieved at the expense of air quality.

There is no way that wealth creation should be for just the happy few.

There is no way that, despite the investments made in global infrastructure in the last 50 years every citizen should not have access to quality water.

There is no way we should not be able to offer proper medical care to anyone who needs it.

There is no way that, after the Glasgow Summit, there should not be a clear plan on how the world will achieve its Net Zero targets.

Of course, I do not underestimate the challenges that leaders of governments, global and local institutions, and corporations face in resolving these 5 very complex challenges to make the world a better and more sustainable place.

Everyone has to contribute, and I believe that leaders of any organisation can play a major role.

It is time for corporate leadership to step up and deliver sustainable performance for all stakeholders.

I know that this is a huge task, particularly as the sometimes irreconcilable interests of different groups can create a conflicted agenda.

It remains however a major responsibility for leaders, given the depth and breadth of the ecosystems in which organisations operate and their responsibilities to all parts of society. Leaders have very little choice in the matter.

When I was running Euro Disney, for example, I had a clear idea about what our stakeholders were expecting from us. And these expectations differed widely from group to group.

Let's start with the consumer. Their expectations were quite straightforward to identify. They essentially wanted better, safer Disney family entertainment, more fun, more magic, more brilliant days out with us. So, when we came up with something new – like the Lion King show – it had to meet some very high expectations. And it had to do so every time; there could be no off-days.

The cast members held some expectations that were closely related to those of the consumers: they wanted a clean and safe workplace that got better every day, helping them to deliver everything the customers were looking for. So their expectations of management were straightforward. Give us the tools we need to improve the workplace, along with the support and training that will make us better at our jobs. And give us the scope to outperform – give us the time to rehearse and don't ask us to do three live shows in a single day during the weekend. Importantly, cast members expect to be rewarded fairly and get access to personal growth opportunities.

When it comes to suppliers, they have clear expectations when working with a company like Euro Disney (or anybody else for that matter). Essentially, they want fair trade. They don't want to be squeezed on price, they want to be paid on time, and they expect everybody to abide by the T&Cs in the contracts in place.

Just like consumers and cast members, regulators want all safety and hygiene standards to be met. Additionally, they expect – and require – the business to operate in accordance with the law.

The large and vibrant east-Parisian community around us simply wanted us to be a good neighbour. While they wanted us to bring investment and commercial opportunities to the area, above all they wanted us to treat them fairly and kindly, respecting their rights and offering them our support whenever necessary.

As for the French government, their interest was straightforward. They wanted us to create jobs, create economic growth and pay our taxes. Essentially, they wanted us to invest.

And finally, what about our shareholders – those stakeholders whom all too many companies place at the top of the agenda to the detriment of other stakeholders? They wanted us to drive consistent earnings growth, to use our cash in a disciplined approach, paying dividends of course and investing wisely to increase customer satisfaction and deliver sustainable growth.

So there are some very real tensions between the diverse and sometimes conflicting interests of different stakeholder groups.

Making sense of all these different expectations is one major aspect of what being a leader is all about.

It's a huge task.

You'll hear some people say that it's simply not possible to reconcile everybody's interests and please all stakeholders.

But that's not good enough.

We have no choice.

We operate in an ecosystem that will only survive if all its constituents get what they expect from the company.

That's the same, wherever you are in the world, whatever your industry. You simply need to work for and with all stakeholders.

First of all, it's part of your duty; and being a force for good for all stakeholders is the right thing to do.

Just as important, you will suffer if you don't. Your reputation depends on your ability to deliver sustainable performance for all, and people will be quick to make your life difficult if you fail to do so.

It's a fact of life that stakeholders are increasingly more and more demanding.

Get used to it.

The world today is unforgiving, and in the shape of social media everybody with a grievance has a clear and easy-to-access route to making their opinions known.

Anybody can go online and start shaking the tree to see what falls out.

Anybody can affect a company's reputation and ultimately undermine its ability to perform.

While social media wasn't a big part of the mix in those days, you can imagine the complexity you face when running an operation like Euro Disney.

Personally, I sometimes felt more like a mayor running a town, with all the health and safety, security, tidiness, and other factors I had to take into account alongside the resort's financial performance.

Sustainability equals legacy

As I have said before, leadership is a privilege. Leading a company into the future is highly energising and very rewarding. It is our responsibility to take the business from A to Z, based not only on a clear vision and a strategy but also on the need to deliver a sustainable performance for all stakeholders.

I would argue that operating with a balanced approach that takes into account the short and long-term considerations of every stakeholder is what this privilege and this responsibility are all about.

I fundamentally believe that sustainability is the only way to define the successful legacy of a leader – sustainability equals legacy.

Delivering sustainable value for every stakeholder is what defines sustainability.

Tracking progress towards your goals

As I have suggested when describing the stakeholders at Euro Disney, stakeholder mapping is an essential part of the strategic-planning process for leadership teams.

Of course, this is just the beginning, and you then have to allocate time to tracking progress towards your goals with each stakeholder group, ensuring you refine and amend your approach as required.

You must ensure you treat this aspect of planning for success with every stakeholder in exactly the same way as you would approach the financial planning process – that is, with absolute precision and honesty.

Many companies that fail to do this can get themselves into difficulty by making bullish statements about their sustainability targets, which they then fail to live up to.

One way of ensuring you stay on track – and I will explain this in greater detail below – is to create empowerment to deliver your sustainability agenda at every level of the organisation. This really embeds responsibility in the wider team, making it systemic in the organisation.

For tracking performance, you will benefit from using a well-defined sustainability scorecard when tracking the Five-Year Strategic Plan, reviewing the Annual Operating Plan, and conducting your Monthly Performance Reviews.

Every management team needs to spend quality time developing their sustainability scorecard and identifying the right metrics to track progress with a systemic approach, which is the only way to deliver sustainable performance for all stakeholders.

Every stakeholder has a different set of expectations and it's interesting to observe how the sustainability agenda is shaping up in the complex ecosystems of corporations.

Companies will often use factories owned by 3rd parties around the world where they do not have direct control on how their products are being manufactured. For many years, brand owners were focused on the quality and safety performance of these 3rd party owned factories. Today, brand owners need to make sure that the working conditions in these factories are of the highest standards as consumers will not buy the products otherwise.

Companies operate a complex global supply chain with a multitude of tier 1, tier 2 and tier 3 suppliers for the components or parts they use to manufacture their products.

Understanding the entire ecosystem of a global supply chain is paramount as the regulators, the trade buyers and the end consumers want to be reassured about the total sustainability of what is being sold by companies.

This is of course hugely complex in terms of data management but it's at the same time mission-critical, as companies have to deliver their Net Zero goals.

It's impossible for any company to calculate their total carbon footprint unless they have decomposed their entire value chain, understanding precisely how many tier 1, 2 and 3 suppliers produce what and where on a daily basis.

I am convinced that the race to Net Zero inside corporations will make a huge difference over time as governments will be able to track progress at the national level and give visibility to all citizens on when they will achieve their own national Net Zero targets.

Importantly, consumers will be able to make decisions based on the carbon footprint of the products or services they buy as I expect carbon labelling to be part of any brand communication moving forward.

Operationalise the strategy with sustainability excellence

To be truly impactful, your effort to deliver sustainable performance for all has to start at the heart of your business. It's the only way of achieving sustainable excellence.

To do this, you need to think about how you can operate sustainably in every aspect of your value chain – products and services, process and systems, facilities, assets and the environment.

By placing a sustainability focus on every core area of your value chain, you will redefine what operational excellence means within your organisation and operationalise your strategy with sustainability excellence.

Until a few years ago, the operational excellence formula was somewhat different from today. What you needed to achieve it was the highest-quality output at the lowest cost, with the best customer service, all on time and within budget.

Today, however, a business that is not demonstrably sustainable would not qualify for operational excellence.

Products & Services

It is, in my view, necessary for organisations to ensure, for example, that their products and services are created with sustainability in mind at every stage of their lifecycle, starting with raw materials and components, through production to transportation, and then to consider how the finished product is used, disposed of, recycled and re-used.

I want to provide an example of one of our clients at Intertek that I think is doing really well in this area.

It has been the norm for many years in the fashion industry that when a designer starts to prepare a collection, the company sources materials from right across the world. Most of them are determined to find the highest quality and most elegant fabrics.

Five years ago, our client decided to do things differently. Now, the designer accurately defines the CO_2 footprint of every garment before agreeing that it will be part of the design and ultimately be part of the value chain.

Our client was a pioneer then and now we see many companies quantify the total CO_2 impact of a garment before designing their collections.

Putting sustainability considerations at the R&D stage is a huge opportunity, not only to reduce the carbon footprint of our planet but also to make products or services even more attractive to environment-conscious consumers.

Operating processes

Turning to processes, sustainability considerations have to be included in the standard operating procedures that govern sourcing, manufacturing and distribution.

The consistent quality, safety and sustainability of products and services in the value chain depend on the sustainability of the processes that support them, which need to be reviewed, benchmarked and verified on a regular basis.

Process re-engineering to deliver higher quality output faster and at lower cost is very well known in the corporate world. It has delivered billions of dollars in the last 5 decades to shareholders.

Process reengineering to improve the sustainability performance of a company is the next big thing inside companies.

Reducing the carbon footprint of a given product or service to have a competitive advantage in the marketplace will only happen through an end-to-end review of the supply, manufacturing and distribution operating procedures with sustainability in mind.

At Intertek, we work with companies across several industries and one of the trends we are seeing is the 'nearshoring' of products to low production cost countries that are closer to the end-consumer markets. This has created significant manufacturing investments over the years in Mexico for the North American market and more recently in Turkey, Morocco and Egypt for the European market.

Systems

In the systems area, the focus needs to be of course on the sustainability of the technology infrastructure that the organisation uses to store and process data.

Obviously, this can range from a single laptop to a worldwide network of data centres and cloud-based repositories. Whatever the case, you need an effective system strategy to ensure you've got the right storage capability with the right data security, 24/7.

Without sustainability systems, no organisation can be sustainable.

I experienced what can go wrong first-hand during my time as a Non-Executive Director at Reckitt Benckiser.

It was June 2017, and we were attacked by a hacker in one of our countries. The hacker did that to get into the heart of the global system and took it down.

Reckitt Benckiser became one of the first companies to have to tell the world that it would be unable to report its financial results on time.

Since then, many companies have been attacked and unable to report their performance properly to shareholders.

Companies must be totally focused on cyber security to ensure their systems are fit for purpose, even in the smallest and most remote offices in their networks.

Facilities

When it comes to the company's facilities, right across its own operations, the sustainability priorities are, on the face of it, straightforward.

All manufacturing, logistics, service, administrative, retail and other consumer-facing locations must be set up to minimise energy and water-consumption, to reduce waste and importantly, to ensure the wellbeing and safety of all employees and visitors.

There is one particular part of the infrastructure in most corporate buildings, hotels, and public buildings that in my view requires much more attention: indoor air quality.

Currently, the regulatory standards that ensure we get access to clean air when we are indoors are not demanding enough. This is an area of sustainability regulation that I believe needs to be urgently addressed.

One of the positive effects of COVID-19 in 2020 and 2021 was a very low incidence of flu globally, as wearing masks in public places increased the world population's protection against flu.

The need for higher air quality standards in all public places has to be addressed quickly!

Assets

A company's assets include the equipment, tools and instruments it uses to manufacture its products and services.

These are at the heart of a company's business model and are an important part of its IP.

It's therefore essential that companies have in place policies and audits that ensure the safety, protection and durability of their assets, making sure they continue to work properly in the organisation's best possible interests.

Companies typically have very good operating systems in place to track the visibility of their assets, given the role these assets play in the value chain.

I expect companies to increase their focus on the sustainability risks of these assets and to report accordingly in their sustainability scorecards.

A lot of manufacturing facilities around the world produce a significant emission of CO_2 and I am very excited about the carbon capture technology that is being developed to remove carbon emissions from the air we breathe every day.

Carbon capture technology will be a major step to capture the carbon emissions at source in every factory.

It's difficult to predict the time required for the carbon capture technology to be ready for scale implementation.

I am sure however, that one day, every factory that produces CO_2 will have a carbon capture unit at the end of their production line.

Environment

Every company is surely aware of the need to monitor and minimise its impact on the environment, reducing carbon and other emissions, preventing pollution, reducing waste, using renewables and conserving natural resources.

Creating the visibility at a local level in every operation is essential to reduce the carbon impact on the environment as making the data available at the local level in every operation will create end-to-end accountability.

We are committed to reaching Net Zero at Intertek and we have precise plans, site by site, on how we will deliver our Net Zero targets.

Over the years we have put in place a comprehensive performance management system and can now track CO_2 emissions like we track revenue, cost, profit and cash, with a monthly scorecard which we use during our monthly performance discussions.

What we can measure, we can reduce.

The race to Net Zero

Following the Paris Agreement a few years ago, a lot of progress has been made to create the right level of awareness and commitment among all nations in the world to achieve Net Zero.

COP26 in Glasgow in the 4th quarter of 2021 was a big success, with many important milestones being achieved.

Unfortunately, COP26 missed a big point: there is no clear plan with precise accountabilities of when and how the world will achieve Net Zero.

This is of course very complex, but the world's leaders need to agree on how they will create a global reporting system and monitor progress country by country, every year.

Transparency is the only way in business or life to create accountability.

That is so true regarding the race to Net Zero.

Creating a mandatory carbon emissions reporting system with well-defined indicators, published every year, by every organisation, private or public, in every city and every country, is what's missing to achieve Net Zero.

Indeed, we quickly need a Net Zero Cockpit for the entire world and I expect the global regulators to work together on this in the next few months.

I truly applaud the efforts of the EU with their taxonomy approach, the current IFRS work on sustainability accounting, and the initiatives of multiple regulators and non-profit organisations, to improve transparency in terms of sustainability reporting.

However, I am concerned by the lack of global cooperation and coordination between all regulators, given the urgent need to create precise mandatory global sustainability reporting for all companies.

Transparency will create accountability and once we have achieved that, we are more likely to achieve Net Zero on time.

The race to Net Zero is real.

Time is not on our side.

The world needs to move faster – much faster.

Lead the company sustainably, end-to-end

Operationalising your strategy with sustainability excellence within your products and services, operating processes, systems, facilities and assets, is indeed paramount to address all operational sustainability risks in your value chain.

However, while it's necessary to have in place the right operational sustainability solutions to address the high-risk sustainability areas, they're not enough on their own.

In a large organisation, it's virtually impossible to have all the operational controls needed at every point of the value chain, 24/7.

Operational sustainability solutions are usually focused on high-risk areas.

In addition to having the right operational sustainability solutions in place, a company needs to have the right corporate sustainability processes to deliver its sustainability goals in a systemic way, end-to-end, and give its stakeholders total peace of mind that they are doing business the right way.

Easier said than done, as it is challenging for any CEO to identify where sustainability starts and where it ends, while defining the right corporate sustainability processes and having the appropriate controls in place to get total sustainability peace of mind.

I have been fortunate over the year to work across multiple industries, which has helped me identify the systemic areas that any company needs to focus on when driving their sustainability agenda at the corporate level.

It starts of course with quality and safety to get to end-to-end assurance that the sustainability standards are met in every part of the value chain.

Risk management is the second area to focus on, as risk awareness and risk management are essential to build resilience in the entire ecosystem of the company.

Enterprise security is the 3rd area to watch carefully, as protecting the safety of all employees, critical assets, data including IP, is mission critical from a sustainability standpoint.

Doing business the right way with the right corporate controls to track compliance every day vis-à-vis the policies in place covering regulations, ethics, corporate policies, cannot be overlooked.

The approach to implement the company's environmental policy to protect the future of the planet plays a central role in the corporate sustainability strategy as the right corporate standards will have to be defined and the appropriate resources have to be put in place.

People and Culture are essential in delivering sustainable performance and the right policy has to be put in place when it comes to qualifications, training, engagement, health, safety and wellbeing.

Community engagement happens locally of course and given its importance in terms of stakeholder engagement, I suggest that the corporate sustainability strategy covers what 'giving back to society' really means for everyone.

Governance is at the heart of ESG – and rightly so – as embedding the right governance across the organisation will create the right alignment and accountabilities on how to manage the expectations of every stakeholder.

The integrity of financial processes with accounting excellence, the appropriate financial plans, the proper treasury policy and a disciplined capital allocation, are of course essential to deliver sustainable financial performance.

Finally, getting the right transparency when communicating with your stakeholders will make a big difference to building trust over time.

Aligning your corporate sustainability strategy and process with the 10 areas I just described will give your company a sustainability advantage over time.

I am very energised to see how corporations are actively stepping up their corporate sustainability agenda.

This is good news!

We spend a lot of time helping our clients at Intertek, offering our sustainability solutions which cover the areas we have just described.

We recently held a survey to truly understand where our clients see their own vulnerabilities in terms of sustainability.

The results showed up how vulnerable to failure and reputational damage corporations feel.

Here are some of the headline results:

* 74% agree that customers and other stakeholders are demanding that corporations do more with relation to sustainability.
* 67% acknowledge they are under significant pressure to improve their sustainability performance.
* 71% agree with the statement: "There are too many sustainability expectations and reporting standards, which leads to confusion."
* 76% agree with the statement: "We take on risk by not assessing our full supply chain."
* 92% acknowledge that some of their supply chain would receive a poor sustainability report if a full audit were to be carried out.

Corporations know indeed they are vulnerable when it comes to sustainability, which means they will do something about it!

The current approach in corporations is not end to end. Most are solely focused on ESG issues which, while necessary, does not come close to being sufficient.

My advice to any leader is simply to invest a disproportionate amount of time to develop the right sustainability strategy for the entire company and all its stakeholders, with three areas in mind:

First, sustainability has to be at the heart of the operational activities inside the value chain and having the right priorities and solutions to mitigate operational sustainability risks in the areas we covered earlier, is where it all starts: products and services, processes, systems, facilities, assets, environment.

Second, the leadership team needs to put in place the right end-to-end corporate processes to make sure the company takes an end-to-end sustainability approach and that these processes are audited on a regular basis. Based on my experience, there are 10 corporate process areas that require attention: quality & safety, risk management, enterprise security, compliance, environment, people & culture, communities, governance, financial and communications.

The third area to focus on is external communications. I mentioned earlier in the book the need for any leader to over-communicate in a transparent and genuine way. This applies to sustainability of course and a key moment in the yearly communication activities of a company is when the company publishes its annual results and sends its annual report to its shareholders.

Right now, companies are only seeing the very beginning of the levels of scrutiny to which their sustainability practices are going to be exposed in years to come. Stakeholders are extremely cynical, and they're going to demand absolute clarity on the data presented, as well as clear evidence that the measurements made and reported on have an effective role in driving down negative impacts and improving the sustainability of operations.

I would suggest that companies start to rethink the way their annual report is presented, by structuring it into three distinct reports: the Strategy report, giving the CEO the opportunity to articulate the way forward; the Financial report, reporting the results for a given financial year – independently audited of course – and the Sustainability report, reporting the performance during the year, with extensive disclosures on non-financial matters, also independently audited.

Empowering teams with self-sustainability management

Having the right sustainability strategy and processus in place will deliver the expected results provided that the execution is seamless.

There is only one way to get across to everybody in a company how important sustainability is and to ensure that individuals and teams take responsibility for their own sustainability agenda and take positive action, right across the organisation.

That is to empower them with the responsibility, the ability, and the resources that enable them to deliver sustainability in action.

Making this happen is not an easy task.

First, the tone from the top has to be authentic. A leadership team cannot fake a commitment to sustainability. So the tone needs to be genuine. It has to be inspirational, focusing on the meaning of sustainability as part of the company's fundamental purpose. This will then help unleash the organisation's natural energy, enabling individuals to embrace its sustainability journey with total commitment.

To achieve this, the leadership team needs to go beyond merely communicating with people. It needs to empower them too.

Clearly, it is vital that the company's sustainability approach works at a local level, both internally and externally. The ecosystem varies in different geographies and at different layers, dependent on the activities the company carries out in different locations.

The right approach is therefore to allow colleagues to develop their own ideas and initiatives to deliver the company's global sustainability agenda in a clearly tailored and targeted fashion. This makes the corporate sustainability agenda properly meaningful for all.

So, in my view, the best way for a leadership team to encourage and enable a commitment to total sustainability is first to lead from the front with authenticity, inspiring and empowering every colleague to join the movement of our time.

In this way, people throughout the organisation will be enabled to make the world ever better, inch by inch, by understanding, meeting and exceeding the expectations of stakeholders in their own parts of the wider corporate ecosystem.

We have discussed earlier in this chapter how at Intertek, we are encouraging and enabling people to 'own' and understand their carbon footprint, inspiring and empowering them to take ambitious action to reduce it.

We provide emissions dashboards at our sites, which help people on the ground understand exactly what their emissions are and what is causing them. As a result, they can implement localised initiatives to directly manage and reduce their environmental impact.

Sustainability from the heart

Some of the community work we did as volunteers at Disney was particularly inspirational, because all volunteers were doing their community work with a big heart.

So whether it involved helping local people in the aftermath of a major storm or bringing a little joy to terminally ill children in their final days, it felt right.

People's desire to be involved was inspired by the same impulse that encouraged them to join Disney in the first place. This could not be faked.

Sustainability from the heart is the only way.

Build Back Ever Better

You might remember that in the preface to this book, I mentioned the need post COVID-19 to build back a better society, based on the idea of working together to create something bigger and better for everybody.

Build Back Ever Better (#BBEB), based on the idea of working together to create something bigger and better for everybody.

Intertek is a purpose led company, fully committed to delivering sustainable value for all of our stakeholders. We are truly committed to making our communities ever better and over the years our teams have demonstrated genuine and authentic support to their communities.

Build Back Better is a very relevant theme for all stakeholders on the planet and at Intertek we made it our central theme post COVID-19 to help our customers build back ever better operations, to make Intertek an ever better workplace and to provide support to our communities to Build Back ever Better.

In April 2021, we launched a bold initiative targeted at our communities with our BBEB.com digital platform, which enables anyone in each of our operations and in our communities to share and read inspirational stories of how people are making a difference to Build Back Ever Better communities.

The idea is simple: your story on how to build back an ever better community will inspire each of us to Build Back Ever Better communities.

#BBEB is a digital platform that's open to everybody. Its aim is incredibly simple: to inspire communities and ultimately everyone in the world to build back following the COVID-19 pandemic in a way that's better than anything that has gone before.

It is a recognition that future generations deserve the best possible legacy we can leave them – something far better than would be possible if we carry on as we are today.

COVID-19 has been a wake-up call for the human race. It has been the biggest crisis of our time.

COVID-19 has brought into clearer view than ever before the challenges we face: from rising temperatures and shifting climates to the ethical and sustainability risks associated with running a business; from challenges to people's physical and mental health and wellbeing to disappearing wildlife and polluted oceans.

COVID-19 has made 2020 the moment when we were collectively forced to rethink how we could make the world a better place. That's why I believe it will prove to be an important turning point in the history of mankind.

And it is why at Intertek we are building a movement to inspire everyone to make a positive difference in their community.

Key points from this chapter:

- Make sure that there is total commitment anchored to your purpose, your vision, your values and your strategy.
- Spend time and energy making sure you understand the sustainability agenda of every one of your stakeholders.
- Operationalise and execute the strategy with sustainable excellence, ensuring that you have the right activities and risk mitigations in place.
- Lead the company sustainably, end-to-end, with the right corporate processes.
- Empower your teams to self-manage and report on their own sustainability agendas.

Conclusion
Lead with Soul. For good

Despite the huge progress made over the years, organisations are underled and, therefore, failing to unleash their full potential.

I firmly believe that the solution is simply Good Leadership.

At the beginning of the book, we have covered the fact that 2.6 billion employees are not engaged every day at the workplace.

One should never believe that the number of disengaged employees will reduce in future on their own. The only solution is for leaders to take their leadership responsibilities seriously and change their approach.

Leading in the 21st century will not get easier; if anything, in the post COVID-19 workplace, with people working remotely more often, such a lack of engagement is likely to be even more prevalent in the years ahead.

It's time for change.

Unless leaders listen to their humanist side, the number of disengaged employees will increase and organisations, big and small, private and public and profit and non-profit, will continue to underperform and fail to unleash their full potential.

I very much hope that Leadership with Soul will inspire today's and tomorrow's leaders to think differently about their roles and responsibilities; recognising of course that Good Leadership is both thrilling and very complex.

The thinking behind Leadership with Soul is based on my fundamental belief that there is only one way to be successful on a sustainable basis when you lead an organisation in the 21st century, no matter its size or nature.

That is always to put people at the heart of your growth strategy and day-to-day operational management, regardless of the specific circumstances you find yourself in, always leading based on your purpose and values.

Leadership with Soul reconciles the interests of the financial markets in delivering sustainable shareholder value, with the desire of employees to make their company a better place to work.

Applying the 10 principles of Leadership with Soul consistently will enable leaders to gain energy and inspiration from their financial performance and the enthusiasm of their people.

Ultimately, this will empower leaders to collectively make their workplace and ultimately the world a better place for future generations.

This is the true heart of the matter: the positive impact Good Leaders have on their companies is significant. Their influence can be huge, because of who they are, the time we all spend at work, and how deep company ecosystems permeate society at every level.

Starting this book with quotes from ancient philosophers was very deliberate. These were people who thought intensely about the role of the individual in society and how the ways that people think and behave can have a positive influence on humanity as a whole.

I have looked for people who today are shedding light on our lives in the way that Socrates, Plato and Aristotle did, or more recently the likes of Voltaire, Diderot and Rousseau in the late 18th century. But I've so far failed to find any big thinkers in the 21st century who are shaping the right 21st century model for our society to make the world a better, safer and more sustainable place.

In fact, if anything, we're going in the opposite direction. Before the COVID-19 pandemic, western and other governments were spectacularly failing to spread the benefits of GDP growth fairly across society. This in turn was widening the wealth gap, fuelling the rise of populism, creating unrest and undermining belief in and respect for politicians and institutions.

At the beginning of this book, I referred to the series of seismic shocks that have hit us during the early years of the 21st century, from 9/11 to COVID-19 and recently, the war in Ukraine. Thinking about the way we started the 21st century, I believe that the institutions which were developed following WWII, to help govern the challenges society faced back then, are no longer fit for purpose in our fast-paced interconnected world.

Today, the checks and balances designed to deliver global governance across and between countries are becoming less effective and less relevant every day. The climate risk facing the future of our planet is possibly the best evidence that today's global institutions are failing to address our number one issue, given the fact that, despite the efforts of many, there is still no clarity, transparency and real accountability to achieve Net Zero.

Given the lack of guidance from big thinkers to help us deal with the challenges we face in the 21st century and given the inability of governments and institutions to resolve some of these challenges, I believe that making the workplace better in order to make the world better is a big idea whose time has come.

Imagine how much better the world could be if the leaders of organisations everywhere – teams in departments, global companies and their subsidiaries, local shops, hospitals and associations – were Good Leaders.

For sure, the level of engagement in any organisation would be much higher than today, creating a workplace that is highly energising for all employees, resulting in sustainable growth and value creation for all stakeholders.

It's a simple vision. If we all make our workplace better every single day, we will ultimately make the world a better place for everybody and the future more sustainable for the generations to come.

So, that is the 'grander purpose' behind Leadership with Soul – I believe in it, and every day I work as hard as I can to show that Leading with Soul helps turn that purpose into something tangible.

But there is another purpose to this book that means a lot to me. I have written Leadership with Soul to provide leaders who are curious and eager to learn how to become a Good Leader, reflecting on a leadership model that works and delivers growth for all stakeholders.

I have been very fortunate throughout my career, having worked in fantastic companies with exceptional colleagues in more than 100 countries around the world. I have learnt so much from every situation and I have never stopped growing to become a better leader and ultimately a better person.

I have written Leadership with Soul for existing and future leaders who believe in continuous learning and who have the energy to immerse themselves in the leadership model I developed to find areas that will inspire them to change and become a Good Leader.

Said differently, Leadership with Soul is an invitation to any leader who wants to stop and think about the effectiveness of her or his leadership style, recognising, of course, that becoming a Good Leader takes time and is hard work.

Right at the beginning of this book, I challenged you to ask yourselves two questions every day: The What: 'Are you focusing your organisation on the right priorities to deliver your goals?' and the How: 'Are you sure you know how your employees feel?'

You will get multiple insights from these two questions and applying the 10 principles of Leadership with Soul consistently will deliver sustainable value for all your stakeholders.

Leadership Principle 1: Lead with emotional intelligence

- If you don't put people at the heart of your growth strategy and day-to-day operations, you cannot lead with EQ. That's because EQ is all about achieving great things through people.
- To create genuine empowerment, it's vital to build a decentralised and well co-ordinated operating model that empowers people close to the customer to make decisions in line with policies set at the highest level.
- It's essential to create a high-performance culture that embraces the values of respect, courage, passion, integrity and responsibility.
- You have to continuously demonstrate your EQ through interacting with people and leading by example.
- And you need always to have the right antennae in place and to sense the pulse of the organisation at all times.

Leadership Principle 2: Imagine the journey and paint the picture for all

- Do your homework to determine the size of the prize for all stakeholders, and understand the different expectations from group to group.
- Articulate a simple vision that clearly defines the journey's ultimate destination and is both inspirational and meaningful for all stakeholders.

- Develop a well-integrated communications plan that paints the picture for all and takes into account the different interests, expectations and aspirations of all different groups.
- Invest your personal time in communicating the vision in a way that will energise your audience, thanks to your own conviction and passion, based on an in-depth preparation.
- Never stop driving home the messages that matter: repeat, repeat, repeat!

Leadership Principle 3: Energise the organisation to outperform

- Make sure everybody understands with total clarity exactly what 'outperform' means for their role, their department and the organisation as a whole.
- Set up daily, weekly and monthly operating systems to empower the organisation with constant insight into comparative performance and progress against targets.
- Commit yourself and make yourself highly visible as you lead from the front with high – and highly visible – energy.
- Always be genuine and authentic as a leader, continually challenging the organisation with ideas and programmes to drive continuous improvement.
- Recognise and celebrate success every day, providing excellent role models and inspiring others to outperform.

Leadership Principle 4: Customer intimacy

- Ensure every part of the organisation has the capability to achieve true zero-defect quality, 24/7.
- Build a truly customer-centric organisation, in which everybody understands that the ability to meet or exceed expectations is the single most important driver of sustainable success.
- Make sure you have an independent source of Total Quality Assurance in your business that helps you manage the conflict between quality and speed to market.
- Listen to the voice of the customer, ensuring you consistently, precisely understand the challenges they face and their views on your products and service levels.

- Ensure you're getting the basics right, offering a differentiated value proposition, with memorable moments that will make the customer experience truly magical. Customer intimacy is the ultimate advantage.

Leadership Principle 5: Reinvent the future

- Create a culture of continuous and vigorous innovation, meaning the moment you launch a new product you start considering how to create something better.
- Focus at local (Zero-to-One) and global (One-to-100) levels to create growth- and margin-accretive innovations.
- Start first with innovation from the core of your business, where you have scale and expertise.
- Identify and invest in fast-growing segments that are adjacent to your core business where you can capitalise on your strengths.
- Ultimately go for the Big Prize, whether organically or inorganically, achieving breakthrough innovations that open up exciting new markets.

Leadership Principle 6: Master complexity

- Understand the 'capability-complexity equilibrium', and appreciate the source of the organisation's energy or pain.
- Formulate a comprehensive capability plan to deliver the strategy, based on your organisation's capital strengths, its technology, assets, processes and people.
- Unleash the full potential of the organisation through the magic of talent planning.
- Ensure you attract the right talent for today, tomorrow and the day after.
- And be sure to sponsor and support the careers of those talents who demonstrate particularly high potential – just as somebody in the past has done for you.

Leadership Principle 7: Embody the strategy at the top

- Create a leadership team around you that embodies the organisational strategy, and that meets your standards.
- Make sure the top team delivers the strategy in action with a single voice.

- Focus on driving short-term performance consistently, which will give you the licence to do the right things strategically.
- Always stay composed under pressure – this is a key leadership characteristic because, no matter what you may think, you're always on stage.
- Operate as a team throughout good and bad times, making the tough calls and difficult decisions when you have to.

Leadership Principle 8: Laser-focused execution

- Identify the core priorities on which the organisation needs to be laser-focused to implement the strategy and deliver the vision.
- Make sure you have a capability plan covering each of these priorities.
- Carry out meticulous planning to ensure a disciplined execution with zero-defect.
- Monitor progress with 360° leading indicators, ensuring you use the right data and operating systems.
- Be certain which part of the business cycle you're in – start-up, business turnaround, corporate activity and good to great journey – as this will influence how you lead the business.

Leadership Principle 9: Ever-better branding glo-cally

- Ensure that your brands have a differentiated, authentic and winning USP.
- Seize growth opportunities by continuing to build and strengthen your brands, step-by-step: this is the road to continuous improvement.
- Realise the global, universal appeal of your business, but ensure that you connect the dots with the local desires and aspirations of your customers.
- When developing your advertising, use a very small, focused and highly creative team that deeply understands the brand and the customer. Take risks, be creative – to open people's minds, you need to be impactful.
- Ensure that you live the brand values internally to build a strong brand externally.

Leadership Principle 10: Sustainable performance for all

- Make sure that there is total commitment anchored to your purpose, your vision, your values and your strategy.
- Spend time and energy making sure you understand the sustainability agenda of every one of your stakeholders.
- Operationalise and execute the strategy with sustainable excellence, ensuring that you have the right activities and risk mitigations in place.
- Lead the company sustainably, end-to-end, with the right corporate processes.
- Empower your teams to self-manage and report on their own sustainability agendas.

Of course, I cannot guarantee that applying these 10 principles consistently will empower you to become the CEO of an organisation – besides, this may not be your ambition.

But I am certain that these principles will help you become a better, more effective leader, to create sustainable growth for all and make your world a better place – whether that world is a small family business, a local charity or a department in a larger organisation or a multinational corporation.

Becoming a successful leader is of course a journey and the success of any leader in any organisation will be visible to all stakeholders for many years to come.

As I said in a previous chapter, a leader who does not leave an organisation with a strong track record of value creation and a truly sustainable platform for future growth, has failed.

Leaving that legacy is all about doing what is right, with the right goals and in the right way.

Said simply, legacy is the ultimate measurement of Good Leadership.

Over the years, I came to a very simple insight on what it means to leave a respected legacy for any Good Leader.

In our pacy and globally-connected society, news is written very fast while history is written very slowly.

Only the most significant moments of our lives will be remembered to inspire future generations.

At its core, Leadership with Soul is about achieving big things that are truly meaningful and enduring.

In his 1962 speech calling on Americans to support the space programme, JFK said: 'We choose to go to the Moon in this decade and do the other things, not because they are easy, but because they are hard, because that goal will serve to organize and measure the best of our energies and skills, because that challenge is one that we are willing to accept, one we are unwilling to postpone, and one which we intend to win, and the other, too'.

Armstrong and Aldrin walked on the Moon less than seven years later.

Kennedy's leadership was a vital factor in this extraordinary achievement: it showed how much can be achieved by understanding people and what motivates them – talking directly to the collective soul of your immediate audience and all your stakeholders. That's Leadership with Soul.

Let's lead with soul – and leave a legacy for good that will make history by putting people at the heart of your growth strategy.

Let's lead with soul. For good.

André Lacroix
2022

Printed in the United States
by Baker & Taylor Publisher Services